D1376478

Confronting Racism in Higher Education

Problems and Possibilities for Fighting Ignorance, Bigotry and Isolation

A volume in
Educational Leadership for Social Justice
Jeffrey S. Brooks, *Series Editor*

Confronting Racism in Higher Education

Problems and Possibilities for Fighting Ignorance, Bigotry and Isolation

edited by

Jeffrey S. Brooks
Iowa State University

Noelle Witherspoon Arnold
University of Missouri–Columbia

INFORMATION AGE PUBLISHING, INC.
Charlotte, NC • www.infoagepub.com

Library of Congress Cataloging-in-Publication Data

A CIP record for this book is available from the Library of Congress
http://www.loc.gov

Printed in the United States of America

CONTENTS

v

ACKNOWLEDGEMENTS

I thank all of my colleagues fighting against racism in schools and society around the world. Though the struggle is daunting, your courage and sacrifice will move us closer to equity. I also thank the many fine scholars and practitioners with whom I have worked and learned from over the past several years: Catherine Marshall, Linda Tillman, Catherine Lugg, Kathleen M. Brown, Fenwick English, Harry Wolcott, Ira Bogotch, Leslie Hazle Bussey, Ernestine Enomoto, Carlos McCray, Floyd Beachum, Sonya Douglass Horsford, Autumn K. Tooms, George Theoharis, Denise Armstrong, Sandy Harris, Whitney Sherman Newcomb, Bradley Carpenter, Sarah Diem, A. J. Welton, Katherine Cummings Mansfield, Terah Venzant Chambers, Elizabeth Ramalho Murakami, Lisa Nieuwenhuizen, Lisa Delpit, Bill Ayers, Anthony H. Normore and Gaetane Jean-Marie. There are many more—I apologize for those omissions.

Thanks to Nicole Fraise, my wonderful graduate assistant who helped coordinate the process of collecting and organizing chapters. I appreciate all of your hard work and your insights.

I reserve a special word of thanks to my co-editor Noelle Witherspoon Arnold. She is an inspiration to me and to many other students, scholars and educators. I am proud to be your friend and colleague, Noelle.

Finally, I cannot thank my family enough for their gift of unconditional love. None of this work is possible without the support and love of another outstanding scholar, my wife Melanie, and my children, Jürgen, Clodagh, Bronwyn and Holland. I love you all deeply. This book is another achievement for Team Rainbow.

—Jeffrey S. Brooks

Confronting Racism in Higher Education, pages vii–viii
Copyright © 2013 by Information Age Publishing
All rights of reproduction in any form reserved.

The writing of this book came at an exciting time. It was exciting because I finally married my husband Bruce Makoto Arnold. Thank you for always making me feel like I can do anything. I love you.

Thank you to Jeffrey S. Brooks who has influenced my professional life in many ways and challenged me to be a better scholar. Thank you to all the race warriors who "trouble the waters" of racism and fight for social justice and equity. You work hard for everyone, every day. Many of you are in this book; some of you are not, but you know who you are. All of you give me energy to protest and the power to persist.

Last but not least, thank you to my mom, Jacqueline, my first influence for justice and antiracism. You have always troubled the waters.

—Noelle Witherspoon Arnold

CONFRONTING RACISM IN HIGHER EDUCATION

Problems and Possibilities for Fighting Ignorance, Bigotry and Isolation

Noelle Witherspoon Arnold and Jeffrey S. Brooks

Ignorance and prejudice are the handmaidens of propaganda. Our mission, therefore, is to confront ignorance with knowledge, bigotry with tolerance, and isolation with the outstretched hand of generosity. Racism can, will, and must be defeated.
— Kofi Annan

Racism and ignorance churn on college campuses as surely as they do in society at large, with a number of high-profile incidents each year serving as a ready reminder that hatred and oppression are all around us—lest anyone forget. Over the past fifteen years there have been many discussions regarding racism and higher education. Some of these focus on formal policies and dynamics such as Affirmative Action or The Dream Act, while many more discussions are happening in classrooms, dorm rooms and in campus communities. Of course, corollary to these conversations, some of which are generative and some of which are degenerative, is a deafening silence around issues of race (Brooks, 2012). This lack of dialogue and action speaks volumes about individuals and organizations, and suggests a complicit acceptance, tolerance or even support for institutional and individual

Confronting Racism in Higher Education, pages ix–xiv
Copyright © 2013 by Information Age Publishing

racism. There is much work to be done if we are to improve the situation around race and race relation in institutions of higher education.

Specifically, there is still much work to be done in unpacking and addressing the educational realities of those who are economically, socially, and politically underserved and oppressed by implicit and overt racism. These realities manifest in ways such as lack of access to and within higher education, in equitable outcomes and in a disparity of the quality of education as a student matriculates through the system. While there are occasional diversity and inclusion efforts made in higher education, institutions still largely address them as quotas, and not as paradigmatic changes. This focus on "counting toward equity rather" than "creating a culture of equity" is basically a form of white privilege that allows administrators and policymakers to show incremental "progress" and avoid more substantive action toward real equity that changes the culture(s) of institutions with longstanding racial histories that marginalize some and privilege others.

Issues in higher education are still raced from white perspectives and suffer from a view that race and racism occur in a vacuum. Some literature suggests that racism begins very early in the student experience and continues all the way to college (Berlak & Moyenda, 2011). This mis-education, mislabeling and mistreatment based on race often develops as early as five to ten years old and "follows" them to post-graduate education and beyond.

Racism is still a chronic and pervasive problem in the educational system. Jones (1972/1997) identified three types of racism

1. *Individual.* An attitude or an act of racism from a singular person or small group of individuals.
2. *Institutional.* Formal and informal policies, practices, and structure of institutions that oppress those of color.
3. *Cultural.* Majority groups assume superiority and impose white norms as standard.

These three types of racism can be interpersonal, collective, symbolic, and sociopolitical (Harrell, 2000). Racism can also be overt, covert, intentional or unintentional (Brooks & Jean-Marie, 2007). In any case, racism still has negative consequences for those who are targets.

This book takes a P–20 approach to examining the continued racial crisis in higher education and to remind us that "racism has come out of the closet again and into our schools" (Pine & Hilliard, 1990, p. 593).

CHAPTER OVERVIEWS

In Chapter 1, *Examining the Blockages of Race-Related Conversations in the Classroom: From Recognition to Action,* Sarah Diem and Bradley W. Carpenter tell us that conversations about race often invoke a litany of reactions, ranging from silence, denial, frustration, anger, passion, hope, and optimism. They highlight how the avoidance of such conversations prevents us from the communal, individual, and reflective learning necessary for our society to address the race-related inequities that continue to mar the enactment of democracy. Conversely, what is often overlooked is how professors within educational leadership preparation prepare for and facilitate social justice oriented conversations within their classrooms, particularly when these conversations are focused on race. The authors also provide a comprehensive examination of why race-related conversations may be derailed, stalled, or blocked all together and are needed by focusing on three concepts that often limit and/or block discussions focused on race from occurring within the classroom:

1. colorblind ideologies
2. myths of meritocracy; and
3. false notions of human difference.

Chapter 2, *Persistence is Chess, Not Checkers: A Counterstory on the Lives and Strategies of Six African American Administrators at One Predominantly White Institution* by Brandon Wolfe highlights a recent study on the narratives of six African American university administrators in an effort to provide a snapshot of their current experiences and challenges in a predominantly White institution (PWI). In this chapter, a theoretical model is proposed to explain this phenomenon. Specifically, a synthesis of existing literature and theories from sociology, psychology, and education along with results from the study suggests that there are five variables in constant interaction that suggests how persistence strategies are formulated among minority institutional leaders. While each component of the proposed model is thoroughly explained, insight into how each variable interacts is also offered. Research and practical implications for researchers, university administrators, and stakeholders who are interested in ways to retain administrators of colored are presented to conclude the chapter.

Chapter 3, *Combat in the Academy: Racial Battle Fatigue, Role Strain, and African American Faculty at Public Community Colleges* by Tamara N. Stevenson reminds us that African Americans remain disproportionately underrepresented in the faculty ranks at institutions of higher education in the United States, specifically community colleges. In consideration of the parallel legacy of racism and discrimination African Americans have endured in society and academia, this chapter draws upon the tenets of Critical Race Theory (CRT), a framework to examine the environment and experiences of African-American community college faculty.

In Chapter 4, *Critical Race Theory and College Readiness: A Review of the Literature,* Chad Kee utilizes a CRT frame to present an extensive literature review particularly in the area of college readiness of students of color.

In Chapter 5, *An Overview of the History, Research, and Culture of Historically Black Greek Letter Organizations,* Andre Brown examines historically Black Greek letter organizations since the early 1900s. Like their predominately White counterparts, historically Black Greek letter organizations identify themselves with Greek letters, have customs, traditions, organizational culture, and require members to take oaths of allegiance and secrecy to their respective organizations. In contrast to their White organizational counterparts, the author argues that historically Black Greek letter organizations have provided Black students with social outlets to address the unique needs and concerns on the campuses where they are represented. Together, these points resulted in the development and advancement of historically Black Greek letter organizations. This chapter explores their history, culture, and existing research on individuals affiliated with historically Black Greek letter organizations.

Chapter 6, *Legal and Educational Foundations in Critical Race Theory* by Evelyn Young, focuses on the phenomenon of racism often overlooked in the shaping of legal and educational policies in the United States. This chapter provides a general overview of the literature in CRT in both law and educational research. In particular, it utilizes a CRT perspective to examine the interplay of racism in the areas of curriculum and instruction, educational policy, school finance, and assessment and accountability.

In Chapter 7, *Critical Race Theory and African American Women's Theoretical Leadership Constructions: Changing Frameworks for Changing Times* by Collette Bloom examines current leadership constructions by using CRT to unpack traditional and enduring leadership paradigms and offer suggestions for paradigmatic change.

In Chapter 8, *(Re)thinking Race: Positioning Multiracial Representations within Critical Pedagogy,* Claire Peinado Fraczek considers the merits, strategies, and limitations of Critical Race Theory (CRT) and antiracist (critical Whiteness) theory as pedagogical tools in higher education contexts. She discusses how CRT and antiracist theory provide opportunities to analyze how power and privilege are deployed, subverted, and repositioned for various constituencies, particularly mono-racial and multiracial students of color; educators can still provide analytical guidance for understanding how his multiracial history provides new, largely unheard, mixed race narratives. Such attentiveness can certainly be extended into classroom and higher education contexts in which participants take a more holistic inventory of their various identities operating within discourse. By centralizing the experiences of mixed race students who might claim White and non-White heritage, this paper pushes educators to consider how curriculum about race might be moved forward in ways that benefit a broad spectrum of diverse students, including a growing multiracial student population.

Chapter 9, *Who's Zoomin' Who? A Critical Race Analysis of Florida's Public High School Graduates* by Terri Watson and Jennifer Sughrue focuses on higher education pipeline issues by reviewing a case where the American Civil Liberties Union (ACLU) of Florida filed a class action lawsuit against The Palm Beach County School Board and its district superintendent on behalf of approximately 176,000 students under their jurisdiction (*Schroeder v. The Palm Beach County School Board,* 2008). The plaintiffs cited the defendants for their failure "to provide a uniform, efficient, safe, secure, and high quality education" (p. 7) as required by the Florida Constitution, Article IX, § 1. They contended that their claim was substantiated by The School District of Palm Beach County's (SDPBC) dismal high school graduation rates. This chapter explores the controversy surrounding high school graduation rates, in spite of decades of school reform measures, and why different calculation methods are utilized in the state of Florida. Critical Race Realism, a methodological framework founded in Critical Race Theory (CRT), was utilized to examine Florida's public high school graduation rates.

Chapter 10, *Neither Latino nor White Enough: Educational Experiences of Meso Hispanic Meso American Urban and Suburban Public High School Students* by Paula Marie Gallegos explores "key factors" associated with academic success. Successful Hispanic students were studied, at the college level, from two different settings (suburban public high schools and urban public high schools), to explore the factors of their success. Experiences were gathered using semi-structured interviews and narrative story telling. Student narratives point to district policies, school policies, daily bell schedules, and low expectations of the school and teachers, as factors that inhibit academic success for some Meso Hispanic Meso American high school students. Conversely, student success was attributed to having at least one strong parental influence (role model, nonjudgmental), a strong teacher influence (role model or caring teacher), and the trait of doggedness to persist in education and achieve a four-year college degree.

This book does not offer "solutions" to the issues of race or racism. What we hope you gain from this collection is learning and (un)learning racism and that you will "become a catalyst for issues of race in educational leadership through your research, teaching and service" (Brooks, 2012, p. 124).

REFERENCES

Berlak, A., & Moyenda, S. (2011). *Taking it personally: Racism in the classroom from kindergarten to college.* Philadelphia, PA: Temple University Press.

Brooks, J. S. (2012). Black school, White School: Racism and educational (mis) leadership. New York: Teachers College Press.

Brooks, J. S., & Jean-Marie, G. (2007). Black leadership, white leadership: Race and race relations in an urban high school. *Journal of Educational Administration, 45*(6): 756-768.

Harrell, S. P. (2000). A multidimensional conceptualization of racism related stress: Implications for the well-being of people of color. *American Journal of Ortho-psychiatry, 70* (1), 42–57.

Jones, J. M. (1972/1997). *Prejudice and racism.* New York: McGraw-Hill.

Pine, G. J., & Hilliard, A. G., III. (1990). Rx for racism: Imperatives for America's schools. *Phi Delta Kappan,* 593–600.

CHAPTER 1

EXAMINING THE BLOCKAGES OF RACE-RELATED CONVERSATIONS IN THE CLASSROOM

From Recognition to Action

Sarah Diem
University of Missouri

Bradley W. Carpenter
University of Louisville

Following the election of President Barack Obama the scrutiny of educational leaders and leadership preparation programs has intensified, as the current administration has placed a significant emphasis on the "strengthening" of "metropolitan areas[1]" (Wilson, 2010, p. 41). Specific to the field of educational leadership preparation, one of the primary goals of the Obama/Duncan education agenda is to "turn around" the nation's chronically lowest performing public schools, the great majority of which are lo-

Confronting Racism in Higher Education, pages 1–20
Copyright © 2013 by Information Age Publishing
All rights of reproduction in any form reserved.

cated in metropolitan areas where poverty is concentrated and students of color are the primary population (Noguera & Wells, 2011). Consequently, as the federal government has become increasingly more assertive in its efforts to address low-performing public schools, significant attention has focused on both the influence of school leaders (Orr & Orphanos, 2011) and the ways in which institutions of higher learning prepare education leaders to serve in diverse settings (Brown, 2004, 2006; Dantley, 2002; Grogan & Andrews, 2002; Jean-Marie, 2010; López, 2003; Marshall & Oliva, 2006; Tillman, 2004).

While the recent movement within educational leadership programs to address issues of social justice (Blackmore, 2009; Jean-Marie, 2010; Jean-Marie, Normore, & Brooks, 2009; Marshall & Oliva, 2006; McKenzie et al., 2008; Theoharis, 2007, 2009, 2010) may provide educational leaders with a number of the skills necessary to achieve success in schools labeled as at-risk for failure, the field of leadership preparation has provided little information as to how professors facilitate social justice-oriented conversations within their classrooms, particularly when such conversations are founded upon anti-racist themes. Certainly, issues pertaining to racism have always been present within schools, both covertly and overtly. Therefore, as Ryan (2003) states, "...racism ought to be a serious concern for educational leaders, particularly those who hold positions of responsibility in schools, like principals and headteachers. This is because the place where racism is often most evident is at the school level" (p. 145). Consequently, we believe the preparation of today's school leaders must include a purposeful focus on building the critical dialogical skills necessary to facilitate anti-racist conversations. The premise of this chapter is educational leaders choosing to work with diverse populations must be provided with a rigorous and critically-oriented curriculum which promotes the critically reflective examination of the ideologies/concepts often limiting and/or blocking anti-racist discussions from occurring.

Encouraged by Milner's (2010) conceptual detailing of the "repertoires of diversity"—elements he suggests should be embedded within any curriculum guiding a teacher preparatory program—we developed a list of five critical concepts we believe must be woven into the curricula and pedagogical practices of programs seeking to prepare educational leaders for diverse settings. Specifically, it is our belief that educational leadership preparatory programs must carefully examine issues/concepts pertaining to:

1. Color-blind ideology
2. Misconceptions of human difference
3. Merit-based achievement
4. Critical self-reflection, and
5. The interrogation of race-related silences in the classroom.

Just as Milner (2010) warns when outlining his repertoires of diversity, the five issues/concepts discussed in this chapter are not intended to represent an all-inclusive listing of the issues pertaining to the preparation of educational leaders for diverse school communities. Rather, the five topics were decided upon after the reflexive examination of findings and feedback revealed during our previous research efforts with professors and students within educational leadership preparation programs. These efforts include the examination of how professors and students conceptualize what is present and/or missing in educational leadership courses with regard to conversations surrounding race, racism, and race relations (Carpenter & Diem, 2010). Additionally, our work examines the ways in which professors plan for and facilitate conversations focused on race and race-related issues within educational leadership preparation programs (Carpenter & Diem, 2011). Over the course of two years, we conducted multiple interviews with six professors, each of whom taught courses responsible for addressing issues relating to race in educational leadership and public schools. We also conducted multiple focus groups with a cohort of educational leadership students during this time, beginning shortly after their entry into the leadership preparation program and ending close to their scheduled graduation, in order to gain a better understanding of how classroom discussions surrounding issues of race, racism, and relations may have (or not) evolved throughout the duration of their involvement within the program. Finally, in an effort to triangulate our research findings and determine how the field has examined the possible contributors to race-related silences within the classroom, we conducted an extensive review of the educational leadership literature, focusing on both the preparation of educational leaders for social justice and equity and the exploration of race-related silences in the classroom. Additionally, unlike Milner's five conceptual repertoires of diversity, two of the five issues we examined—critical self-reflection and the interrogation of silenced voices—are practice-specific concepts that, if acted upon, may help preparation programs develop transformative curricula and pedagogical experiences for educational leaders.

We begin this chapter by highlighting a number of issues related to the preparation of today's educational leaders for diverse settings. Next, we examine three conceptual issues we believe must be embedded within the curricula of leadership preparation programs. We then illustrate how two practice-specific concepts provide the foundation for a number of normative strategies that, if enacted, will help move the field of leadership preparation towards developing the anti-racist educational opportunities leaders of diverse communities deserve. Next, we describe how such a project offers a number of implications for the field of educational leadership preparation. We then conclude the chapter with a discussion of the tangible implementation suggestions for programs seeking to prepare educational leaders for diverse school communities.

PREPARING EDUCATIONAL LEADERS
FOR DIVERSE SETTINGS

Today's educational leaders must navigate a variety of social complexities (Horsford, 2010), as they will likely encounter a school population in which 25% of the students live in poverty, 10% to 20% struggle with specific learning differences, 15% speak English as a second language, and 40% identify as members of racial/ethnic groups (Darling-Hammond, 2006). Moreover, the leaders most often serving these students have been predominately White (Aud et al., 2011), often overlook and are hesitant to acknowledge issues of race and racism in their schools as they believe them to be individual issues (Ryan, 2003; Young & Laible, 2000), and have not been prepared to engage students, teachers, and their school communities in conversations related to diversity, race, culture, and inequality (Dantley, 2002; Hawley & James, 2010; hooks, 1994; Jean-Marie, 2010; Milner, 2010; Parker & Shapiro, 1992; Tillman, 2004; Young & Laible, 2000). The cultural, racial, and ethnic divide between teachers, leaders, and school communities makes the examination of how leadership preparation programs equip leaders of diverse communities of paramount importance and presents a myriad of implications for academic achievement. Yet, as Hawley and James (2010) explain, such divides receive far too little attention in the examination of the factors that contribute to poor student achievement.

> It is ironic, given the gap between the achievement of students of different races and ethnicities, that school leaders and advocates for school improvement rarely look at explanations for the gap that might be related to race and ethnicity. It seems absolutely sensible, for example, to conclude that the achievement gap cannot be substantially narrowed unless we eliminate gaps in opportunities to learn. (p. 1)

The impetus for these statements was provided by a study in which Hawley and James (2010) examined a number of University Council for Educational Administration (UCEA) member universities to better understand how preparation programs structured courses, resources, and strategies to prepare educational leaders to meet the needs of diverse student populations. Overall, while the programs addressed issues pertaining to the sociological, economic, discriminatory, and inequity-related difficulties encountered by students of color, Hawley and James found curricular offerings failed to adequately provide educational leadership students with the contextually specific strategies necessary to address issues of diversity. Thus, while programs address the variety of conditions contributing to societal inequities, they rarely provide substantive guidance as to how leaders should address diversity issues within the contextual environments in which they work.

The disconnect between the complexities faced by current administrators and the inattention of preparation programs regarding the ways in which race and ethnicity are related to the historically persistent gap in student achievement are disturbing. Yet, simply calling attention to this problematic irony is not enough. As hooks (2003) suggests, naming the problem without a "constructive focus on resolution" will only serve to lessen the "hope" of those seeking transformational change by marginalizing such critiques as mere expressions of profound cynicism (p. xiv). Consequently, the following sections examine each of the five critical concepts we believe deserves further attention as preparation programs move toward crafting the transformative and anti-racist curricula and pedagogies required to prepare the social justice-oriented educational leaders our children deserve.

RECOGNITION: THREE CRITICAL COMPONENTS OF AN ANTI-RACIST CURRICULUM

In an increasingly complex and changing society, research suggests educational leaders must be exposed to the following three conceptual issues if expected to effectively lead within diverse school communities. Each of the concepts discussed in the subsequent sections were chosen based upon the relationship of two factors: each surfaced as dominant themes within our previous research efforts and each appeared frequently in the body of literature pertaining to the preparation of socially just educational leaders for diverse settings. These concepts include:

1. Color-blind ideology
2. Misconceptions of human difference, and
3. Merit-based achievement.

Color-Blind Ideologies

Those subscribing to a color-blind ideology believe in order to create a more just and inclusive society, racial differences among individuals should not be emphasized. Color-blind proponents believe people should enact race-neutral approaches to politics, education, law, and all other aspects of our lives. "They oppose race-conscious solutions on the grounds that racial inclusion requires only that individuals be treated similarly under the law— no more, no less" (Brown et al., 2003, p. 4). Color blindness works to maintain an appearance of formal equality among individuals without paying much attention to the inequality existent in our everyday lives (Guinier & Torres, 2002). When comparing what he conceives as a new form of "racial ideology" to Jim Crow racism, Bonilla-Silva (2010) describes color blindness as "racism lite." As opposed to . . .

> relying on name calling (niggers, Spics, Chinks), color-blind racism otherizes softly ("these people are human, too"); instead of proclaiming God placed minorities in the world in a servile position, it suggests they are behind because they don't work hard enough. . . . Yet this new ideology has become a formidable political tool for the maintenance of the racial order. (p. 3)

While the idea of color blindness may come with good intentions, and may even be appealing given its alignment with the importance of focusing on the individual when measuring success (Flagg, 1993), in the field of education it causes harm to students of color, and perpetuates the inability to create classroom environments acknowledging the importance of race (Howard, 2010). Research has shown using a color-blind discourse not only allows Whiteness to remain invisible as the measure of comparison to other races/ethnicities, it also disavows the importance of the histories and cultures of underrepresented groups (Applebaum, 2006). Moreover, as our schools continue to operate from a Eurocentric, middle-class framework, color blindness requires students of color to act upon the ideals of Whiteness while simultaneously allowing Whites to maintain their privilege (Bergerson, 2003; Guinier & Torres, 2002). Furthermore, operating from a color-blind ideology may misrepresent the realities of racism and promote acts of prejudice and discrimination toward persons of color (Schofield, 2010). Although color-blind policies claim to negate race as a consideration, in reality, the color-blind structures enable racism and even allow it to persist in more subtle ways (Bergerson, 2003). In a society as color conscious as ours, operating from a color-blind ideology is simply unrealistic (Pollock, 2004).

Educational leaders, and the programs preparing them, must be familiar with the theoretical constructs of color-blind ideologies. As one professor told us, "It's one thing to teach racial sensitivity and cultural understanding, but I feel like the students need something to anchor that in a little bit more and a deeper education in some of these issues . . . in terms of the understanding about the why." The acceptance of a color-blind agenda has serious ramifications for educational practitioners, as it inhibits the purposeful confrontation of critical issues concerning race and racism (Guinier & Torres, 2002). Such paralysis only exacerbates the inequities still present within today's public schools. Although it is important to name and become familiar with color-blind ideologies, it is even more important that preparation programs provide educational leaders with a pragmatic guide on how to confront these issues.

Misconceptions of Human Differences

Talking critically about the misconceptions of human differences is another important concept of diversity that should be integrated into the curriculum of leadership preparation programs. For many centuries, scientists have constructed the false notion that abilities are race-based. Thus social, economic, and educational disparities exist because certain races (Whites) are more intellectually capable than other races (non-Whites) (Pollock, 2008). This myth of intellectual capability is ever-present in contemporary society. Most notably, in their highly controversial book *The Bell Curve*, Richard Hernstein and Charles Murray (1996) suggest a correlation between race and intelligence, insinuating IQ is genetic. This notion falls in line with the idea of deficit thinking in education, where it is believed students, predominately low-income students of color, fail to succeed in school because of their family structure and background (Valencia, 1997).

In reality, the differences existing amongst the socially constructed categories of people we label as "races", from education to wealth to health, have nothing to do with genetics but rather with history and our social lives (Goodman, 2008; Haney Lopez, 1994; Pollock, 2008). Indeed, when the social construction of race was first employed, a racialized social structure was created to provide Europeans (Whites) with systemic privileges over non-Europeans (non-Whites). Over time, such structures spread globally allowing Europeans to "extend their reach" (Bonilla-Silva, 2010, p. 9). Within her work, Britzman (1998) cites Freud when explaining how the "narcissms of minor differences" determine how individuals imagine themselves as "members of a particular collectivity." She describes how tensions are not necessarily inherent within the actual joining of people, but in the actions taken to establish group differences. Not to dismiss differences, Britzman claims focusing on "minor" differences is not meant to trivialize the historical violences of hatred; instead, this focus highlights how such differences should signify the idea there is "no biological ground to the cultural dynamics and hatreds between and within communities" (p. 98). Exploring Freud's concern with the psychic investments of distinguishing self from other, Britzman considers how "differences within communities fashion relations between communities" (p. 101).

Today, the reproduction of White privilege and racial structures continue to exist so those in power are able to maintain their privilege and benefit from a position of dominance. Britzman (1998) claims if "anti-racist pedagogy is to be more than a consolation, it must make itself inconsolable by engaging with what it excludes, namely the complex and contradictory debates within communities over how communities are imagined and made subject to their own persistent questions" (p. 111). This challenge to anti-racist pedagogy must be acknowledged in the preparation of educational leaders. As leaders grapple with the differences in community, their own and others, it is important they "incite identifications and enlarge the geography of memory" so they are able to create environments that seek to address the exclusivities created through the narcissisms of minor difference (p. 111).

Merit-Based Achievement

The misconception resources are distributed based upon the merit of individuals (meritocracy) is another concept we believe should be included in the curriculum of educational leadership preparation programs. The theory behind education-based meritocracy looks at the relationship between the origin of individuals' socioeconomic status, their educational attainment levels, and their socioeconomic status in society. As individuals attain ideal education-based meritocracy, social mobility gradually increases; where it fails to do so can be attributed to "meritocratic reasons" (Goldthorpe, 2003, p. 235). Stated simply, if you work hard enough and "pull yourself up by your bootstraps," you can lift yourself out of a dire situation and ultimately achieve your personal and professional goals. However, what is often not taken into consideration is the realization not everyone is afforded the same opportunities to "rise to the top," and racial and socioeconomic privilege play fundamental roles in people's ability to "get ahead" in society. Individuals do not approach the starting line with the same economic, educational, and social opportunities (Milner, 2010), and discriminatory practices continue to shape institutions within our society. Indeed, the system currently in place does not operate to benefit everyone. Yet, many educational leaders believe success is merited, and thus consider the plight of those struggling to succeed to be a direct consequence of the choices they make and the lack of effort they put forward.

In her review of the literature on the role of principals meeting the needs of diverse students, Riehl (2000) found administrators to be "steeped in a structural-functionalist perspective viewing the existing social order as legitimate, that espouses the values of democracy and meritocracy, and that adopts a managerial orientation instead of a socially transformative one" (p. 58). School leaders often fail to recognize discriminatory structures built upon the social constructions of race are purposefully reproduced so the dominant race (Whites) is able to maintain their privileges in society. Maher and Tetreault (1998) state, "among the most powerful frameworks for maintaining the superiority of dominant voices, in the classroom and elsewhere, is the failure to understand the workings of Whiteness: how assumptions of Whiteness shape and even dictate the limits of discourse" (p. 138, as cited in Hytten & Warren, 2003). Further, many administrators avoid publicly admitting to the race-related problems that exist within their schools, even when they personally recognize the presence of such issues (Riehl, 2000).

In order to have a truly meritocratic society, increases in social mobility would *always* be directly correlated with individual achievement rather than social background. However, we know this to be false as children from more advantaged socioeconomic backgrounds that do not perform well educationally still manage to increase their social mobility due to their privileged access to resources (Goldthorpe, 2003). Further, educational opportunities for children across different racial/ethnic and socioeconomic groups continue to be unequal. Schools serving low-income students and students of color receive fewer resources, and thus have a more difficult time attracting highly qualified teachers which challenges their ability to address students' needs (Lee & Burkam, 2002). Thus, no matter how hard a student works toward achieving his/her goals, the systemic barriers existent within the educational system actually work to perpetuate inequalities within schools. Indeed, it would be false and detrimental on the part of school leaders to subscribe to a discourse promoting merit-based achievement as it fails to recognize the many complexities undergirding the ability for students to succeed in school and beyond.

The following sections examine the two practice-specific issues—*critical self-reflection* and *silences*—preparation programs must consider as they seek to address, both curricularly and pedagogically, each of the conceptual issues previously mentioned. More specifically, in order to successfully facilitate the rigorous examination of color-blind ideologies, misconceptions of human difference, and merit-based achievement, professors within leadership preparation programs must provide course offerings where critical self-reflection and the informed exploration of race-related silences are essential components.

BEYOND RECOGNITION: TWO PRACTICE-ORIENTED COMPONENTS OF AN ANTI-RACIST CURRICULUM

The historically present gap between theory and practice prompted hooks' (2003) remark that it is "easier for everyone in our nation to accept a critical written discourse about racism that is usually read only by those who have some degree of educational privilege than it is for us to create constructive ways to talk about White supremacy and racism, to find constructive actions that go beyond talk" (p. 29). Therefore, the following sections examine two practice-oriented concepts that provide the foundation necessary for educational leadership preparation programs to develop and implement the curricula and pedagogies able to provide school leaders with the dialogical skills necessary to facilitate anti-racist conversations.

Critical Self-Reflection

The field of adult learning has long addressed the importance of critical self-reflection in the education of democratic citizens (e.g., Brookfield, 1991, 1995; Mezirow, 1985, 1990; Taylor, 1993, 1998). In fact, Mezirow (2003) suggests the mere possibility of critically-oriented discourse is dependent upon two learning capabilities specific to adults: *critical self-reflection* (Kegan, 2000) and *reflective judgment* (King & Kitchner, 1994). It is the nurturing of each of these cognitive exercises that lead to "transformative" learning experiences, the learning that allows for the development of adult educators and activists able to foster the "social, economic, and political conditions required for fuller, freer participation in critical reflection and discourse by all adults in a democratic society" (Mezirow, 2003, p. 63).

The valued role of critical self-reflection in the development of socially conscious educators and activists has also been an important topic within the field of educational leadership. Dantley (2008), in a speech challenging the traditional paradigms historically structuring leadership preparation programs, suggested principled leadership[2] cannot exist without the presence of its most essential ingredient, critical self-reflection. For Dantley, critical self-reflection is viewed as a specific type of cognitive exercise that "questions the democracy of decisions and administrative practices" in ways that trouble the "perpetuation of classism, racism, homophobia, ageism, ableism, and other markers of individual or collective identity" (p. 456). Brown (2004, 2006) and Ridenour (2004) also promote critical self-reflection, asking future school leaders to examine their own values and beliefs through the writing of cultural autobiographies and reflective analysis journals. Such activities allow students to gain insight into their feelings about race, social class, gender, sexual orientation, and inclusion, hopefully altering a priori values and beliefs in ways that can impact social change. Hernandez and Marshall (2009) use self-reflections in their educational leadership preparation classrooms much in the same way as Brown (2004, 2006), posing questions to students that force them to consider their values and beliefs, how these values and beliefs were learned, and how this learned knowledge translates into their leadership practices in schools. However, if preparation programs expect to facilitate the development of what Dantley (2008), Brown (2004, 2006), Hernandez and Marshall (2009), and Ridenour (2004) consider to be socially just leaders, professors within such programs must learn *how* to better facilitate conversations encouraging the persistent exercise of critical self-reflection in a way that extends well beyond the walls of their university classrooms.

While the field of educational leadership has often addressed the importance of *why* a socially conscious and critically reflective pedagogy is important, there must be a more concerted effort to examine *how* this type of pedagogy can be developed and implemented within leadership preparation programs. With this in mind, the re-visiting of Paulo Freire's (2000) notion of a "problem-posing" education is necessary as scholars seek to push the field toward the more active development and implementation of critically conscious curricula and pedagogies. Freire's notion of a problem-posing pedagogy is based upon his broader critique of the "banking concept of education."

> In the banking concept of education, knowledge is a gift bestowed by those who consider themselves knowledgeable upon those whom they consider to know nothing. Projecting an absolute ignorance onto others, a characteristic of the ideology of oppression, negates education and knowledge as a process of inquiry. (p. 72)

Thus, Freire's argument is a student's "critical consciousness" is unable to develop appropriately in an educative setting where she/he is simply considered to be the objective recipient of a teacher's deposited knowledge. Viewed as a critical alternative to educational banking, Freire suggests the possibilities of a problem-posing pedagogy that facilitates the collaborative development of the critically cognitive conscious. Within this model, students/teachers must realize their roles as "critical co-investigators" in a reflexive dialogue founded upon the persistent questioning of social realities. A problem-posing pedagogy replaces the traditional authoritative dichotomy between teacher/student with a collaborative model where both students and teachers cooperate in the critical intervention of social injustices. As educational leadership preparation programs seek to develop critically conscious and self-reflective practitioners, the professors involved must recognize and understand how to navigate the ways in which race-related silences can stymie such efforts.

The Interrogation of Silenced Voices

Critical self-reflective practices, while an essential component of anti-racist efforts in the classroom, often emphasize the "out loud" consideration of race-related issues. Consequently, such conversations may overshadow the meanings that underlie race-related silences. Researchers have identified a number of issues that may contribute to existence of silences in conversations concerning race, such as feelings of oppression or fear (Ladson-Billings, 1996; Mazzei, 2007), desires to resist (Ladson-Billings, 1996), maintenance of privilege (Mazzei, 2007, 2011), and feelings of guilt (Giroux, 1997).

Recognizing the detrimental consequences of silenced voices in an anti-racist classroom, scholars have acknowledged the importance of developing pedagogical practices that allow practitioners to examine how and why race-related silences occur (e.g., Ladson-Billings, 1996; Mazzei, 2007; Schultz, 2003). Yet, while such practices may contribute to a more purposeful focus on race within educational leadership preparation courses, the critical penetration of race-related silences in the classroom, though important, must be approached in a cautious manner. As highlighted in the conversation between Freire and Macedo (1995), the structural inclusion of a dialogical model where all students are forced to move beyond silence may in fact interfere with the intended purposes of such silences, thus imposing an inauthentic enactment of democracy.

Ladson-Billings (1996), noting not all race-related silences should be construed as a negative occurrence, suggests while teachers have a responsibility to probe the silences of students they must also consider the ways in which they are themselves complicit in the creation of such silences. Therefore, educational leaders in the twenty-first century must skillfully interact with diverse populations (Tatum, 2007). The failure to equip leaders with the conversational skills necessary to interrogate race-related silences may prevent the critical addressing of racial biases that continue to obstruct excellence and equity in diverse school communities (Singleton & Linton, 2005).

IMPLICATIONS FOR THE FIELD

In 2009, President Barack Obama and Secretary of Education Arne Duncan unveiled their revision of the Title I School Improvement Grant (SIG) program. As a $3.5 billion commitment to the improvement of chronically low-performing public schools, the issuance of the revised SIG heightened the already existent scrutiny of educational leaders and principal preparation programs. Subsequently, as educational leaders continue to be scrutinized on their ability to "turn around" schools most often nested in metropolitan areas where students of color are the primary population (Noguera & Wells, 2011), leadership preparation programs must address the fundamental gap existing between theories which *recognize* the importance of preparing leaders to meet the needs of diverse populations, and actions that *ensure* the development and implementation of curricula and pedagogies necessary for leaders of diverse school communities.

Although a great deal of research has addressed how issues of social justice should be included in educational leadership programs to successfully prepare school leaders to lead in diverse settings (Blackmore, 2009; Brown, 2004, 2006; Dantley, 2002; Grogan & Andrews, 2002; Jean-Marie, 2010; Jean-Marie, Normore, & Brooks, 2009; Marshall & Oliva, 2006; McKenzie et al., 2008; Theoharis, 2007, 2009, 2010; Tillman, 2004), less research has focused on how such programs implement and center anti-racist curricula and pedagogies within their coursework to prepare school leaders to discuss issues of race and racism within the schools they will eventually lead.

We have proposed in this chapter five critical concepts we believe must be addressed in leadership preparation programs when preparing leaders to engage in and practice every day anti-racism (Pollock, 2008). Both conceptual and practical, we believe these concepts can help transform leadership preparation programs in regards to how future leaders are asked to think about issues of race and racism (e.g., color-blind ideology, merit-based achievement, misconceptions of human difference) as well as provide tools (e.g., critical self-reflection, interrogation of silenced voices) assisting them in working through and wrestling with their own assumptions about diversity and its impact on education. Although challenging at times, conversations confronting the dilemmas of race, culture, and diversity in education must be focal points in preparation programs if we are truly committed to equity and equality for all students. Although not inclusive, these concepts can serve as a guide for faculty seeking to develop an anti-racist curriculum for leadership preparation programs able to address issues germane to the changing landscape of today's public schools.

IMPLEMENTATION STRATEGIES: PREPARING LEADERS FOR DIVERSE COMMUNITIES

Revisiting the importance of the conceptual and practice-oriented concepts we consider to be essential for those programs preparing educational leaders for diverse communities reinforces the premise of this chapter: educational leaders choosing to work in diverse schools settings must be provided with a rigorous and critically-oriented curriculum that promotes the critically reflective examination of the ideologies/concepts that often limit and/or block anti-racist discussions from occurring. Thus, it is important we conclude the chapter by addressing hooks' (2003) call to move beyond recognition by providing a constructive focus on strategies that can be implemented within educational leadership programs.

The critical examination of issues pertaining to race and racism must be a central component to all courses within leadership preparation programs. Although educational leaders are likely to encounter a school population in which

15% of the students speak English as a second language and 40% identify as members of racial/ethnic groups (Darling-Hammond, 2006, p. 301), research from the 2007–2008 school year shows approximately 82.9% of public school teachers were White, 6.9% Black, 7.2% Hispanic, and 2.9% other, which includes Asian, Native Hawaiian/Pacific Islander, American Indian/Alaska Native, and two or more races. These statistics have remained stable since the 1999–2000 school year, as approximately 84.6% of public school teachers were White, 7.3% Black, 5.6% Hispanic, and 2.4% other (Aud et al., 2011). Racial/ethnic demographics for public school principals in the 2007–2008 school year closely mirror those of public school teachers with 82.4% of these leaders being White, 9.7% Black, 5.9% Hispanic, and 2.1% other. Again, as is the case with public school teachers, the racial/ethnic demographics for public school principals has remained nearly the same since the 1999–2000 school year; approximately 83.9% of principals were White, 9.8% Black, 4.7% Hispanic, and 1.6% other (Aud et al., 2011).

Persons responsible for the further development of educational leadership preparation programs must recognize the cultural, ethnic, and racial disconnect that exists between the populations of students being served and the population of leaders being prepared. Beyond the purposeful recruitment of a more diverse group of educational leaders, programs must conduct a detailed audit of their programmatic offerings to determine if spaces to address race and racism exist and are in operation. Programs must also seek to establish spaces in *all* of their courses, not just the few focused on diversity, multiculturalism, and social justice, for their students to grapple with their own assumptions as to how racism continues to permeate the discourse of educational leadership.

Three conceptually critical issues—color-blind ideology, misconceptions of human difference, and merit-based achievement—must be embedded in the curricula structuring leadership preparation classes. The curricular offerings of educational leadership preparation programs often fail to provide students with the contextually specific knowledge necessary to address issues of diversity (Hawley & James, 2010). Therefore, educational leaders must be exposed to contextually relevant issues such as color-blind ideology, misconceptions of human difference, and merit-based achievement if they are expected to effectively lead diverse school communities. Avoiding the critical examination of these three concepts can contribute to the creation of hostile learning environments that disallow the development of an anti-racist education.

Programs should conduct a detailed audit of their course offerings in order to determine how contextually specific issues pertaining to the three aforementioned concepts are specifically addressed within the curricula structuring the program. Upon determination, curricular gaps must be addressed by weaving the examination of such concepts throughout the entire scope and sequence.

Professors seeking to implement an anti-racist curriculum must incorporate two-practice specific concepts—critical self-reflection and interrogation of silences—into their pedagogical offerings. Mezirow (2003) suggests transformative learning experiences are dependent upon the development of two learning capabilities specific to adults: *critical self-reflection* (Kegan, 2000) and *reflective judgment* (King & Kitchner, 1994). Yet, while employing practices that encourage the "out loud" critical-self examination of race-related issues in the classroom is a necessary component of anti-racist educational offerings, such practices may preclude the thoughtful examination of meanings underlying the race-specific silences of both professors and students.

Programs desirous of establishing an anti-racist focus for developing school leaders must provide professional development that further exposes faculty to the pedagogical constructs required to successfully facilitate the implementation of critically self-reflective conversational strategies and those strategies allowing professors and students to thoughtfully examine the existence of race-related silences in the classroom.

Scholars within the field of educational leadership must conduct research efforts that move beyond the naming of race-related problems by conducting research efforts that contribute to the active development and implementation of anti-racist strategies in the classroom. Though a number of scholars within the field of educational leadership have addressed the importance of preparing leaders for social justice (Blackmore, 2009; Jean-Marie, 2010; Jean-Marie, Normore, & Brooks, 2009; Marshall & Oliva, 2006; McKenzie et al., 2008; Theoharis, 2007, 2009, 2010), there is an absence of research focused upon *how* educational leaders should plan for and implement social justice oriented conversations, particularly conversations founded upon anti-racist themes. The failure to translate anti-racist concerns from theory to practice contributes to the development of educational leaders that, while cognizant of racial inequities in educational attainment, attribute educational such gaps to external factors (Singleton & Linton, 2005). Consequently, the externalization of blame allows educational leaders to sidestep critical reflections about their personal and professional responsibilities, further institutionalizing the racial biases already present within school communities.

Scholars in the field of educational leadership should revisit the work of innovative scholars who have attempted to cross the divide between anti-racist theory and anti-racist practice (e.g., Milner, 2010; Pollock, 2010; Singleton & Linton, 2005; Theoharis, 2010). Additionally, scholars must conduct more empirically driven research projects that seek to assess and refine anti-racist strategies already in existence.

NOTES

1. According to the U.S. Census Bureau, a "metropolitan area contains a core urban area of 50,000 or more population, consists of one or more counties, and includes the counties containing the core urban area, as well as any adjacent counties that have a high degree of social and economic integration (as measured by commuting to work) with the urban core." Retrieved July 19, 2011 from *http://www.census.gov/population/www/metroareas/metroarea.html*

2. Principled leadership is one of the three categories—principled, pragmatic, purposeful—of educational leadership Dantley (2008) believes to be grounded in Cornel West's prophetic spirituality. In principled leadership there is an "ethic of justice and critique" where the standard is rooted in treating "all students, and in fact all members of the learning community, in a socially just way" (p. 455).

REFERENCES

Applebaum, B. (2006). Race ignore-ance, colortalk, and white complicity: White is...white isn't. *Educational Theory, 56*(3), 345–362.

Aud, S., Hussar, W., Kena, G., Bianco, K., Frohlich, L., Kemp, J., & Tahan, K. (2011). The condition of education 2011 (NCES 2011–033). U.S. Department of Education, National Center for Education Statistics. Washington, DC: U.S. Government Printing Office.

Bergerson, A. A. (2003). Critical race theory and white racism: Is there room for white scholars in fighting racism in education? *Qualitative Studies in Education, 16*(1), 51–63.

Blackmore, J. (2009). Leadership for social justice: A transnational dialogue. *Journal of Research on Leadership Education, 4*(1), 1–10.

Bonilla-Silva, E. (2010). *Racism without racists: Color-blind racism and the persistence of racial inequality in America.* (3rd ed.). Lanham, MD: Rowman & Littlefield Publishers, Inc.

Britzman, D. (1998). *Lost subjects, contested objects: Toward a psychoanalytic inquiry of learning.* Albany, NY: State University of New York Press.

Brookfield, S. (1995). *Becoming a critically reflective teacher.* San Francisco, CA: Jossey-Bass.

Brookfield, S. D. (1991). The development of critical reflection in adulthood. *New Education, 13*(1), 39–48.

Brown, K. M. (2004). Leadership for social justice and equity: Weaving a transformative framework and pedagogy. *Educational Administration Quarterly, 40*(1), 77–108.

Brown, K. M. (2006). Leadership for social justice and equity: Evaluating a transformative framework and andragogy. *Educational Administration Quarterly, 42*(5), 700–745.

Brown, M. K., Carnoy, M., Currie, E., Duster, T., Oppenheimer, D. B., Shultz, M. M., & Wellman, D. (2003). *Whitewashing race: The myth of a color-blind society.* Berkeley, CA: University of California Press.

Carpenter, B. W., & Diem, S. (2010). *Narrative explorations of race and racism: Interrogating the education of tomorrow's leaders.* Paper presented at the 2010 American Educational Research Association Annual Meeting, Denver, CO.

Carpenter, B. W., & Diem, S. (2011). *Talking about race in the classroom: An examination of the ways professors facilitate critical conversations with future educational leaders.* Paper presented at the 2011 American Educational Research Association Annual Meeting, New Orleans, LA.

Dantley, M. E. (2002). Uprooting and replacing positivism, the melting pot, multiculturalism, and other impotent notions in educational leadership through an African American perspective. *Education and Urban Society, 34*(3), 334–352.

Dantley, M. E. (2008). The 2007 Willower Family Lecture reconstructing leadership: Embracing a spiritual dimension. *Leadership and Policy in Schools, 7*(4), 451–460.

Darling-Hammond, L. (2006). Constructing 21st-century teacher education. *Journal of Teacher Education, 57*(3), 300–314.

Flagg, B. J. (1993). "Was blind but now I see": White race consciousness and the requirement of discriminatory intent. *Michigan Law Review, 91*(5), 953–1017.

Freire, P. (2000). *Pedagogy of the oppressed* (M. B. Ramos, Trans., 31 ed.). New York, NY: The Continuum Publishing Company.

Freire, P., & Macedo, D. P. (1995). A dialogue: Culture, language, and race. *Harvard Educational Review, 65*(3), 377–402.

Giroux, H. A. (1997). Rewriting the discourse of racial identity: Towards a pedagogy and politics of whiteness. *Harvard Educational Review, 67*(2), 285–320.

Goldthorpe, J. (2003). The myth of education-based meritocracy: Why the theory isn't working. *New Economy, 10*(4), 234–239.

Goodman, A. H. (2008). Exposing race as an obsolete biological concept. In M. Pollock (Ed.), *Everyday anti-racism* (pp. 4–8). New York, NY: The New Press.

Grogan, M., & Andrews, R. (2002). Defining preparation and professional development for the future. *Educational Administration Quarterly, 38*(2), 233–256.

Guinier, L., & Torres, G. (2002). *The miner's canary: Enlisting race, resisting power, transforming democracy.* Cambridge, MA: Harvard University Press.

Haney Lopez, I. F. (1994). The social construction of race: Some observations on illusion, fabrication, and choice. *Harvard Civil Rights—Civil Liberties Law Review, 29*(1), 1–62.

Hawley, W., & James, R. (2010). Diversity-responsive school leadership. *UCEA Review, 52*(3), 1–5.

Hernandez, F., & Marshall, J. M. (2009). "Where I came from, where I am now, and where I'd like to be": Aspiring administrators reflect on issues related to equity, diversity, and social justice. *Journal of School Leadership, 19*(3), 299–233.

Hernstein, R. J., & Murray, C. (1996). *The bell curve: Intelligence and class structure in American life.* New York, NY: Free Press Paperbacks.

hooks, b. (1994). *Teaching to transgress: Education as the practice of freedom.* New York, NY: Routledge.

hooks, b. (2003). *Teaching community: A pedagogy of hope.* New York, NY: Routledge.

Horsford, S. D. (2010). *New perspectives in educational leadership: Exploring social, political, and community contexts and meaning.* New York, NY: Peter Lang Publishing Group.

Howard, T. (2010). *Why race and culture matter in schools: Closing the achievement gap in America's classrooms.* New York, NY: Teachers College Press.

Hytten, K., & Warren, J. T. (2003). Engaging whiteness: How racial power gets reified in education. *International Journal of Qualitative Studies in Education, 16* (1), 65–89.

Jean-Marie, G. (2010). "Fire in the belly": Igniting a social justice discourse in learning environments of leadership preparation. In A. K. Tooms & C. Boske (Eds.), *Bridge leadership: Connecting educational leadership and social justice to improve schools* (pp. 97–124). Charlotte, NC: Information Age Publishing, Inc.

Jean-Marie, G., Normore, A., & Brooks, J. S. (2009). Leadership for social justice: Preparing 21st century school leaders for a new social order. *Journal of Research on Leadership in Education, 4*(1), 1–31.

Kegan, R. (2000). What "form" transforms? A constructive-developmental approach to transformative learning. In J. Mezirow (Ed.), *Learning as transformation: Critical perspectives on a theory in* progress (pp. 35–69). San Francisco, CA: Jossey-Bass.

King, P. M., & Kitchener, K. S. (1994). *Developing reflective judgment.* San Francisco, CA: Jossey-Bass.

Ladson-Billings, G. (1996). Silences as weapons: Challenges of a Black professor teaching white students. *Theory Into Practice, 35*(2), 79–85.

Lee, V. E., & Burkam, D. T. (2002). *Inequality at the starting gate.* Washington, DC: Economic Policy Institute.

López, G. R. (2003). The (racially neutral) politics of education: A Critical Race Theory perspective. *Educational Administration Quarterly, 39*(1), 68–94.

Maher, F., & Tetreault, M. K. T. (1998). "They got the paradigm and painted it white": Whiteness and pedagogies of positionality. In J. L. Kincheloe, S. R. Steinberg, N. M. Rodriguez, & R. E. Chennault (Eds.), *White reign: Deploying whiteness in America* (pp. 137–158). New York, NY: St. Martin's Press.

Marshall, C., & Oliva, M. (2006). *Leadership for social justice: Making revolutions in education.* Boston, MA: Pearson.

Mazzei, L. A. (2007). *Inhabited silence in qualitative research: Putting poststructural theory to work* (Vol. 318). New York, NY: Peter Lang Publishing Group.

Mazzei, L. A. (2011). Desiring silence: Gender, race, and pedagogy in education. *British Education Research Journal, 37*(4), 657–669.

McKenzie, K., Christman, D., Hernandez, F., Fierro, E., Capper, C., Dantley, M., Gonzalez, M., Cambron-McCabe, N., & Scheurich, J. (2008). Educating leaders for social justice: A design for a comprehensive, social justice leadership preparation program. *Educational Administration Quarterly, 44*(1), 111–138.

Mezirow, J. (1985). A critical theory of self-directed learning. In S. Brookfield (Ed.), *Self-directed learning: From theory to practice* (*New directions for continuing education, Number 25),* (pp. 63–74). San Francisco, CA: Jossey-Bass.

Mezirow, J. (1990). *Fostering critical reflection in adulthood: A guide to transformative and emancipatory learning.* San Francisco, CA: Jossey-Bass.

Mezirow, J. (2003). Transformative learning as discourse. *Journal of Transformative Education, 1*(1), 58.

Milner, IV, R. H. (2010). What does teacher education have to do with teaching? Implications for diversity studies. *Journal of Teacher Education, 61*(1–2), 118–131.

Noguera, P. A., & Wells, L. (2011). The politics of school reform: A broader and bolder approach to Newark. *Berkeley Review of Education, 2*(1), 5–25.

Orr, M. T., & Orphanos, S. (2011). How graduate-level preparation influences the effectiveness of school leaders: A comparison of the outcomes of exemplary and conventional leadership preparation programs for principals. *Educational Administration Quarterly, 47*(1), 18–70.

Parker, L., & Shapiro, J. (1992). Where is the discussion of diversity in educational administration programs? Graduate student voices addressing an omission in their preparation. *Journal of School Leadership, 2*(1), 7–33.

Pollock, M. (2004). *Colormute: Race talk dilemmas in an American school.* Princeton, NJ: Princeton University Press.

Pollock, M. (2008). *Everyday antiracism: Getting real about race in school.* New York, NY: The New Press.

Pollock, M. (2010). Engaging race issues with colleagues: Strengthening our professional communities through everyday inquiry. *MASCD Perspectives*—Online, Winter 2010. Publication of the Massachusetts Association of Supervision and Curriculum Development.

Ridenour, C. S. (2004). Finding the horizon: Education administration students paint a landscape of cultural diversity in schools. *Journal of School Leadership, 14*(1), 4–31.

Riehl, C. J. (2000). The principal's role in creating inclusive schools for diverse students: A review of normative, empirical, and critical literature on the practice of educational administration. *Review of Educational Research, 70*(1), 55–81.

Ryan, J. (2003). Educational administrators' perceptions of racism in diverse contexts. *Race Ethnicity and Education, 6*(2), 145–164.

Schofield, J. W. (2010). International evidence on ability grouping with curriculum differentiation and the achievement gap in secondary schools. *Teachers College Record, 112* (5), 1490–1526.

Schultz, K. (2003). *Listening: A framework for teaching across difference.* New York, NY: Teachers College Press.

Singleton, G. E., & Linton, C. (2005). *Courageous conversations about race: A field guide for achieving equity in schools.* Thousand Oaks, CA: Corwin Press.

Tatum, B. (2007). *Can we talk about race? And other conversations in an era of school resegregation.* Boston, MA: Beacon Press.

Taylor, E. W. (1993). A learning model for becoming interculturally competent. *International Journal of Intercultural Relations, 18*(3), 389–408.

Taylor, E. W. (1998). Transformative learning: A critical review. *ERIC Clearinghouse on adult, career, and vocational education* (Information Series No. 374), 80 pages.

Theoharis, G. (2007). Social justice educational leaders and resistance: Toward a theory of social justice leadership. *Educational Administration Quarterly, 43*(2), 221.

Theoharis, G. (2009). *The school leaders our children deserve: Seven keys to equity, social justice, and school reform.* New York, NY: Teachers College Press.

Theoharis, G. (2010). Sustaining social justice: Strategies urban principals develop to advance justice and equity while facing resistance. *International Journal of Urban Educational Leadership, 4*(1), 92–110.

Tillman, L. C. (2004). (Un)Intendend consequences? The impact of the *Brown v. Board of Education* decision on the employment status of Black educators. *Education and Urban Society, 36*(3), 280–303.

Valencia, R. R. (Ed.). (1997). *The evolution of deficit thinking: Educational thought and practice.* London: Falmer Press.

Wilson, W. J. (2010). The Obama administration's proposals to address concentrated urban poverty. *City & Community, 9*(1), 41–49.

Young, M. D., & Laible, J. (2000). White racism, antiracism, and school leader preparation. *Journal of School Leadership, 10,* 374–415.

CHAPTER 2

PERSISTENCE IS CHESS, NOT CHECKERS

A Counterstory on the Lives and Strategies of Six African American Administrators at One Predominantly White Institution

Brandon L. Wolfe
Auburn University

There seems to be a growing conspiracy of silence surrounding the experiences of the disproportionate number of African American administrators working in predominantly White colleges and universities. For many African American administrators, the silenced narrative is a gauntlet of retention and professional advancement seemingly undermined by keywords such as diversity and affirmative action. A close examination of the research aimed at the status of African Americans in higher education reveals a large proportion has been directed towards the areas of retention for students and faculty only (Holmes, 2004; Jackson, 2001; 2002; Perna, Gerald, Baum, & Milem, 2007). Scholarship on African American administrators in higher

Confronting Racism in Higher Education, pages 21–41
Copyright © 2013 by Information Age Publishing
All rights of reproduction in any form reserved.

education has been relegated to either student affairs practitioners or to administrative roles directly related to the diversity mission of the institution (Rolle, Davies, & Banning, 2000; Holmes, 2004; Jackson, 2004; Watson, 2001). As a result, I beg the question, "Why are there so few African American administrators at Primarily White Institutions (PWIs), and how are they persisting?" Upon review, the literature suggests that either there is a small African American graduation pipeline for administrators, or the challenges of certain "isms" have deterred their decision to persist within the academy (Perna et al., 2007; Holmes, 2004; Jackson, 2002, 2004). With this being accepted as the dominant narrative on the poor representation of African American administrators, a scholarship gap exists. In particular, how are the few remaining African American administrators at PWIs able to persist?

STATEMENT OF PURPOSE

The purpose of this study is to gain an understanding of the experiences and persistence strategies used by African American administrators serving at a PWI located in the South. Because this topic involves a subjective state of knowing—an exploration of strategies developed as a response to the participants' interpreted experiences—a qualitative study was the most appropriate choice. The results of this study will provide more insight into the experiences and the persistence strategies employed by African American administrators at a PWI. To do so, however, it is essential to contextualize the African American administrator experience in higher education by providing a historical overview. Researchers such as Gregory (1995) and Wilson (1989) have advocated that in order to understand the uniqueness of the African American experience in higher education, a historical framework is needed to situate their academic life within an institutional culture originally designed to benefit White males (Brubacher & Rudy, 1997; Holmes, 2004). Furthermore, a historical overview provides an illustration of the culture, habits, decisions, practices, and policies that have perpetuated White privilege within higher education (Stanley, 2006).

HISTORY

Evidence suggests that there is a long-standing connection between historical ideologies of injustice and higher education access, equal opportunity, and career mobility related to people of color (Holmes, 1999, 2003). Prior to the 1960s it was understood that the small number of African American faculty and administrators represented in higher education at PWIs was most likely attributed to deliberate exclusionary practices (Smith, 1980).

The rise of African American administrators on college campuses originated out of the student civil rights protests of the 1960s (Jones, 1997). As Smith (1993) notes:

> Black administrators were hired to pacify the Black community and/or to demonstrate that the hiring institution is an "equal opportunity employer," neither of which is legitimate; the leadership which they could provide based on their knowledge of a given issue is neither accepted not respected by those who must be influenced. (p. 64)

Furthermore, the impetus for hiring African American administrators resulted from affirmative action orders backed by the federal government. All employers, including institutions of higher education, who received federal contracts of at least $50,000 and had 50 employees were required to end discrimination based on race, creed, national origin, or sex and were required to develop affirmative action programs to ensure that all groups of people were hired at a rate their availability in the workforce would suggest (Fleming, Gill, & Swinton, 1978). In 1971, Executive Order 11246 united affirmative action mandates to higher educational institutions to provide broad-based access to all areas of the academy for African Americans and other minority groups (Washington & Harvey, 1989).

Access through affirmative action did not always translate into ongoing acceptance or guaranteed access within PWIs. As the federal government became involved in higher education during the 1970s, there have been improvements in minority participation (Brubacher & Rudy, 1997). However, many of the executive orders ratified in the mid1960s and early 1970s were nullified in the 1980s during the Reagan administration (Washington & Harvey, 1989). Furthermore, Washington and Harvey (1989) contend that historically White institutions have regressed in their efforts to retain African Americans and other people of color in all areas of the academy. Kawewe (1997) adds that colleges and universities began to devise sophisticated internal mechanisms to subvert affirmative action in recruitment, hiring, retention, and promotion. Meanwhile in some states, such as California and Texas, the institutions' reliance on affirmative action has been called into question and even suspended (McCutcheon & Lindsey, 2004).

In the 1990s, reports from national conferences, symposia, workshops, and research findings revealed that African Americans in all areas of the academy were exiting the academy as fast as they entered because of certain "-isms" against them (Holmes, 2004; Holmes, Ebbers, Robinson, & Mugenda, 2000; Phelps 1995). Further, when explored, African Americans have cited inhospitable campus environments, isolation, alienation, marginalization, unrealistic role expectations, limited advancement opportunities, feelings of powerlessness, tokenism, and the lack of mentoring and sponsorship as reasons for leaving (Burgess, 1997; Gregory, 1995; Holmes,

1999; Moses, 1997; Phelps, 1995; Watson, 2001). Oliver and Davis (1994) also noted that the retention of African American administrators in PWIs is short-lived because of the personal harassment and indignity they face in the discharge of normal duties. These findings are important because they reveal areas of needed improvement and enable us to examine the current status of African American administrators within a historical context.

RESEARCH DESIGN

The study utilizes a phenomenological approach to qualitative inquiry that focuses on understanding and describing the "lived experiences" of individuals who all share the experience of a common phenomenon, or have been exposed to a parallel set of conditions (Creswell, 2003, 2007). The phenomenon is a narrative of underrepresented African American administrators persisting at the same PWI. The goal of the phenomenological account is to gather the essence of a person or group of people and describe what they have experienced, how they have experienced it, and how they internalize and interpret various effects relative to the phenomenon (Moustakas, 1994). As Collins (1990) and Leedy (1997) contend, a person's reality is shaped within a cultural, social, political, and economic landscape that determines how they perceive their reality in relation to the events that occur around them.

In addition to phenomenology, the study also employed the use of a Critical Race Theory (CRT) element called *counter-storytelling*. Solórzano and Yosso (2002) define counter-storytelling as a "method of telling the stories of those people whose experiences are not often told" including people of color, women, gay men, lesbians, and the poor (p. 26). There are three different types of counter-stories: personal stories, other people's stories, and composite stories. The third was selected for this chapter because it relies on data collected from multiple individuals of color who have experienced a phenomenon within a particular context. The aim of composite stories is to represent the often disregarded experiences of a larger group through a subset of "characters" who represent them. Overall, the goal is to challenge the aspect of White privilege that claims 'neutral' research and "objective" researchers, while exposing the *majoritan narratives* that silences and distorts epistemologies of people of color (Ladson-Billings, 1998). Majoritan narratives are dominant accounts that are often accepted as universal truths about particular groups which results in negative characterizations (e.g., African Americans males are irresponsible and lazy). While majoritan narratives speak from a standpoint of authority and universality in which the experiences of one group (Whites) are held to be normal, standard, and universal; counter-stories serve to undermine racist, sexist, homophobic, and classist narratives. Counter-stories facilitate social, political, and cultural cohesion, as well as survival and resistance among marginalized groups (DeCuir & Dixson, 2004). In this study, counter-storytelling is used to gain insight into the experiences of full-time African American administrators and their persistence strategies (which are not often shared).

Given that the majoritan narrative on African American administrators focuses almost exclusively on the challenges that cause them to exit the academy, counter-stories demonstrating their persistence was the aim of this study. Therefore, the composite characters in this study reject commonly held assumptions regarding their ability to persist in spite of the challenges faced as African American administrators in a PWI. Instead, they show how each experience has honed their persistence strategy to move forward.

Sample and Data Collection

The six contributing participants were solicited via the purposeful sampling method of criterion sampling (Patton, 2002). Six mid to high level full time African American administrators were selected as participants for the study (Patton, 2001). A small sample size is generally used by qualitative researchers because of the rigorous and systematic methodology. Six participants were chosen because it is the recommended sample size for a phenomenological study (Creswell, 1998; Morse, 1994). Also, according to Polit, Beck, and Hungler (2001), phenomenology studies are typically based on samples of 10 or fewer.

The site university's Office of Institutional Research helped to identify African American administrators with a minimum of mid level standing and at least four years service as a university administrator—which served as the criteria. The term *university administrator* refers to an individual in a managerial or policy-making capacity that may have a line or staff function (Jackson, 2004). Typically, administration levels of higher education are broken down into three specialty areas: academic affairs (president, academic dean, vice president, or provost of research), student affairs (vice president of student affairs, dean of students, and director of financial aid), and administrative affairs (vice president of finance, director of alumni affairs, and director of computer services) (Sagaria, 1988). Participants were selected from all university administration areas from the same institution: three academic affairs administrators, two student affairs administrators, and one administrative affairs administrator. Of the participants, three are male and three are female. Each participant offered rich information and personal accounts of their experiences with the majority culture, and how that influenced their method of persistence as one of the few African American administrators within a PWI. Assuming that the criteria hold true, it is conceivable that much can be learned from accessing the narratives of these participants.

Open ended interview questions (both semistructured and informal in depth) were the primary method of data collection (Patton, 2002). The researcher used an audio recorder to obtain and ensure interview data accuracy. Each participant was interviewed at least twice. Each interview lasted between 60 and 90 minutes in the participant's office. A journal was kept to document the descriptions, thoughts, and interpretations of the interviews. Both the audio recordings and the journal assisted in the follow up interview and analysis. After each interview, the researcher transcribed the audio recording into a Word document verbatim, and e-mailed each participant's individual transcript interview to the appropriated participant for their review, verification, and validation (document review). A corresponding letter was attached requesting that each participant review the document, make changes, and note any questions they may have from personal reflection between then and the follow-up interview. Follow-up interviews were conducted for *member checking*, clarity, data validation, and additional questions. Member checking is a term used to determine the trustworthiness of the data analysis. By participating in member checking, study participants have the opportunity to review the researcher's conclusions to ensure that they accurately depict the participants' personal experiences (Creswell, 1998). Also, this second interview is an opportunity for participants to provide any additional information that was not provided in the previous meetings (commentary).

Data Analysis

Data analysis in qualitative research can be defined as consisting of three action steps: *data reduction, data display,* and *conclusion drawing and verification* which are present in parallel during and after the collection of data (Miles & Huberman, 1994). First, data reduction refers to the process of selecting, focusing, simplifying, abstracting, and transforming the collected data. It must be reduced and simplified in order to make the data more readily accessible and understandable (Kvale, 1996). Second, data display is used to organize the collected data in such a way that it permits conclusion drawing (Miles & Huberman, 1994). Lastly, the third component of the data analysis process is conclusion drawing and verification. During the collection of data, there should not be made any definitive conclusions, and these preliminary conclusions should be verified during the process (Miles & Huberman, 1994).

Once the interviews were completed and all other data had been collected, participant code names were changed, information was separated into color-coded folders, and all other possible identifiers were removed. This aforementioned method is introduced in order to minimize potential bias while analyzing and interpreting data. Afterwards, each interview was transcribed verbatim, the researcher engaged in data reduction to better analyze and code transcriptions for themes. As Krueger and Casey (2000) contend, the analysis should be systematic, sequential, verifiable, and continuous. Following this path provides a trail of evidence, increases the extent of dependability, consistency, and conformability of the data (Lincoln & Guba, 1989).

The first step in providing a trail of evidence is using a clear procedure of data analysis so that the process is clearly documented and understood. Interviews are separated into segments by reading and re-reading the transcripts thoroughly for readily identifiable themes and patterns as related to the phenomenon. Notes were generated in the margins and categorized as the analysis transitioned into the second step—coding. According to Bogdan and Biklen (1998):

> Developing a coding system involved several steps: You search through your data for regularities and patterns as well as for topics your data cover, and then you write down words and phrases to represent these topics and patterns. These words and phrases are coding categories. They are a means of sorting the descriptive data you have collected so that the material bearing on a given topic can be physically separated from other data. (p. 171)

Once initial codes were developed, audio recorded interviews were replayed while following transcripts in order to understand and recapture what was being discussed in the interviews. Close attention was paid to the comments and the manner in which they were stated.

Further, transcribed interviews were reviewed multiple times for emerging patterns and themes. Following the procedures outlined by Moustakas (1994), I extracted significant statements from each transcript and organized these statements into clusters of meanings (vertical analysis). An initial analysis, or summary, was written for each interview and given back to the participants for member checking purposes. Once the initial analysis for each participant was reviewed, all significant statements were analyzed across interviews (horizontal analysis). The clusters of meanings were then identified as fitting into two separate categories, *textural* or *structural*. The textural cluster describes *what* happened (Creswell, 1998). The textural cluster is simply considered the content information, merely the answer to the question about the experience of persisting as an African American administrator in a PWI. However, a structural cluster describes *how* the phenomenon is experienced (Creswell, 1998). Once this process was employed through each transcript, data matrices were formed, the researcher combined the clusters from all transcripts by theme (textural and structural), conclusions were drawn, and interviews underwent cross comparisons for verification. The individual descriptions were used to develop composite descriptions of the meanings and essence of the experience representing the sampled population (Moustakas, 1994). The findings of these analyses are introduced in the next section. First, I will introduce the participating university administrators.

ABOUT THE PARTICIPANTS

Timothy Wright is a high level administrator who is very determined and driven, and who owes his academic and intellectual influences to his university professors. Wright's ultimate goal is to become a university president; something for which he has been grooming, since graduate school. Wright attributes his persistence as an administrator to being a good listener and communicator, a hard worker, a teacher, an empathizer, a critical thinker, having a desire to constantly learn, and his ability to take in tons of information to process and make data driven decisions. He also views himself as a lifelong learner—constantly driving towards improving his craft as an administrator.

Mary Moore is currently a mid level administrator who is also one of the longest serving African American administrators in the interview group. Moore considers herself "old school" and feels a strong alliance to the African American community because she knows that she not only represents herself, but her church, race, and community through her actions. Moore's frame of reference for persistence comes from being familiar with individuals involved in civil rights desegregation and litigation cases against the university. She believes this resulted in her administrative hiring. She credits her persistence strategies to the older African American administrators who welcomed her when she first arrived. From them, she learned the importance of punctuality, accountability, doing her very best, hard work, keeping proper appearances, and being an activist.

Jason Williams is a mid level administrator. He was born and raised in the city where he currently works. In addition, Williams received both his undergraduate and doctoral degrees from this university. Williams was once a high level administrator who attributes his persistence to being politically savvy and being able to make good friends and connections with individuals in high places. Williams feels that he is in his current administrator post because of university politics gone wrong, and betrayal from executive level administrators who have served as allies and political safeguards in the past. Despite the incident(s), he continues to persist.

Joe Clark is currently a high level administrator. Like Jason Williams, he grew up in the community where his host institution is located, and received all of his postsecondary education and training. Clark owes his persistence to having a great mentor and staying true to his core convictions of fairness and integrity. He feels that his racial identity does not influence who he is as an African American administrator. Clark views himself the same as all other administrators regardless of race.

Margaret Rayford is a high level administrator. She is also one of the highest ranking African American female administrators among all participants. Rayford claims that she chose to become a university administrator because she was looking for opportunities to engage in challenging work. She feels that her unique experience as staff, faculty, and now as administrator, gives her a well rounded perception of how the university functions. She feels that she has honed her skills as an administrator through an "internship of observation" in which she watched, observed, and learned from those who were really good at their craft. In terms of persistence, Rayford does not see herself as doing such because she knows that she can leave at any time. Rayford attributes her sustainability to taking ownership of her own happiness within the workplace. A comfortable work place, she suggests, is something that you have to create and work at.

Susan Johnson is a mid level administrator. She spent a large part of her career as a professor at an historically Black college until she decided to go into university administration. Since arriving at her current institution, Johnson decided to stay in administration because she did not want to undergo the pressures and politics of receiving tenure again. She also wanted to expand her role in helping as many students as possible inside and outside of the classroom. In addition to doing good work, Johnson attributes her persistence to understanding how to blend in and use a tactic that she refers to as *playing the game*—which she learned as a professor in an historically Black college while matriculating to tenure.

FINDINGS AND THEMES

The participants were asked to share their experiences and persistence strategies as it pertains to their status as African American administrators at a PWI. Within this context, the structure of persistence strategies relegates to actions taken to sustain or strengthen career mobility. The themes were verified across a majority of the six participants' transcripts. Because the nature of the study relies on individual experiences, there is not a "prototypical case". Therefore, the approach is to place the narratives in the most appropriate context to provide an expansive illustration of general experiences using criteria for the best fit rather than exact fit (Strauss & Corbin, 1998). The seven themes that emerged are all worthy of examination: (a) Maintain Professionalism, (b) Manage Your Brand, (c) Deconstruct to Understand Culture,

(d) Deconstruct to Understand Race, (e) Maintain Personal Values, (f) Master University Politics, and (g) Develop/ Sustain Support Networks.

Maintain Professionalism

Participants referenced their ability to maintain professionalism as a theme used as a persistence strategy allowing them to navigate the academy. According to them, one has to maintain a business-like manner within the workplace via appearances, preparation, and competency to accomplish the task at hand. Respondents often cited how the minority administrator label is a double-edged sword. On one hand, they are advocates for underrepresented groups. But, for some of the African American administrators, there is a sense of *minority pigeon holding*. Minority pigeon holding refers to the generated assumption of being the authoritative minority voice (in this case, the "Black voice") in the conversation or in the boardroom. Williams best sums up the assumption in stating, "You will be perceived as the minority person that does the minority thing, whatever that thing is."

In addition to the minority label, participants noted their consciousness of the cultural and institutional barriers held against them as racial minorities. Administrators felt that in spite of such knowledge they must remain professional and perform their job as if unaffected. Williams concludes this notion by stating, "You got to have thick skin because you will hear a lot of stuff a lot of things about us that are inappropriate. A lot of those White attitudes that you go up against—you just have to roll on through." On the other hand, Wright adds that although he is aware of his race as a minority administrator, he places more emphasis on his values; professional preparation and competence on the job.

> I think less about my race and I tend not to judge things that happen to me or for me based on my race. I don't even try to think about it that way, but I try not to let it come to my mind that they made that decision because I am Black. It can, I'm not suggesting that I'm ignorant to that, but if they did I don't care. I'm going to bring so much data to the table that whatever decision we need to make they are going to say, "'Gosh, this brother thought the issue all the way through.' And it's going to be tough for them to say yes or no based on what I brought to the table." I pride myself on that.

Manage Your Brand

Managing your brand refers to being able to maintain a positive image in one's field beyond the hosting institution. For the administrators, that meant gaining what they felt were "proper" credentials such as professional certifications and educational degrees. Another component of managing your brand resides in active participation in (a) national and international conferences, (b) professional development workshops, and (c) referred scholarship contribution to their field. Johnson feels that because she is an African American female, she has to have more credentials than her male counterparts. "I may not or can't just have a master's degree or a certificate. I have to have more than the next person, and that's why I decided to get my Ph.D." Wright, a high level African American male administrator agrees and often feels the need to stand out as a professional in comparison to his colleagues. Therefore, he communicates his brand by constantly raising the professional standard for administrators. He understands that some may see that as, "showing off," but, he does not care. "I rather have them say that about me than 'here comes some slack presentation again'."

Deconstruct to Understand Culture

The administrators in this study shared their experiences, and the knowledge gained from observing the culture around them has helped them persist in their leadership role. They suggest that being able to read and deconstruct culture is vital to understanding and contextualizing the institution in relation to their status. Rayford recalls her first impression of her institution and the push for tradition over change:

> It's a complicated culture to me. You have to know when to dig in or say, "You know what? I'm going to let that go." You know what I mean? Sometimes, it's not worth the fight. There is a culture here where people really do take pride in saying that this is how we really do things in terms of tradition. "That's our way." However, at the same time, they talk about change, but refuse to let go of the traditional ways.

As a result, Rayford notes that it is very important to constantly pay attention to the consistency between individuals' words and actions. Wright agrees, and suggests that he also observes people in order to avoid being plotted against—something that he cautions others to do as well.

> I think that's where people of color make the mistake in that they get so committed to the craft they fail to notice their surrounding environment. While you are working your tail off, suddenly people around you are plotting. If you are not paying attention, you won't even realize what's going on until the hammer falls.

In addition to protecting themselves, a number of administrators address lessons gained from watching other colleagues depart the institution. Johnson, after witnessing another African American associate's career cut short, incorporates a persistence strategy of blending in among her White counterparts, which she calls *playing the game*. "You have to be like one of them. You have to allow them to feel comfortable around you to be permitted in their environment. And that's playing the game." Williams understands Johnson's point of view, and adds that refusing to blend in with his White counterparts can result in an exclusion from the decision making process.

> You want to be known as one who is not going to make too much of fuss. That's not a bad thing, but it's inappropriate because fussing about wrong is something I have the right to fuss about it. However, they don't expect you to challenge authority and the decision making. If you do, then one of the things they do is exclude you from the meeting. That sends another message. If you talk too loud you won't be invited back.

Although telling, not everyone agrees with Williams and Johnson's method. Other administrators feel that they would rather not become involved with their White counterparts if it means assimilating or accommodating themselves to that degree. Instead, the remaining participants prefer to take note and use that information in order to formulate a strategy to navigate beyond the challenge.

Deconstruct to Understand Race

Like culture, being able to deconstruct and understand the complexities of race within the institution was revealed as an ongoing theme that undergirds most responses. According to participants, being able to deconstruct and understand race relates to identifying and navigating beyond the institutional (covert) and face-to-face (overt) notions of racism. In particular, the respondents pointed to institutional traditions, perceptions, and every day practices that sustain White privilege. By identifying and understanding the racism within the university, participants felt better prepared to address it while navigating their day-to-day practices. Moore speaks for the group when she instructs, "Don't take racism personally." They suggest that race and racism are not a correlation to job their job performance. Wright provides his perspective on the influence of understanding racism in relation to the institution:

> People feel like this is a racist environment and "I can't do this or do that". Racism is their problem. That's your problem if you are challenged by my race. That's not my problem, and I'm not about to make it my problem. If

there is something that I need, I am going to make a case for it. I'll go for it. I'll rally the troops, and I'll do whatever I need to attain it. Once again, let me state that my race is not my problem. I've lived with it (being an African American) all my life and I have no problem with it. It might be your problem and that's fine. And you have the right to have your own problem, but it's not going to be my problem. I try to tell young African American men, women, and other administrators of color to stop getting caught up in their problems. Stop limiting yourself because people don't like you due to your race. If you don't, then you have accepted their problem. Now you have made it your problem.... Listen, work ethic is personally motivated. It's not race driven, and they can't take my work ethic away from me.

While a majority of the African American administrators in this study agreed with Wright, there were two administrators who thought otherwise. Williams felt that race does play a role in his position and as a result has influenced his persistence strategies in the past. However, in stating so, Williams provided a more unique account that differs from other participants. Due to the nature of his position, Williams felt that other African Americans viewed and unfairly judged him as an "Uncle Tom". Consequently, he associates more closely with his White counterparts.

> I basically felt that if I was to be treated like that by my own kind, then I should make me a new set of friends and see what I can get out of it. And guess what? I benefitted to a point because I didn't have to do anything but my job.

Johnson, the second administrator who disagrees, admittedly code switches—a phenomenon associated with shifting linguistic styles to fit the culture one is in communication with (Cross & Fhagen-Smith, 2001). Johnson knows that her code-switching is intentional because she is aware of general negative stereotypes held against African Americans. Therefore, Johnson is more sensitive to her own racial perception around her White counterparts in comparison to her African Americans peers:

> Say for instance, if I was at a meeting with a Black administrator and my brother just got put in jail. I can tell him or her that. However, I can't tell the White administrator that, because "us" going to prison is already a stereotype with Black people anyway. As a result, I always keep it professional around them.

Additionally, Johnson admits to further assimilating herself among her peers within the institution by removing aspects of her "Blackness":

> I think that when it comes to the business environment you have to take away the social characteristics of a Black person. Take that out, put it aside, and be "normal". You need to be the normal person that dresses nice, looks and act the part, and actually does the job.

Maintain Personal Values

Having the ability to maintain personal values is a theme that addresses one's ability to sustain a strong sense of self with regard to their ethics. A strong sense of self helps to combat the pressures of assimilation on minority administrators by majority groups (Cross, 1991; Helms 1990). For respondents, maintaining personal values means "doing the right thing" takes precedence over persistence. In general, participants agree with Clark's definition of "doing the right thing" as relying on core values and convictions built upon fairness, appreciation for equity, building community, and listening to others. Rayford states, "There are things that I value in terms of who I am as a professional, and I don't compromise those for anybody." Wright adds that he does not worry about losing his job as an administrator because he has always performed well. "I feel like I worked my tail off here, so my next job is going to take care of itself because my reputation is going to proceed me in whatever I do next."

Master University Politics

Another theme that surfaced as a contributor to the persistence strategies of African American administrators resides in the ability to master university politics. According to the respondents, university politics varies from the traditional politics of corporate America.

> The politics of decision making in a university is very different from the politics of decision making in corporate America. It's not always about what the data says, or what the most efficient process is, or what the right thing is. Sometimes, we have to make decisions based on image, reputation, and who's friends with whom (Wright).

As a result, Wright often finds himself asking the question, "What are the colors of the employees that I'm getting ready to make these decisions on, and how is this decision going to be played out in the media?" Wright also notes that even if the resolution is financially sound or a data driven decision, which is in the best interest of the university, he may not be permitted to do make the decision.

For other administrators, they view mastering university politics in two ways: political correctness and alliance building. Johnson, having spent most of her career at historically Black colleges/universities (HBCU), contrasts her observations on political correctness between the two institutions:

> You have to know what to say and when to say it. You can say different things in a Black environment than you can say in a White environment. They are not

the same. Working in a Black institution, there are a lot of things that I said to students that I can't say to students on this campus because the culture is different. That's what I mean by politically correct. I had a boss at my old HBCU and he was Black, and my boss here is White. The way we speak and interact is completely different. At a Black institution, they are more professional. You have the "doctor this and doctor that" (Johnson).

Williams, as with a majority of the participating administrators, contributes his persistence to having developed political alliances within the institution. "My political savvy and astuteness has allowed me to be able to make good friends and good connections in high places. Those allegiances have protected me when situations didn't go according to plan." Formulating high powered alliances has proven to be a positive contributor to every administrator's persistence strategy. However, sometimes that can backfire.

Williams, once a high level administrator, recalls a time where politics caused a setback in his career. While at one time he felt immune to other administrators within the institution, a change at the executive level left him vulnerable to those who were not supportive of Williams. "Those individuals created a nasty situation for me. When we got a new president, the person who hired me was no longer employed. Therefore, the new president owed me no commitment, and so there I was."

Not everyone engages in politics to the extent that Williams has. Rayford chooses to minimize her involvement as much as possible. Outside of garnering support, Rayford is cautious when it comes to forming alliances because she does not want others to take advantage of her. "I think that a lot of people want to pair up or be connected because they see something they can gain from you, or it's the other way around. That's not something that I want to be a part of."

Develop/ Sustain Support Networks

The final theme that emerges in the persistence strategies of African American administrators at a PWI is in the establishment of support networks. In particular, the participants addressed the various ways that they use their mentors. Traditionally, mentors either serve their purpose through role modeling or by providing advice. However, many of the administrators admit to using their mentor (and in most cases, more than one mentor) to contribute to their professional development, or to troubleshoot their socialization within the academy. For instance, Williams credits his mentors with providing access and guidance to positions for which he would not have been considered, otherwise. In other words, his mentors advocated on his behalf. Therefore, Williams strongly advises attaining a mentor within the institution with the power to do so.

> This is why your mentor should be a person that's already established on the campus, has a little clout, credibility, and has the ability to pick up a phone and say, "Hey, I'm calling on behalf of Jason Williams" and that door ought of open just to give you the opportunity. Now, you may not get the position, but you will at least have the opportunity. Sometimes, as African Americans we don't even get the opportunity because there is no one to advocate for us to say, "You can trust him. He's okay. He qualifies. He has degree training and experience. He'll be okay" (Williams).

As previously mentioned, other administrators willingly used more than one mentor. Wright professes to have an advisory board that offers a different perspective on what he feels are critical issues and decisions.

> I have identified a group of people internal and external that I can turn to and share my concerns. I also turn to them for critical advice. Building an advisory team is important because you can turn to this group and tell them your most controversial decisions and ask for their input outside of your work. Before you make the final decision you need a group of people that will tell you, "Don't go that route. It will cause you that problem." Sometimes, you may not have anticipated that problem; therefore, you need other people who can look at it from a different lens or perspective and help you think it through.

In addition to having mentors, some participants spoke of building up a support network through investing in trusting relationships with their staff to facilitate office efficiency. Well trained staff supported systems create a community of trust and mutuality that sustains a sense of pride and a positive cycle of contribution. Therefore, the role of building staff support creates a trusting culture that increases workplace efficiency, loyalty, and dependability.

SUMMARY OF THEMES

The above themes evolved out of the experiences and persistence strategies of six African American mid to high level administrators who participated in this study. Seven themes emerged and were noted: (a) maintain professionalism, (b) manage your brand, (c) deconstruct to understand culture, (d) deconstruct to understand race, (e) maintain personal values, (f) master university politics, and (g) support networks. Taken as a composite, these themes represent the phenomenon of being an African American administrator persisting at a PWI. Furthermore, these themes serve to add to the already existing body of work on African American administrators in higher education.

CONCLUSION AND IMPLICATIONS

A number of suppositions about African American administrators in higher education were addressed in this study. My overriding assumption was shaped by the discourse (Critical Race Theory, postmodernism, and social dominance theory) that suggests that the experiences of African American administrators in higher education (specifically at PWIs) are largely constructed by race, class, culture, and historical knowledge of PWIs. Thus, the persistence strategies employed by the participants were guided by at least one of those factors. Another assumption refers to the hierarchal construction of social institutions in American society, and how it was manifested by the role of non-White groups in relation to their White counterparts. While my assumptions may have guided the initial inquiry, I asked questions that not only allowed the administrators to share their narratives, but explored my assumptions as well.

Overall, my assumptions have been validated, but not exactly as I had imagined. The participants in the study support the assumption that issues of race, class, culture, and historical knowledge of their PWI are salient factors that may undergird the poor representation of African American administrators and other administrators of color. These factors influence the type of positions African American administrators are able to obtain in addition to the amount of power delegated for each. The research revealed that while some African Americans have the title of university administrator, their lack of power due to being underrepresented encourages them to use persistence strategies based on building support networks first. Consequently, a majority of them are consumed with maintaining a positive image and brand in the eyes of their peers. The participants understood the value of maintaining their brand by carefully observing their PWI culture. These findings suggest institutions must find ways to become more open, inviting, and supportive to administrators of color if diversity is truly a core value. This means that more university officials and administrators must make it a point to re-examine and challenge institutional traditions, policies, and organizational roles to ensure that more administrators of color have a voice at the table.

The second assumption regarding the social construction of PWIs was not supported specifically as I had imagined by the administrators of this study. I thought that the administrators were all knowledgeable of the roles that White privilege plays within the hierarchal construction of their social institution. While some alluded to their knowledge of the aforementioned concept, others did not. As a result, administrators in this study held mixed feelings on whether their race caused them to accommodate, assimilate, or resist the social hierarchy within the institution. Those who accommodate themselves sought to do so by way of engaging in university politics. The one administrator who chose to assimilate, purposely code switched and shed aspects of her "Blackness" that might have "distracted" her White peers. Those who chose resistance focused more on increasing their own professional competence to advance. Some participants chose neither. They noticed the racial factors, but refused to engage, citing that their race has no correlation on job performance. Thus, they did not adopt the concept of racial hierarchies and White privilege within the institution. This finding suggests that self-identity and internalization play a large role in influencing persistence in the face of a dominant culture.

Overall, the primary findings of this study suggest that the persistence strategies of African American administrators are guided by their own identity and how they choose to internalize their institutional environment. This means that the persistence strategies of African American administrators participating in this study are merely responses to the environment and culture around them. However, in order to understand "why", we must continue to generate counter-stories and narratives that illustrate how the participants create their persistence strategies. Further, in highlighting the experiences of African American administrators, we gain insight on salient factors that may adversely contribute to their poor underrepresentation due to the normalization of institutional traditions defined and held by the majority. Consequently, more intuitiveness is offered on the cultural factors that could attribute to improving minority recruitment, retention, policy formation, and ultimately minority career mobility and success. However, because these narratives provide an illustration into the professional experiences of other African American administrators in similar PWI settings, these accounts should not be perceived to represent or explain the experiences of all African American administrators in higher education or all PWIs. Research must continue. Therefore, let this be a call to scholarship.

REFERENCES

Bogdan, R., & Biklen, S. (1998). *Qualitative research in education* (3rd ed.). Boston: Allyn and Bacon.

Brubacher, J., & Rudy, W. (1997). *Higher education in transition: A history of American colleges and universities, 1636–1976* (4th ed.). New Brunswick: Transition.

Burgess, N. (1997). Tenure and promotion among African American women in the academy: Issues and strategies. In L. Benjamin (Ed.), *Black women in the academy: Promises and perils* (pp. 227–234). Gainesville, FL: University Press of Florida.

Collins, P. (1990). *Black feminist thought: Knowledge, consciousness, and the politics of empowerment.* New York: Routledge.

Creswell, J. (1998). *Qualitative inquiry and research design: Choosing among five traditions.* Thousand Oaks, CA: Sage.

Creswell, J. (2003). *Research design: Qualitative, quantitative and mixed methods approaches.* Thousand Oaks, CA: Sage.

Creswell, J. W. (2007). *Qualitative inquiry and research design: Choosing among five approaches* (2nd ed.). Thousand Oaks, CA: Sage.

Cross, W. (1991). *Shades of Black: Diversity in African-American identity.* Philadelphia, PA: Temple University Press.

Cross, W. E., Jr., & Fhagen-Smith, P. (2001). Patterns of African American identity development: A life span perspective. In C. L. Wijeysinghe & B. W. Jackson, III (Eds.). *New perspectives on racial identity development.* New York: New York University Press.

DeCuir, J. T., & Dixson, A. D. (2004). "So when it comes out, they aren't that surprised that it is there": Using critical race theory as a tool of analysis of race and racism in education. *Educational Researcher, 33*(5), 26–31.

Fleming, J., Gill, G., & Swinton, D. (1978). *The case of affirmative action for Blacks in higher education.* Washington, DC: Howard University Press.

Gregory, S. (1995). *Black women in the academy: The secrets to success and achievement.* New York: University Press of America.

Helms, J. (1990). An overview of Black racial identity theory. In J. Helms (Ed.), *Black and White racial identity: Theory, research, and practice* (pp. 9–32). New York: Greenwood Press.

Holmes, S. L. (1999). *Black women academicians speak out: Race, class, and gender in narratives of higher education.* Unpublished doctoral dissertation, Iowa State University, Iowa.

Holmes, S. L. (2003). Black administrators speak out: Narratives on race and gender in higher education. *National Association of Student Affairs Professionals, 6,* 47–67.

Holmes, S. L. (2004). An overview of African American college presidents: A game of two steps forward, one step backwards, and standing still. *The Journal of Negro Education, 73*(1), 21–39.

Holmes, S. L., Ebbers, L., Robinson, D., & Mugenda, A. (2000). Validating African American students at predominantly White institutions. *Journal of College Student Retention: Research, Theory, & Practice, 2,* 41–58.

Jackson, J. (2001). A new test for diversity: Retaining African American administrators at predominantly white institutions. In L. Jones (Ed.), *Retaining African Americans in higher education: Challenging paradigms for remaining students, faculty, and administrators* (pp. 93–109). Sterling: Stylus Publications.

Jackson, J. (2002). Retention of African American administrators at predominantly White institutions: Using professional growth factors to inform the discussion. *College and University, 78*(2), 11–16.

Jackson, J. (2004). Engaging, retaining, and advancing African Americans in executive-level positions: A descriptive and trend analysis of academic administrators in higher and postsecondary education. *The Journal of Negro Education, 73*(1), 4–20.

Jones, (M. (1997). Does leadership transcend gender and race? The case of African American women college presidents. In L. Benjamin (Ed.) *Black women in the academy: Promises and perils* (pp. 201–209). Gainesville: University Press of Florida.

Kawewe, S. (1997). Black women in diverse academic settings: Gender and racial crimes of commission and omission in academia. In L. Benjamin (Ed.), *Black women in the academy: Promises and perils* (pp. 263–269). Gainesville, FL: University Press of Florida.

Krueger, R., & Casey, M. (2000). *Focus groups: A practical guide for applied research.* Newbury Park, CA: Thousand Oaks.

Kvale, S. (1996). *Interviews: An introduction to qualitative research interviewing.* Thousand Oaks, CA: Sage.

Ladson-Billings, G. (1998). Just what is critical race theory and what's it doing in a nice field like education? *International Journal of Qualitative Studies in Education, 11*(1), 7–24.

Leedy, P. D. (1997). *Practical research.* Upper River: Prentice Hall Saddle.

Lincoln, Y., & Guba, E. (1989). *Fourth generation evaluation.* Newbury Park, CA: Sage Publications.

McCutcheon, S. R., & Lindsey, T. (2004). The last refuge of official discrimination: The federal funding exception to California's Proposition 209. *Santa Clara Law Review, 44.*

Miles, M., & Huberman, A. (1994). Qualitative data analysis (2nd ed.). Thousand Oaks, CA: Sage Publications.

Morse, J. (1994). *Designing funded qualitative research.* In N. Denzin & Y. Lincoln (Eds.), Handbook of qualitative research (pp. 220–235). Thousand Oaks: Sage.

Moses, Y. (1997). Black women in academe: Issues and strategies. In L. Benjamin (Ed.), *Black women in the academy: Promises and perils* (pp. 23–37). Gainesville, FL: University Press of Florida.

Moustakas, C. (1994). *Phenomenological research methods.* Thousand Oaks, CA: Sage.

Oliver, B., & Davis, J. (1994). Things they don't teach you about being a dean. In J. Davis (Ed.), *Coloring the halls of ivy: Leadership & diversity in the academy* (pp. 59–70). Boston, MA: Anker Publishing Company.

Patton, M. Q. (2001). *Qualitative research and evaluation methods.* Thousand Oaks, CA: Sage Publications.

Patton, M. Q. (2002). *Qualitative research and evaluation* (3rd ed.). Thousand Oaks, CA: Sage Publications.

Perna, L., Gerald, D., Baum, E., & Milem, J. (2007). The status of equity for Black faculty and administrators in public higher education in the south. *Research in Higher Education, 48*(2).

Phelps, M. (1995). What's in a number?: Implications for African American female faculty at predominantly White colleges and universities. *Innovative Higher Education, 19,* 255–268.

Polit, D., Beck, C., & Hungler, B. (2001). *Essentials of nursing research: Methods, appraisal, and utilization* (5th Ed). Philadelphia: Lippincott.

Rolle, K., Davies, T., & Banning, J. (2000). African American administrators' experiences in predominantly White colleges and universities. *Community College Journal of Research and Practice, 24,* 79–94.

Sagaria, M. (1988). Administrative mobility and gender: Patterns and prices in higher education. *Journal of American History, 59,* 306–326.

Smith, C. (1980). The peculiar status of Black educational administrators: The university setting. *Journal of Black Studies, 10*(3), 323–334.

Smith, Y. (1993). Recruitment and retrenchment of African American and other multicultural physical educators. *Journal of Physical Education, Recreation & Dance, 64*(3), 66–70.

Solórzano, D., & Yosso, T. (2002). Critical race methodology: Counter-storytelling as an analytical framework for education research. *Qualitative Inquiry, 8*(1), 23–44.

Stanley, C. (2006). Coloring the academic landscape: Faculty of color breaking the silence in predominantly White colleges and universities. *American Educational Research Journal, 43*(4), 701–736.

Strauss, A., & Corbin, J. (1998). *Basics of qualitative research: Techniques and procedures for developing grounded theory.* Thousand Oaks, CA: Sage Publications.

Washington, V., & Harvey, W. (1989). *Affirmative rhetoric, negative action: African-American and Hispanic faculty at predominantly White institutions.* Washington, DC: School of Education and Human Development, The George Washington University.

Watson, L. W. (2001). In their voices: A glimpse of African-American women administrators in higher education. *National Association of Student Affairs Professionals Journal* (4), 7–16.

Wilson, R. (1989). Women of color in academic administration: Trends, progress, and barriers. *Sex Roles, 21*, 99–112.

CHAPTER 3

COMBAT IN THE ACADEMY

Racial Battle Fatigue, Role Strain, and African American Faculty at Public Community Colleges

Tamara Nichele Stevenson
Westminster College of Salt Lake City

In the academy, race is a difference that makes a difference.
—Moore, 1987

When the doors of Harvard College first opened in 1636, access to formal higher learning in the United States was exclusive to those who were White, male, and wealthy. About 375 years and more than 6,600 colleges and universities later [as of 2009 (NCES, 2011)], postsecondary educational options have, in several aspects, expanded and evolved from their homogenous beginnings, including the racial demographic of the student body. However, only slight change has occurred within a pivotal sphere of American higher education: the racial demographic of the faculty.

While teaching is a core faculty function at both two- and four-year institutions, community colleges (also known as two-year colleges) are often described as teaching colleges; quality instruction is the chief expectation and teaching excellence is a defining component of the community col-

Confronting Racism in Higher Education, pages 43–66
Copyright © 2013 by Information Age Publishing
All rights of reproduction in any form reserved.

lege mission (Bower, 2002; Grubb, 1999; Hardy & Laanan, 2006; Harvey, 1994; Harvey & Valadez, 1994; Outcalt, 2002; Somers et al., 1998; Townsend & Twombly, 2007; Turner, Myers, & Creswell, 1999). Community colleges are accredited, open-admission, publicly or privately controlled institutions that provide a range of educational options, including vocational/technical training, remedial education, continuing education, and general education classes (e.g., courses that transfer to four-year institutions and can be applied to baccalaureate degree requirements). Along with awarding certificates in a variety of occupational fields, the associate degree is the highest degree conferred by a community college (Cohen, 2001; Cohen & Brawer, 1994, 2008; McCormick & Cox, 2003). One of the main contributions of the community college to American higher education is its charge to expand access to postsecondary education for students who might not have participated otherwise (Cohen & Brawer, 1994, 2008). For example, the two-year college historically has been a major postsecondary option for African American[1] students and continues to be a viable and attractive gateway into higher education for Blacks (Bower, 2002; Lewis & Middleton, 2003; Lovell, Alexander, & Kirkpatrick, 2002; Solmon, Solmon, & Schiff, 2002; Zamani, 2006). Nearly half (i.e., 46%) of African American undergraduates are enrolled at community colleges (Chronicle of Higher Education, 2010).

As of Fall 2009, African Americans comprised 6.6% of the American college and university professoriate (NCES, 2010). This is a relatively slight increase from 5.3% in Fall 2005 and 4.9% in Fall 1998 (Johnson & Pichon, 2007, NCES, 2007). These numbers demonstrate a largely disproportionate underrepresentation of African American faculty in higher education, who compose approximately 13% of the general U.S. population (U.S. Census Bureau, 2011). In comparison, more than 75% of the full-time college and university faculty posts were held by Whites in Fall 2009. Overall, African American faculty are the least proportionately represented, less promoted and tenured, positioned in lower academic ranks, and under researched, especially at historically White institutions[2] (Alexander-Snow & Johnson, 1998; Allen et al., 2002; Allison, 2008; Altbach, Lomotey, & Kyle, 1999; Bower, 2002; Bowman & Smith, 2002; Branch, 2001; Brown, 1988; Cole et al., 2003; Cross & Slater, 2000; Evans & Chun, 2007; Feagin, Vera, & Imani, 1996; Harvey, 2007; Harvey & Scott-Jones, 1985; Jayakumar et al., Jackson & Phelps, 2004; 2009; Kayes, 2006; Laden & Hagedorn, 2000; Lewis & Middleton, 2003; Smith, 1992, Smith et al., 2004; Smith & Witt, 1993; Tuitt et al., 2009; Villalpando & Delgado, 2002). Nationwide, African Americans constitute close to 7% of full-time, public, two-year faculty (Chesler, Lewis & Crofoot, 2005; Townsend & Twombly, 2007).

For the African Americans (along with other faculty of color) who eventually attain teaching positions, their experiences in academe are dramatically different from their White colleagues (Harlow, 2003; Laden & Hagedorn, 2000), largely impacted by a campus racial climate that perpetuates an unwelcome and unsupportive environment. Campus racial climate refers to the overarching racial temperature or atmosphere of a college or university campus, inclusive of concurrent societal, institutional, and interpersonal exchanges that occur with and beyond the campus, as considered by Hurtado (1992) and colleagues (Hurtado et al., 1998, 1999). Turner and Myers (2000) describe a "chilly" campus climate as the underrepresentation of Black faculty and other faculty of color in higher education and a "White-male-dominated institutional culture that undervalues the contributions and/or presence of women and people of color" (p. 78).

African American faculty experience isolation, course overload, excessive committee work, racial, gender and language biases, and minimal guidance or mentoring relating to promotion, tenure, and reappointment (Cooper & Stevens, 2002; Harvey, 1994; Jayakumar et al., 2009; Johnson & Pichon, 2007; Laden & Hagedorn, 2000; Sutherland, 1990; Turner & Myers, 2000; Turner, Myers, & Creswell, 1999). Distinctive race-related issues include dealing with perceptions of tokenism, being typecast as an "ethnic specialist", idealized expectations to fulfill certain race-related assignments (including mentoring students of color, attending to diversity-related courses and committee work) the devaluing of research focused on race, and negotiating a conflicted path to promotion and tenure due to ambiguous and wavering expectations, requirements, and evaluation criteria (Banks, 1984; Feagin, Vera, & Imani, 1996; Laden & Hagedorn, 2000; Patitu et al., 2000; Somers et al., 1998; Turner & Myers, 2000; Tuitt et al., 2009; Turner, Myers, & Creswell, 1999).

African American faculty function within "chilly" or racially hostile campus climates inclusive of racism, discrimination, and an anti-Black sentiment, as academia is a microcosm of the larger society. Such environments are problematic for Black faculty and can have a negative impact on their social, professional, and personal expectations of and subsequent behaviors in their faculty role, likely resulting in race-related role strain. This chapter will highlight findings from an exploratory qualitative dissertation research study of the perceptions and lived experiences of African American public community college faculty; specifically, the nature and extent to which these Black faculty members experience strain in the faculty role exacerbated by race.

CONCEPTUAL FRAMEWORK

Critical Race Theory

Critical Race Theory (CRT) is a useful lens to consider and understand the "more subtle, but just as deeply entrenched, varieties of racism that characterize our times" (Delgado & Stefancic, 2001, p. xvi) by "studying and transforming the relationship among race, racism, and power" (Delgado & Stefancic, 2012, p. 3). The basic tenets of CRT illuminate the cryptic patterns and practices of race, racism, and racial exclusion and call for the voices and perspectives of African Americans and other people of color to "reexamine the terms by which race and racism have been negotiated in American consciousness" (Crenshaw et al., 1995, p. xiv). Arising from the Civil Rights Movement's grassroots traditions of resistance, the scholarly articulation of this framework emerged through two social movements—Critical Legal Studies and radical feminism—which, in the mid1970s by legal scholars Derrick Bell and Alan Freeman, was a response to the seemingly sluggish progress of civil rights legislation to produce meaningful racial reform (Delgado & Stefancic, 2001; Roithmayr, 1999; Tate, 1997, Villalpando & Delgado, 2002). Gloria Ladson-Billings and William Tate (1995) ushered CRT into educational research because of the necessity to discover ways to discuss race which, they claimed, was not a theorized subject of inquiry in educational scholarship. In the second edition of *Critical Race Theory: An Introduction*, Delgado and Stefancic (2012) identify four generally accepted CRT propositions: (a) racism is an ordinary, normal, permanent fixture in American society, (b) interest convergence (the alleviation of racism is contingent upon the advancement of the self-interests of Whites), (c) the social construction of race, reveals the dominant society's manipulative strategy to racialize minority groups to gain or maintain economic, social, or political advantage, and (d) counter-storytelling, or the "voice-of-color" thesis records and analyzes the lived experiences of race and racism.

Racial Battle Fatigue

Racial Battle Fatigue (RBF) is a person of color's reaction to the troubling conditions that occur from dealing with racism on a daily basis (Smith, 2004). CRT's clarion call about the ingrained, endemic existence of racism in society (and subsequently, education) and the importance of detailing the stories of people of color to challenge the long-standing notions of race and racism bridge and inform the philosophical underpinnings of CRT to RBF, with the RBF model functioning as the depiction of those embedded actions and outcomes outlined in CRT (William A. Smith, personal communication, July 28, 2006). Symptoms of RBF are physiological, psychological, and emotional/behavioral in nature, ranging from tension headaches, constant anxiety, and ulcers to increased swearing and complaining, insomnia, rapid mood swings, difficulty thinking or speaking, and social withdrawal (Smith, 2004; Smith, Hung, & Franklin, 2011; Smith, Yosso, & Solórzano, 2006, 2007). RBF is the physical, mental, and emotional response to racial microaggressions: subtle, conscious or unconscious, intentional or unintentional, layered, cumulative, verbal and nonverbal, behavioral, and environmental insults directed at people of color based on race and other distinguishing characteristics that cause unnecessary stress upon people of color, including African Americans, while benefiting Whites (Smith, 2004; Smith, Yosso, & Solórzano, 2006; Solórzano, Ceja, & Yosso, 2000; Solórzano et al., 2002; Sue et al., 2007; Sue et al., 2008[a]; Sue et al., 2008[b]; Sue et al., 2009; Sue, 2010). Accumulated over time, racial microaggressions can cause various forms of mental, emotional, and physical strain. For African Americans and other populations of color, the ongoing exposure to and accrual of racial microaggressions generates RBF. The constant threat of racial microaggressions can cause RBF to remain "switched on" and symptoms can occur in anticipation of a racist event: rapid breathing, upset stomach, frequent diarrhea or urination (Smith, 2004). Not only does the constant battle with racial stress agitate the lives of people of color, the subsequent psychological and physiological symptoms of RBF can be lethal when gone unnoticed, untreated, misdiagnosed, or dismissed (Smith, Yosso, & Solórzano, 2006).

Role Strain

Role Strain is defined by Goode (1960) as "the felt (or perceived) difficulty in fulfilling role obligations" (p. 483). This concept derives from role theory, the organization of individual and collective social behavior functioning in positions and roles (Biddle, 1986; Turner, 2002). Role Strain is normal because of the impossibility for a person to meet every demand of one's total role network (Goode, 1960). Role Strain occurs when an individual believes or actually experiences tension or struggle when satisfying expected or actual attitudes and behaviors (tasks and responsibilities) in a particular role. Role Strain is framed by three dimensions: (a) role ambiguity (lack of information or clarity about expectations to meet role obligations), (b) role conflict (role expectations from one role are incompatible with the role expectations of another role), and (c) role overload (perceived or actual lack of time to fulfill role obligations (Goode, 1960; Kahn et al., 1964). The inclusion of the Role Strain construct in this study contributes to the exploration of the racialized aspects of role stress uniquely associated with the African American public community college faculty role.

METHODS

A multiple case research design was utilized for this qualitative research study. Qualitative research has been described as an overarching form of inquiry that leads to understanding, explanation, and meaning of social phenomena with as little disruption as possible (Merriam, 1998). Pioneering Racial Battle Fatigue scholar William A. Smith (2004) affirms this exploratory approach to examining African Americans and racial stress: "[t] he research field is wide open for understanding how racism affects folks of color.... Qualitative inquiry should be our first line of defense" (p. 186).

Respondents

Respondents in this multiple case study were purposively sampled, male and female, full-time, African American faculty members at public two-year institutions of higher education situated in a metropolitan locale of a state in the Midwestern region of the United States. The two determining criteria for inclusion in this research study were:

1. to hold a full-time faculty role at a public community college, and
2. to be a native-born citizen of the United States with ancestry from any of the Black racial groups of the continent of Africa.

American citizenship was determined as self-reported by the respondent. This criterion was essential to include in relation to respondents' exposure to and interaction with the distinctive complexities of race relations in the United States. A total of 20 respondents from six public two-year colleges (7 male, 13 female) were interviewed for this research study. One respondent withdrew from the study weeks later, citing "professional and ethical reasons". All respondents were tenured or under long-term contract with their respective institutions.

Data Collection

In-depth interviews were conducted in person with the 20 respondents with a series of semi-structured, open-ended questions informed by the extant literature, elements of the conceptual framework, and the researcher's curiosity. All face-to-face interviews were audio-recorded and transcribed for data analysis. Data collection took place from April 2009 to December 2009. Time lengths for interviews ranged from a minimum of 30 minutes to more than three (3) hours. Follow-up interviews occurred with approximately half of the 19 respondents, either in person or by email. Prior to the initial interview, respondents completed a brief questionnaire to gather general demographic and work-related information (e.g., institution, teaching discipline, educational attainment, academic rank, etc.) along with a survey question and open-ended inquiries to self-report general health status.

Data Analysis

The data generated for this research study (transcripts of in-depth interviews with respondents) were multitudinously explored, inclusive of the identified tenets of Critical Race Theory, the stress responses that compose Racial Battle Fatigue, and the three dimensions of Role Strain. For this multiple case study, data analysis occurred both within and across cases to observe actions and outcomes in alignment with Miles and Huberman's (1994) three-part method of data reduction, data display, and conclusion drawing with the aid of NVivo 9, a qualitative data management program.

HIGHLIGHTS FROM THE FINDINGS

The major themes that emerged from respondents' interviews characterize a variety of attitudinal and behavioral responses while functioning in their faculty roles within hostile campus racial climates. A portion of the findings from three themes are highlighted in this chapter: Representation (respondents' experiences in entering their full-time faculty positions), Rigor (navigating traditional and race-related role expectations), and Resilience (recovering from racially eruptive confrontations with students and colleagues).

Theme: Representation

The theme of Representation attends to the notion of the African American public community college faculty member as an actual (active) and/or figurative (passive) symbol of racial diversity on the public community college campus. A number of participants in this research study either completely integrated their public community colleges and/or academic departments, being among the first African American faculty members hired as recently as the late 1980s to the early 1990s. For example, Albert H. was the first African American male hired into a full-time faculty role at his public community college in 1989. His background in public administration and civil rights shaped his perspective about the context of his employment, the significance of his new full-time role, and the lack of diversity at the college, especially at that time.

And I found out two months after I was hired from one of the adjuncts, part timers, that he [another African American male] had been offered a position back in the '60s, but he had his own practice as a psychologist, and so he wouldn't give that up to come here. So, I found that interesting because out of all the departments, all the disciplines—I didn't know that coming in. See, I found out afterwards. And by training, I have a habit of looking around the room—I worked at civil rights for 10 years. And so the very first training we had was that whenever you enter a setting, you make sure you have a full view of who's there, and that's by race and gender. That was the first thing I learned in 1970. And so I always do that. So, I'm conscious of who's there, gender, ethnic—all that I see. And my very first day here, the meeting here, I just looked. We had our organizational meeting, the whole school, I said, "My God". We did have one Black administrator then, though. That was [name of African American administrator] that they got rid of. They find a way of getting rid of people if they—but that's about how I started.

Similar to Albert, Bill H. was the first African American altogether to be hired into a full-time faculty position in his academic department in the early 1990s. Bill's competitor for the position was a White male with a doctorate compared to his master's degree and length of adjunct instruction.

> ...I had my master's and had been teaching part-time in [name of city] since '74. I was still teaching there. All those things were attractive and when I interviewed, the interview team and especially my department chair, she and the dean, they liked me right away so—they had a couple of more people...he had a Ph.D., or something, but they were—and I came at the right time, too [because] they were looking for some diversity because—and you know we were equal. I don't know if that guy taught. He might have taught part time, I don't know for how long but even though he had a Ph.D., we were both equal other than the educational level and they needed the diversity because our dean, she was telling me that they never had a Black person teaching Criminal Justice over at the academy and they wanted to attract minority applicants in an all-White faculty and so that was part of the reason plus they felt I was qualified.

Gloria S. was the first full-time African American female hired into her academic department, and the second African American woman hired at the campus location of her multisite public community college system. She was concerned about the broader ramifications if she were deemed as unsuccessful in her new faculty role, and the pressures of representation as an undue burden on the Black faculty member.

> I have to put things in the context of time. I think when I first hired in at [name of public community college], because I was the first, or one of the first, that was a huge weight that was placed on me because if I failed, you kind of felt that the race had failed. It wasn't just I as an individual had failed, but

that I was letting the whole race down if I failed. Or, even that I was letting women down if I failed. So, it was a very, very, heavy load that I carried.

In consideration of respondents' awareness and willingness to commit to and engage in the virtuous aspects of African American representation (e.g., integrating departments and/or institutions, serving as role models, etc.), the corresponding sensibility relating to the existence of racial stereotypes and subsequent concern to either dismantle, or at least avoid their perpetuation, influences how they chose to conduct themselves in their faculty roles. Interestingly, along with the anticipated, yet unfounded, expectation of an intuitive camaraderie with Black students based on race, April N's innate physical and cultural attributes, namely her complexion and manner of speech, provoke assumptions about her persona and values.

> I think people expect me to be able to identify with my African American students more, and I don't think that we have common backgrounds often enough for me to make that connection with them that I think perhaps people are subconsciously expecting me to make. So, that's something. And I know a lot of students are put off by me in certain ways—and faculty too—because, 'oh, she talks like a White person'. Now, I think it has a lot to do with where I was born, in [name of city on the West Coast], for the reason, for the way that I talk and my whole body language and my exposure to ideas. So, I don't know, I find that people expect me to be different than how I am because of my skin color, generally speaking.

While CG understands and welcomes the opportunity to encourage and motivate students toward success, he confesses it can be burdensome when people presume that by his race alone, his perspectives and actions are exclusively oriented according to race, and is applicable to all African Americans.

> To me, it's quite taxing that people look at you by your race rather than your content. They don't know anything about you but they stereotype you. Many times, I represent the whole Black community. You speak—you don't speak for yourself. You speak for everyone. Many times, that has occurred.

THEME: RIGOR

Rigor delves into the stated or implied mandate for higher standards of accountability and performance—either willingly embraced by oneself or demanded by others. One of the requirements that respondents determined for themselves included maintaining stringent measures of instructional quality in their faculty roles. Requirements imposed by others include strict scrutiny of and challenges to respondents' educational and professional qualifications and instructional proficiency along with comparisons to White faculty.

Work Ethic

Winifred T. devotes a significant amount of her faculty role to curriculum development and course preparation to uphold her standards of quality instruction and sustain her interests in the course content.

> Sometimes I think—my colleagues laugh at me but I don't care because I'm hard on myself. I'm always trying to figure out, "Now, how can I best—I'm always looking for best practices. So, I'm the one who's always changing the textbook or trying something new, or adopting this new idea. So, I probably could spend less time and sit there and say, "Why don't I just consistently do this and just get happy with what I'm doing?" But, then I'm thinking, "Oh, God, I did that topic [for the last] two semesters. God, I'm bored, or I need something else." So, for me, I'm always working on my teaching, how to be a better teacher, how to be a better instructor, how to keep my standards high when sometimes you're kind of forced to maybe kind of lower those standards.

A hostile encounter or the possibility (or actuality) of critical feedback can be a motivational boost to one's role function. Annette V's inverse reaction to adjusting to a new work environment and a troubling situation with her new (Black) secretary exemplifies her work ethic.

> It didn't affect my work in terms of... performance. No. When people around me think that I can't do it, I dig in. There were nights when I would stay here 'til 12 o'clock at night to make sure it worked. And, I didn't really—and I knew I was by myself and I needed to do it to make it work. And, to this day, I still am like that. I don't let—just because you don't wanna do it—stop me. So, in that respect, it did—that's just the nature of my personality and so the misconception was as I had blockers and obstacles, that is—the assumption in their mind was that they were stopping me. The assumption in my mind is that I can always come up—as an out-of-the-box thinker—I'll come up with a plan to work around you, and it's gonna work.

Teaching/Course Content

In an example of strict scrutiny with regard to instructional competence, Mark T's unexpectedly different delivery of the curriculum in a particular course early in his new full-time teaching position at his public community college prompted students to divert and escalate their concerns to his dean.

Mark considered that his being new and inexperienced with the course, students' resistance to his teaching style, or his race might have motivated the complaints. Mark's subsequent conversation with his dean about the students' complaints concluded with his assumption that the students "did not have the experience that they thought they were going to get."

> I had a bunch of students at one point—the first time I taught Human Sexuality—they complained to the dean about how I was teaching. The class in the past had a history of being very salacious and I was teaching it very academically. I think that made them really upset that they were not having their carnival. But they didn't come to me directly about that. They went to my boss. That bothered me. That was a hurtful experience. But, I did wonder. I was like, well, gosh, would they have done this if I was White? Or, if they perceived me in the majority, maybe they would have or maybe not. I guess we'll never know. I was like, gosh, I wonder what that's about.

Theresa H's descriptions about her teaching experiences and encounters with White students in her classes illustrate her rationale for having to make pedagogical adjustments to her course curriculum as a consequence of her race, gender, and age. She believes that White faculty members (especially those who are male) are exempt from having to downplay such salient aspects of their identity in the classroom for the sake of the teaching and learning process and to maintain student rapport.

> ...I want to say, I have three strikes against me, not including sociology. I look younger than I am, so there's an age issue, ageism issue. With me being a woman, again, that's an obstacle, as well as being Black, that is an obstacle. There are times when, especially when I'm teaching Race and Ethnicity, that I consciously, when we cover African Americans, I consciously do not say "we" or "us" or "we used to." I say "they" or "they would" or "their history," to remove myself because I know as a sociologist if I were to put myself in the conversation then it would make it difficult for some students to really say what they have to say. It doesn't mean I always like what they say, but I've learned to remove myself from the conversation, which I don't think White or male, White male instructors would ever think about doing. So we have to be very aware of our race, very aware of our gender when talking about certain subjects, absolutely.

THEME: RESILIENCE

The theme of Resilience explores respondents' abilities and tactics to rebound and recover from racially hostile exchanges and to adapt to the equally antagonistic conditions to function effectively in their faculty roles. The instances featured in this theme include respondents' descriptions of formidable scenarios where personal and professional safety and welfare were implicitly or explicitly threatened.

Language, Lynching, Longevity

Khallid H's candid yet controversial comments during a campus event generated visceral reactions. During the panel discussion following a lecture on a celebrated historical figure, Khallid's remarks incited two calls for his termination: charges for his dismissal from his faculty position, and wishes for his murder, established by the presence of a racist graphic image at his office.

> So, I'm up on the panel and I didn't think I had said anything so profound. I just started my statement, and I just said, "Only in a country as wicked as the United States could you all honor pedophiles, rapists, slave-holding terrorists or murderers." The whole audience looks crazy. Several people went to the president to demand I be fired. Now this is where I think it was profound: someone slid a picture of a lynching under my door. A picture. Now, of course I don't know—we have to take the meaning for ourselves, but it wasn't some flowers. It was [a picture of] a lynching. Several folks called, left bad, you know, naughty messages on the phone. And, after that I think it really, really came out, you know, he doesn't fit in. He's not like the rest of the Black folk on campus. He's not one of us.

The aftermath of Khallid's outspoken yet sincere counterpoints consisted of explicit insolent words and acts to discourage his future participation in campus events, silence his challenging rhetoric to the mainstream discourse about the well-known historical figure and ultimately, to remove his very presence from the institution. Interestingly, in contrast to the racially intimidating messages and a photograph of a lynching, (a form of punishment and death by hanging of Blacks by White slave owners during chattel slavery in North America) Khallid received in response to his remarks, those who sought to kindly counsel him noted that he was the source of fear and anxiety on campus.

> I even had a couple people who came to me, "Look, I'm just coming as your friend. I want to let you know you have people on campus nervous. (Laugh) You know people are afraid of you." And, I said I've never fought anyone, I've never jumped up in the middle of a meeting and threatened anyone. I said, in fact I ought to be nervous about all y'all. Look at your history, right? And there's no history of us lynching anybody, putting on White sheets and raiding any towns. I should be nervous every day I walk on this campus.

"You're Nothing But a ... Nigger ... Let's Begin Class"

While the racially targeted affronts sent to Khallid were anonymous, a racial epithet that is delivered in person, attached with a face, a name, escalates the intensity of the impact to the instructor, the classroom, and the process to recovery, as Sharon C. experienced. Ongoing tension with a White female student during one semester peaked with the student's use of a racial slur that Sharon claims she has never been called in her 50 years of life, plus having lived in the South for a while.

> The only thing I can tell you is the student used to come to class late. And, of course, on my first-day handout if you come late you can't take the quizzes if the quizzes are being offered on that day or being given on that day. And, she came to class a few minutes late. She didn't finish the quizzes because she came in late. Again, that's not my issue so the day that I was passing back—I usually pass back the quizzes and that changed the whole procedure for me, another procedure I've changed—I would pass back the quizzes to them in the beginning of the next class. The one day she snatched the quiz from me and I said, "You didn't snatch that from me, did you?" And, she rolled her eyes and I said, "Please don't snatch anything from me." So, the next day she came in late again, and I'm passing back the quizzes from the previous day and she snatched it and I said, "I asked you not to snatch the quiz from me" and she said, "You're nothing but a fucking nigger!" and I thought, "Please leave my classroom."

After the student left the classroom, Sharon continued to distribute the quizzes to the students in the midst of her own astonishment, anxiety, anger, and subsequent struggle to regain self-control to face her students and continue with the class meeting. In the aftermath of the student's racial slur, Sharon said that she could not recall if she made any visible movements. "I don't know ... if I made any large gestures or was doing anything with my face ... but, inside I know I was steaming. I was angry as I could be because it never happened to me before ... I was just perplexed." The ruling from the combined administrative and faculty union investigation noted that the student had to take an online cultural sensitivity class, apologize (by letter) to Sharon and never take another class with her. Sharon insisted that the apology take place publicly (to the classmates in the classroom), equivalent to the original racist outburst. In response to the student's fear of Sharon's reaction, Sharon said, "if I didn't do anything to her that day, I'm not going to do anything to her on this day." Sharon agreed to remain in her office until after the student made the apology to the class, expecting to have about 10 minutes and "a chance to sit down and drink some water or something. Two minutes later, they came and got me and I said, 'it's over?' And they said, 'Yes' and I said, 'Ok. Let's begin class.'"

DISCUSSION

"Let's begin class," or its derivative, reflects respondents' persevering choice to remain in the public community college faculty role in spite of the racially hostile campus environment that mirrors the racist, discriminatory and anti-Black sentiment of society-at-large. The instances of compulsory expectations, tasks, and responsibilities imposed along with the interrelated components of racial stress (racial microaggressions) can lead to multiple manifestations of Racial Battle Fatigue and Role Strain, affecting both the personal (mental, emotional, and physical health) and the professional (faculty role performance) of the African American public community college faculty member. Portions of three themes from the study highlighted in this chapter characterize the range of descriptions from the 19 respondents indicative of the three RBF stress responses and Role Strain.

RBF Stress Responses to Racial Microaggressions

Respondents' accounts indicated multiple, concurrent, and cumulative RBF stress responses from either a single racial microaggression or a series of subtle and obvious racially assaultive encounters. One male respondent noted that student complaints made to his dean about his teaching during his first few semesters "bothered" him and that it "was a hurtful experience" that they bypassed him about their concerns, wondering if the students would have proceeded differently if he were White. This account is suggestive of the psychological RBF stress responses of frustration and disappointment. Stereotype threat was one emotional/behavioral RBF stress response that emerged from respondents' accounts relating to racial stereotypes. Briefly, stereotype threat is a framework developed by noted psychologist Claude Steele and his colleagues to explain the process and consequences of contending with negative stereotypes pertaining to aspects of one's social identity to avoid confirming, fulfilling, or perpetuating them and being judged by them for the sake of the individual and/or groups to which the negative stereotypes are associated (Steele & Aronson, 1995).

The relationship of RBF to racial microaggressions embodies the insidious, layered, accumulative words or acts conveyed by White students or colleagues toward the respondents with the possibility, intentional or otherwise, to cause harm. Respondents' accounts noted in the theme of Resilience describe a range of words and actions intended to intimidate the Black faculty member at both individual and environmental levels. Environmental microaggressions are visible or invisible, conscious or unconscious words and behaviors that systemically convey racially derogatory messages and insult or invalidate people of color (Sue, 2010). The streamlined presence of (full-time) Black faculty is suggestive of an environmental microaggression against African Americans.

Role Strain Dimensions

For the Black public community college faculty member, racial stress aggravates what extant literature has identified as the conventional stressors of the faculty role, such as time and resource constraints, substandard compensation and working conditions, lack of reward and recognition, unfulfilling or unrealistic career goals and expectations, and work/life imbalance (Dey, 1994, Gmelch, 1986, 1988; Larkin & Clagett, 1981; Seldin, 1987; Sorcinelli, 1992). Consistent with respondents' descriptions suggestive of racial microaggressions and subsequent RBF stress responses, instances of racialized role strain were linked to perceived or actual race-related expectations, tasks, and duties imposed upon respondents by students, colleagues, or administrators. Respondents in this study did not indicate difficulty in fulfilling the responsibilities of their faculty roles, and acknowledged the need to wisely appropriate time and attention to maintain optimal levels of role performance.

IMPLICATIONS

Campus Racial Climate and Interest Convergence

The pattern of Black faculty underrepresentation has persisted in historically White institutions despite the desegregation of higher education institutions resulting from the Brown v. Board of Education decisions nearly 60 years ago. The only exception to this pattern occurs at historically Black colleges and universities (HBCUs) (Cross & Slater, 2000; Smith, 1992). As of Fall 2001, African American faculty composed nearly 60% of the full-time faculty at HBCUs (NCES, 2004). Along with the civil rights legislation, Black student demand incited the sluggish yet subsequent incorporation of African Americans in the faculty ranks at historically White institutions (and eventually public community colleges), despite resistance and disregard for Black faculty (Banks, 1984; Sutherland, 1990). Attention and scrutiny from civil rights activists and "[t]he threat to institutional calm posed by student militance" prompted the recruitment of "selected" Black scholars to these historically White institutions "in the hope of demonstrating to the protestors that their schools were sensitive to and concerned about the historic absence of [B]lacks from university faculties" (Banks, 1984, p. 326).

Critical Race Theory's tenet of interest convergence sheds light on the causes of the past and present minimal inclusion of African American faculty at historically White colleges and universities and clarifies the rationale for the recruitment and retention of African American faculty. Conceptualized by the late Critical Race Theory scholar Derrick Bell, interest convergence attends to the notion that racial progress occurs when "the interests of Blacks in achieving racial equality will be accommodated only when it converges with the interests of Whites" (Bell, 1995, p. 20). Corresponding to the reasoning for the passage of civil rights legislation to desegregate schools in that "civil rights advances for Blacks always coincided with changing economic conditions and the self-interest of elite Whites" (Delgado & Stefancic, 2001, p. 18), historically White public community colleges gained from the integration of African American faculty in many ways: higher enrollments and tuition dollars from the new Black students, easing of tensions that incite racial unrest (and an improved public image), and a contingent of Black faculty members delegated to appease Black students with minimal interruption to the status quo. Banks (1984) speculated that the historically White institutional response to recruit Black faculty during the 1960s and 1970s might have occurred due to "the moral force that accompanied much of the protest." In actuality, it was more likely as Banks (1984) surmised: "perhaps simple political necessity was paramount" (p. 326). To note, three respondents in the research study highlighted in this chapter integrated their programs, departments, or institutions altogether with their appointment to their full-time faculty positions at their respective two-year colleges, most recently as the late 1980s and early 1990s. Other respondents became and remain one of only a few Black faculty members or faculty of color at all at their institutions.

Along with CRT's interest convergence principle serving to explain the motivation for historically White colleges and universities to diversify its faculties, Hurtado et al.'s (1998) framework draws attention to an institution's campus racial climate to materialize and examine environmental (or campus-wide) patterns of racial/ethnic diversity. The framework consists of a combination of external and internal (institutional) forces. Governmental policy, programs, and initiatives and sociohistorical components comprise the external forces, such as financial aid programs, state/ federal legislation and judicial decisions (e.g., affirmative action, higher education desegregation), and differentiation across state and institutional contexts. The legal and activist pursuits to desegregate public colleges and universities and the resulting civil rights legislation exemplify governmental initiatives. Sociohistorical forces include the past and present racially hostile conditions of the larger society that manifest similarly on college/university campuses. The campus racial climate is generated by the coupling of the aforementioned external domains with the following four internal forces as expressed through an institution's educational programs and practices: structural diversity (numerical representation); historical legacy of inclusion or exclusion; psychological environment (perceptions and attitudes), and behavioral climate (intergroup relations). Milem, Dey and White (2004) added "organizational/structural" as a fifth component and renamed structural diversity as "compositional diversity" to bring clarity with the incorporation of "a more accurate descriptor of the phenomenon that it represents" (p. 15). Hurtado et al. (1999) note that these dimensions are not mutually exclusive, but their interconnections challenge institutions to avoid the focus on numerical diversity "without recognizing how this change affects the psychological climate, or for opportunities across different groups on campus" (p. 6). The past and present-day disproportionate representation and participation of Black faculty at both two- and four-year institutions illustrate the internal forces of campus racial climate.

Most of the research literature on campus racial climate to date has explored through the student perspective, inclusive of in- and out-of-class encounters between faculty and students across race with the bulk of scholarly interest attending to undergraduates at four-year historically White institutions (Harper & Hurtado, 2007; Hurtado, 1992; Hurtado et al., 1998, 1999; Hurtado, 2001; Milem et al., 2005). However, these works call attention to the importance of faculty diversity as part of a college or university's comprehensive efforts toward student development and learning, diversification of the student body, and a commitment to the fulfillment of the community college mission. For educational leaders at public community colleges, especially deans and department/program chairs who work directly with faculty, these implications can inform strategies to address, alleviate, and resolve significant problems pertaining to racism, racial prejudice, and discrimination in the teaching and learning environment. Specific steps include implementing swift, impartial, and thorough investigations of race-related conflicts within and beyond the classroom, developing resolutions that emphasize an institutional intolerance for any words or actions that seek to or actually intimidate or cause harm to others due to race (or any other personal characteristics).

CONCLUSION

In his Fall 1987 article, "Black Faculty in White Colleges: A Dream Deferred," William Moore Jr. wrote, "In the academy, race is a difference that makes a difference" (p. 119). This prophetic sentiment still reverberates throughout the classrooms, halls, buildings, and campuses of America's colleges and universities 25 years later. Sadly, little progress has been made in increasing the numbers of full-time African American faculty in the academy, especially at public community colleges. Further exploration is greatly needed to examine the manifestation and impact of the racialized environment on the participants of the teaching and learning process, specifically, the perspectives of African American faculty at public community colleges to examine the working conditions of the faculty role. Additional in-depth inquiry can inform and guide educational leaders to set and adjust policies and practices that foster an optimal campus racial climate conducive to teaching and learning.

NOTES

1. African American and Black will be used interchangeably throughout this chapter.
2. The use of historically White institutions versus predominantly White institutions addresses the historical and present racialized environment, inclusive of campus climate and institutional structure that favorably serves Whites while disadvantaging African Americans and other populations of color, in addition to the numerical composition of the majority group on campus (Smith, Allen, & Danley, 2007).

REFERENCES

Alexander-Snow, M., & Johnson, B. J. (October1998). *Faculty of color and role performance.* Paper presented at the annual meeting of the Association for the Study of Higher Education, Miami, FL.

Allen, W., Epps, E., Guillory, E., Suh, S., Bonous-Hammarth, M., & Stassen, M. (2002) Outsiders within: Race, gender, and faculty status in U.S. higher education. In W. Smith, P. Altbach, & K. Lomotey (Eds.), *The racial crisis in American higher education: continuing challenges for the twenty-first century* (pp. 189–220). Albany, NY: State University of New York.

Allison, D. C. (2008). Free to be me? Black professors, white institutions. *Journal of Black Studies, 38*(4), 641–662.

Altbach, P. G., Lomotey, K., & Rivers Kyle, S. (1999). Race in higher education: The continuing crisis. In P. G. Altbach, R. O. Berdahl, & P. J. Gumport (Eds.), *American higher education in the twenty-first century: Social, political, and economic challenges.* Baltimore, MD: The Johns Hopkins University Press.

Banks, W. M. (1984). Afro-American scholars in the university: Roles and conflicts. *American Behavioral Scientist, 27*(3), 325–338.

Bell, W. A. (1995). Brown v. Board of Education and the interest convergence dilemma. In Crenshaw, K., Gotanda, N., Peller, G., & Thomas, K. (Eds.), *Critical race theory: The key writings that formed the movement.* (pp. 20–29). New York, NY: The New Press.

Biddle, B. J. (1986). Recent development in role theory. *Annual Review of Sociology, 12,* 67–92.

Bower, B. (2002). Campus life for faculty of color: Still strangers after all these years. *New Directions for Community Colleges, 118,* 79–87.

Bowman, P. J., & Smith, W. (2002). Racial ideology in the campus community: Emerging cross-ethnic differences and challenges. In W. Smith, P. Altbach, & K. Lomotey (Eds.), *The racial crisis in American higher education: Continuing challenges for the twenty-first century.* (pp. 103–120). Albany, NY: State University of New York.

Branch, A. J. (2001). How to retain African American faculty during times of challenge for higher education. In L. Jones (Ed.), *Retaining African Americans in higher education: Challenging paradigms for retaining students, faculty, &administrators.* (pp. 175–191). Sterling, VA: Stylus.

Brown, S. (1988). *Increasing minority faculty: An elusive goal.* NJ: Educational Testing Service.

Chesler, M., Lewis, A., & Crowfoot, J. (Eds.). (2005). *Challenging racism in higher education.* Lanham, MD: Rowman & Littlefield.

Chronicle of Higher Education (2010, December 12). *Who are the undergraduates?* Retrieved from http://chronicle.com/article/Who-Are-the-Undergraduates-/123916/

Cohen, A. M. (2001). Governmental policies affecting community colleges: A historical perspective. In B. K. Townsend & S. B. Twombly (Eds.), *Community colleges: Policy in the future context.* (pp. 3–22). Westport, CT: Ablex Publishing.

Cohen, A. M., & Brawer, F. B. (1994). *Managing community colleges: A handbook for effective practice.* San Francisco, CA: Jossey-Bass.

Cohen, A. M., & Brawer, F. B. (2008). *The American community college* (5th ed.). San Francisco, CA: Jossey-Bass.

Cole, S., Barber, E., Bolyard, M., & Linders, A. (2003). *Increasing faculty diversity: The occupational choices of high-achieving minority students.* Cambridge, MA: Harvard University Press.

Cooper, J. E., & Stevens, D. D. (2002). The journey toward tenure. In J. E. Cooper & D. D. Stevens (Eds.), *Tenure in the sacred grove: Issues and strategies for women and minority faculty.* Albany, NY: State University of New York Press.

Crenshaw, K., Gotanda, N., Peller, G., & Thomas, K. (Eds.). (1995). *Critical race theory: The key writings that formed the movement.* New York, NY: The New Press.

Cross, T., & Slater, R.B. (Eds.). (2000). African Americans in faculty posts: Still tapping the glass and hoping to get in. *The Journal of Blacks in Higher Education, 28,* 22–23.

Delgado, R., & Stefancic, J. (2001). *Critical race theory: An introduction.* New York: New York University Press.

Delgado, R., & Stefancic, J. (2012). *Critical race theory: An introduction* (2nd ed.). New York: New York University Press.

Dey, E. (1994). Dimensions of faculty stress: A recent survey. *Review of Higher Education, 17*(3), 305–322.

Evans, A., Chun, E. B., & Association for the Study of Higher Education. (2007). *Are the walls really down?: Behavioral and organizational barriers to faculty and staff diversity.* San Francisco, CA: Wiley Subscription Services at Jossey-Bass.

Feagin, J. R., Vera, H., & Imani, N. (1996). The agony of education: Black students at White colleges and universities. New York, NY: Routledge.

Gmelch, W. H., & Wilke, P.K. (1988, April). *Toward a comprehensive view of faculty stress in higher education.* Paper presented at the annual meeting of the American Educational Research Association, New Orleans.

Gmelch, W. H., Wilke, P. K., & Lovrich, N. P. (1986). Dimensions of stress among university faculty: Factor-Analytic results from a national survey. *Research in Higher Education, 24*(3), 266–490.

Goode, W. J. (1960). A theory of role strain. *American Sociological Review, 25*(4), 483–496.

Grubb, W. N. (1999). *Honored but invisible: An inside look at teaching in community colleges.* New York, NY: Routledge.

Hardy, D. E., & Laanan, F. (2006). Characteristics and perspectives of faculty at public 2-year colleges. *Community College Journal of Research and Practice. 30,* 787–811.

Harlow, R. (2003). "Race doesn't matter, but" . . . : The effect of race on professors' experiences and emotion management in the undergraduate classroom. *Social Psychology Quarterly, 66*(4), 348–363.

Harper, S. R., & Hurtado, S. (2007). Nine Themes in Campus Racial Climates and Implications for Institutional Transformation. *New Directions for Student Services, 120,* 7–24.

Harvey, W. B. (1994). African American faculty in community colleges: Why they aren't there. *New Directions for Community Colleges, 87,* 19.

Harvey, W. B. (2007). Maximizing higher education attainment: The critical factor to improving African American communities. In J. Jackson (Ed.), *Strengthening the African American educational pipeline: Informing research, policy, and practice.* Albany, NY: State University of New York Press.

Harvey, W. B., & Scott-Jones, D. (1985). We can't find any: The elusiveness of Black faculty members in American higher education. *Issues in Education, 3*(1), 68–77.

Harvey, W. B., & Valadez, J. (Eds.). (1994). *Creating and maintaining a diverse faculty.* San Francisco, CA: Jossey-Bass.

Hurtado, S. (1992). The campus racial climate: Contexts of conflict. *Journal of Higher Education, 63*(5), 539–569.

Hurtado, S., Milem, J. F., Clayton-Pedersen, A. R., & Allen, W. R. (1998). Enhancing campus climates for racial/ethnic diversity: Educational policy and practice. *Review of Higher Education, 21*(3), 279–302.

Hurtado, S., Milem, J., Clayton-Pedersen, A., & Allen, W. (1999). *Enacting diverse learning environments: Improving the climate for racial/ethnic diversity in higher education.* ASHE-ERIC Higher Education Report Volume 26, No. 8. Washington D.C.: The George Washington University, Graduate School of Education and Human Development.

Jackson, J., & Phelps, L. (2004). Diversity in the two-year college academic workforce. *New Directions for Community Colleges, 127,* 79–88.

Jayakumar, U. M., Howard, T. C., Allen, W. R., & Han, J. C. (2009). Racial privilege in the professoriate: An exploration of campus climate, retention, and satisfaction. *The Journal of Higher Education, 80*(5), 538–563.

Johnson, B. J., & Pichon, H. (2007). The status of African American faculty in the academy: Where do we go from here? In J. Jackson (Ed.), *Strengthening the African American educational pipeline: Informing research, policy, and practice* (pp. 97–114). Albany, NY: State University of New York Press.

Kahn, R. L., Wolfe, D. M., Quinn, R. P., & Snoek, J. (1964). *Organizational stress: Studies in role conflict and ambiguity.* New York, NY: John Wiley & Sons.

Kayes, P. (2006). New paradigms for diversifying faculty and staff in higher education: Uncovering cultural biases in the search and hiring process. *Multicultural Education, 14*(2), 65–69.

Laden, B., & Hagedorn, L. (2000). Job satisfaction among faculty of color in academe: individual survivors or institutional transformers. *New Directions for Institutional Research, 105,* 57–66.

Ladson-Billings, G., & Tate, W. (1995). Toward a critical race theory of education. *Teachers College Record, 97*(1), 47–68.

Larkin, P., & Clagett, C. (1981). *Sources of faculty stress and strategies for its management.* Largo: Prince George's Community College, Office of Institutional Research.

Lewis, C., & Middleton, V. (2003). African American in community colleges: A review of research reported in the Community College Journal of Research and Practice: 1990–2000. *Community College Journal of Research and Practice, 27,* 787–798.

Lovell, N. B., Alexander, M. L., & Kirkpatrick, L. A. (2002). Minority faculty at community colleges [Fastback 490]. *Phi Delta Kappa Educational Foundation,* 2–36.

McCormick, A. C., & Cox, R. D. (2003). Classifying two-year colleges: Purposes, possibilities, and pitfalls. *New Directions for Community Colleges, 122,* 7–15.

Merriam, S. B. (1998). *Qualitative research and case study applications in education.* San Francisco, CA: Jossey-Bass.

Milem, B. J. F., Chang, M. J., & Antonio, A. L. (2005). Making Diversity Work on Campus : A Research-Based Perspective. *Association of American Colleges and Universities,* (pp.13–18). Association of American Colleges and Universities.

Miles, M. B., & Huberman, A. (1994). *Qualitative data analysis: An expanded sourcebook* (2nd ed.). Thousand Oaks, CA: Sage Publications.

Milem, J. F., Dey, E. L., & White, C. B. (2004). Diversity considerations in health professions education. In B. D. Smedley, A. S. Butler, & L. R. Bristow (Eds.), *In the nation's compelling interest: Ensuring diversity in the health care workforce,* (pp. 345–90). Washington, DC: National Academies Press.

Moore, W. (1987). Black faculty in White colleges: A dream deferred. *Educational Record, 68*(4), 117–121.

National Center for Education Statistics. (2004). *Historically black colleges and universities, 1976 to 2001.* Washington, D.C.: U.S. Department of Education.

National Center for Education Statistics. (2007). Digest of Education Statistics *(2003 and 2005 Integrated Postsecondary Education Data System).* Washington, D.C.: U.S. Department of Education.

National Center for Education Statistics. (2010). Digest of Education Statistics *(2009 Integrated Postsecondary Education Data System).* Washington, D.C.: U.S. Department of Education.

National Center for Education Statistics. (2011). Digest of Education Statistics *(Institutional Characteristics Survey (IPEDS-IC:90–99), and Fall 2001 through Fall 2008).* Washington D.C.: U.S. Department of Education.

Outcalt, C. L. (Ed.). (2002). *Community college faculty: Characteristics, practices, and challenges.* San Francisco, CA: Jossey-Bass.

Patitu, C. L., Young-Hawkins, L., Larke, P., Webb-Johnson, G., & Sterling, K. (2000). African American faculty balancing the triumvirate: Teaching, research & service. *NASAP Journal, 3*(1), 46–65.

Roithmayr, D. (1999). Introduction to critical race theory in educational research and praxis. In L. Parker, D. Deyhle, & S. Villenas (Eds.), *Race is...race isn't: Critical race theory and qualitative studies in education.* (p. 1). Boulder, CO: Westview Press.

Seldin, P. (1987). Research findings on causes of academic stress. *New Directions for Teaching and Learning, 29,* 13–21.

Smith, D. G., Turner, C. S., Osei-Kofi, N., & Richards, S. (2004). Interrupting the usual: Successful strategies for hiring diverse faculty. *Journal of Higher Education, 75*(2), 133–160.

Smith, E. (1992). *A comparative study of occupational stress in African American and White university faculty.* Lewiston, NY: Edwin Mellen Press.

Smith, E., & Witt, S. L. (1993). A comparative study of occupational stress among African American and White university faculty: A research note. *Research in Higher Education, 34*(2), 229–241.

Smith, W. A. (2004). Black faculty coping with racial battle fatigue: The campus racial climate in a post-civil rights era. In D. Cleveland (Ed.), *A long way to go: Conversations about race by African American faculty and graduate students.* (pp. 171–190). New York, NY: Peter Lang Publishing.

Smith, W. A., Allen, W. R., & Danley, L. L. (2007). "Assume the position . . . you fit the description": Psychosocial experiences and racial battle fatigue among African American male college students. *American Behavioral Scientist, 51*(4), 551–578.

Smith, W. A., Hung, M., & Franklin, J. D. (2011). Racial battle fatigue and the miseducation of Black men: Racial microaggressions, societal problems, and environmental stress. *The Journal of Negro Education, 80*(1), 63–82.

Smith, W. A., Yosso, T. J., & Solórzano, D. G. (2006). Challenging racial battle fatigue on historically white campuses: A critical race examination of race-related stress. In C. A. Stanley (Ed.), *Faculty of color: Teaching in predominantly white colleges and universities.* (p. 299). Bolton, MA: Anker Publishing Company, Inc.

Smith, W. A., Yosso, T. J., & Solórzano, D. G. (2007). Racial primes and black misandry on historically white campuses: Toward critical race accountability in educational administration. *Educational Administration Quarterly, 43*(5), 559–585.

Solmon, L., Solmon, M., & Schiff, T. (2002). The changing demographics: Problems and opportunities. In W. Smith, P. Altbach, & K. Lomotey (Eds.), *The racial crisis in American higher education: continuing challenges for the twenty-first century.* (pp. 43–75). Albany, NY: State University of New York.

Solórzano, D. G., & Yosso, T. J. (2002). A critical race counterstory of race, racism, and affirmative action. *Equity & Excellence in Education, 35*(2), 155–168.

Solórzano, D., Ceja, M., & Yosso, T. (2000). Critical race theory, racial microaggressions, and campus racial climate: The experiences of African American college students. *Journal of Negro Education, 69*(1/2), 60.

Somers, P., Cofer, J., Austin, J. L., Inman, D., Martin, T., Rook, S., & Stokes, T. (1998). Faculty and staff: The weather radar of campus climate. *New Directions for Institutional Research, 98,* 35–52.

Sorcinelli, M. D. (1992). New and junior faculty stress: research and responses. *New Directions for Teaching and Learning, 50,* 27–37.

Steele, C. M. & Aronson, J. (1995). Stereotype threat and the intellectual test performance of African-Americans. *Journal of Personality and Social Psychology, 68*(5), 797–811.

Sue, D. W. (2010). Microaggressions, marginality and oppression: An introduction. In D. W. Sue (Ed.), *Microaggressions and marginality: Manifestation, dynamics, and impact.* (pp. 3–22). Hoboken, NJ: John Wiley & Sons.

Sue, D. W., Capodilupo, C. M., & Holder, A. M. (2008a). Racial microaggressions in the life experience of Black Americans. *Professional Psychology, Research and Practice, 39*(3), 329–336.

Sue, D. W., Capodilupo, C. M., Torino, G. C., Bucceri, J. M., Holder, A. M., Nadal, K. L., & Esquilin, M. (2007). Racial microaggressions in everyday life. *American Psychologist, 62*(4), 271–286.

Sue, D. W., Lin, A. I., Torino, G. C., Capodilupo, C. M., & Rivera, D. P. (2009). Racial microaggressions and difficult dialogues on race in the classroom. *Cultural Diversity and Ethnic Minority Psychology, 15*(2), 183–190.

Sue, D. W., Nadal, K. K., Capodilupo, C. M., Lin, A. I., Torino, G. C., & Rivera, D. P. (2008b). Racial microaggressions against Black Americans: Implications for counseling. *Journal of Counseling and Development, 86*(3), 330–338.

Sue, D. W., Lin, A. I., & Rivera, D.P. (2009). Racial microaggressions in the workplace: Manifestation and impact. In J. L. Chin (Ed.), *Diversity in mind and in action: Disparities and competence: Service delivery, education, and employment contexts.* (pp. 157–172). Santa Barbara, CA: Praeger/ABC–CLIO.

Sutherland, M. E. (1990). Black faculty in white academia: The fit is an uneasy one. *The Western Journal of Black Studies, 14*(1), 17–23.

Tate, W. F. (1997). Critical race theory and education: History, theory, and implications. *Review of Research in Education, 22,* 195–247.

Townsend, B. K., & Twombly, S. B. (2007). Community college faculty: Overlooked and undervalued. In K. Ward, & L. E. Wolf-Wendel (Eds.). *ASHE Higher Education Report.* Hoboken, NJ: Association for the Study of Higher Education.

Tuitt, F., Hanna, M., Martinez, L. M., del Carmen Salazar, M., & Griffin, R. (2009). Teaching in the line of fire: Faculty of color in the Academy, Thought and Action, Fall, 65–74.

Turner, C, & Myers, Jr., S. (2000). *Faculty of color in academe: Bittersweet success.* Needham Heights, MA: Allyn & Bacon.

Turner, C., Myers, S., & Creswell, J. (1999). Exploring underrepresentation: The case of faculty of color in the Midwest. *The Journal of Higher Education, 70*(1), 27–59.

Turner, R. H. (2002). Role theory. In J. H. Turner (Ed.), *Handbook of sociological theory.* New York, NY: Kluwer Academic/Plenum.

U.S. Census Bureau. (2011, June 3). State and county quickfacts. website: http://quickfacts.census.gov/qfd/states/00000.html

Villalpando, O., & Delgado B. D. (2002). A critical race theory analysis of barriers that impede the success of faculty of color. In W. Smith, P. Altbach, & K. Lomotey (Eds.), *The racial crisis in American higher education: Continuing challenges for the twenty-first century* (pp. 243–269). Albany, NY: State University of New York.

Zamani, E. (2006). African American student affairs professionals in community college settings: A commentary for future research (Reprint). In B. Townsend, & D. Bragg (Eds.), *ASHE Reader on Community Colleges.* (pp. 173–180). Boston, MA: Pearson Custom Publishing.

CHAPTER 4

CRITICAL RACE THEORY AND COLLEGE READINESS

A Review of the Literature

Chad Everett Kee
Iowa State University

The review of the literature search was undertaken to gain a better understanding of college readiness among minoritized populations through a Critical Race Theory (CRT) lens. A brief review of the literature relevant to CRT was established to identify major tenets of CRT that are germane to education and the topic of college readiness. It is hoped that this chapter will help in addressing the growing issues present within our educational systems that limit college preparation and consequently college access, and college completion, among minoritized students. More importantly, an examination of CRT and college readiness will uncover possibilities, inform teaching strategies, and challenge current policies that promote dominant cultural practices while failing to legitimize other cultures that possess less capital. This chapter is organized using three tenets of CRT as reported by multiple scholars, particularly Ladson-Billings (1998) that demonstrated a relationship between CRT and college readiness: curriculum and instruc-

Confronting Racism in Higher Education, pages 67–82
Copyright © 2013 by Information Age Publishing
All rights of reproduction in any form reserved.

tion, assessment, and school funding. A brief review of the literature relevant to CRT and college readiness is presented to provide a foundational understanding prior to addressing the three tenets.

CRITICAL RACE THEORY

Toni Morrison, a Nobel Prize and Pulitzer Prize-winning American novelist, editor, and professor who thoroughly captures social issues through writing, eloquently argued that race and racism can be found in every social interaction and structure. Morrison (1992), through a short but substantive statement, adequately conceptualized the work of critical race theorist and the Critical Race Theory movement. Acknowledging the impact and influence throughout American society, the early work of critical race scholars and activists sought to provide the language and challenge needed to push the civil rights movement and transform the social constructs of race, racism, and power (Delgado & Stefancic, 2001). In doing so, the underlying goal and motivation among the activists and scholars were to advance the civil rights movements of the1960s. Delgado and Stefancic highlighted the significant differences between the civil rights movement and CRT as an opportunity to expand the perspective to include history and economics, and move beyond incrementalism to questioning the foundation of liberal order (p. 3).

It is important to note that CRT was not birthed out of the civil rights movement, nor to weaken the civil rights movement, but to expand beyond critical legal studies (CLS) in order to examine and challenge the influence of race and racism in educational practice and policy development. In addition, CRT emerged from a failure to adequately include racism in the CLS agenda, which was argued by some of the founding fathers and early writers of CRT such as Derrick Bell and Alan Freeman (Delgado, 1995; Delgado & Stefancic, 2001). Therefore, CRT became an outgrowth of the civil rights movement, CLS, and radical feminism during the 1970s, but as a separate entity with a unique set of guiding principles specific to race and racism (Delgado & Stefancic, 2001; Ladson-Billings, 1998).

At this time, a clear and shared definition of CRT does not exists. However, the core tenets of CRT are clear and have expanded significantly addressing multiple issues of race and racism within American society. Despite multiple tenets, critical race scholars and activists share two areas of interests: to understand the history and relationship between white supremacy and marginalized populations, and to challenge the connection between racial power and law (Ladson-Billings, 1998). The two areas of interests reveal the ongoing need posed by CRT supporters to reflect on American history and the power differential between races, as well as acting on "lessons learned" to inform future practice. It is important to note that critical race theorists and activists seek to establish a balance of power between racial groups, by applying multiple disciplinary areas such as law, sociology, ethnic studies, and history to inform reflection and critique of policies through a CRT lens (Bell, 1987; Delgado & Stefancic, 2001).

I do not intend to offer a comprehensive review of CRT due to the expansive literature that currently exists since the origin of the movement during the early 1970s; rather I use the four tenets of CRT posed by leading scholars in order to conceptualize the relationship between CRT and college readiness among minoritized populations. The four tenets are: unmasking racism (Delgado, 1995; Ladson-Billings, 1998), employing storytelling (Barnes, 1990; Delgado, 1995; Ladson-Billings, 1998), challenging liberalism (Crenshaw, 1988; Ladson-Billings, 1998), and acknowledging that whites are primary beneficiaries of civil rights legislation (Ladson-Billings, 1998). The four tenets will serve as an informal guide to conceptualize the relationship between CRT and college readiness challenges, and to provide recommendations that may lead to policy changes and liberatory potential of schooling (hooks, 1994) that will support college readiness among minoritized populations.

Yosso (2005) argued that "CRT in education refutes dominant ideology and White privilege while validating and centering the experiences of People of Color" (p. 74). The majority of the literature reviewed examined the issue of college readiness for the minoritized students from a dominant culture ideology. Using CRT will advance the conversation to examine the experiences of students of color from a race lens, not the individual and definitely not from a deficit mentality. Following a brief literature review of college readiness the four tenets of CRT will be applied to conceptualize the educational practices that limit college preparation among minoritized students.

COLLEGE READINESS

A considerable amount of research has been published on college readiness, and the barriers to gaining access to college for minoritized populations due to a lack of readiness. It is important to provide an overview of research and reports on "college readiness" among minoritized populations. The purpose of this analysis is to review the research supporting college readiness while identifying information that aligns with CRT.

Although an extensive amount of literature exists many researchers continue to ask, "What is college readiness?" An agreed upon understanding and shared definition of college readiness has not entered the literature at this time. Many researchers stated the difficulty of defining college readiness is due to the complexity of the subject matter (Byrd & Macdonald,

2005). The complex issues mentioned throughout the literature include measures of academic and intellectual skills, emotional aptitude, and being equipped to socially adjust to a college environment. Although somewhat different, each definition includes some component of preparation. For this review, college readiness will be defined as "the level of preparation a student needs in order to enroll and succeed, without remediation, in a credit-bearing general education course at a postsecondary institution that offers a baccalaureate degree or transfer to a baccalaureate program" (Conley, 2008).

Consistently, a students' level of readiness is often juxtaposed against ones' level of preparation for college which illuminates the concept of college readiness. Conley (2008) presented "a broader, more comprehensive conception of college readiness built on four facets: key cognitive strategies, key content knowledge, academic behaviors, and contextual skills and knowledge" (p. 3). All of which can be determined by grades and standardized tests scores. The use of quantitative measures in isolation can create barriers for minoritized students to gain access to college.

The literature and data revealed a significant need to analyze the complex issue of college readiness, particularly for minoritized students. The achievement gap demonstrated throughout K-12 education between White students and non-White students continue to widen. Thus, students who are members of racial minority groups or low-income communities are less likely to be prepared for the academic, emotional, and social demands encountered throughout postsecondary education and especially during the early years. Although emotional and social readiness are significant areas in need of exploration and examination, the review of the literature focused on the academic and intellectual readiness among minoritized populations. The investigation included the aforementioned topics as a means of highlighting the different experiences and diverse learning needs among minoritized populations using a CRT framework.

One of the measures of college readiness is a students' ability to handle the rigor of college level work. In order to be adequately prepared for college coursework, the K-12 curriculum must be directly connected to the college curriculum. Consequently, students will have a better understanding of what to expect beyond high school, and be intellectually prepared to handle the college environment. A rigorous high school curriculum is a clear predictor of college success and completion of the baccalaureate degree (Martinez & Klopott, 2003).

However, one of the many challenges of connecting the curricula is the inconsistent course titles. Analyses of college courses reveal that although a college course may have the same name as a high school course, college instructors pace their courses more rapidly, emphasize different aspects of the material taught, and have very different goals for their courses than do high school instructors (Conley et al., 2008). As a result, students (especially minoritized students) enter a course with a false sense of confidence, assuming a level of comprehension for college coursework that could negatively influence a student's academic success.

Also, college instructor expectations are drastically different from K-12 instructors. "The college instructor is more likely to expect students to support arguments with evidence, solve complex problems that have no obvious answer, and generally think deeply about what they are being taught" (National Research Council, 2002). College instructors indicate an interest in students entering with a "voice" and critical thinking skills in order to effectively engage with the curriculum.

Two significant themes that emerged from the literature review on college readiness are: the need to examine teacher expectations and beliefs of students, and parental involvement that will support student engagement.

TEACHER EXPECTATIONS AND BELIEFS

A common theme distinct throughout the literature was the influence of teacher (e.g., teacher, counselor, and school administrator, etc.) expectations of, and beliefs about, students. Reid and Moore (2008) conducted interviews which identified students' interests for teachers with high expectations and to challenge them (the student) to use higher level thinking and problem solving skills (p. 242). Beyond expectations, challenging their beliefs including internalized stereotypes, judgments, and overt forms of racism is important to students' academic success.

Assuming that knowledge and understanding produces change, it has been suggested that educators increase their familiarity with daily life experiences of the minoritized students in order to overcome stereotypes and assumptions. Upon recognition of their daily challenges at home and school, it becomes imperative to provide interventions that prepare all students to succeed (Reid & Moore, 2008) and seek to thoughtfully support their academic and personal needs. Critical Race theorists and activists alike propose including in the curriculum the opportunity for multiple voices to be heard which can be incorporated as an intervention tool.

PARENTAL INVOLVEMENT AND SOCIOECONOMIC STATUS

Moving beyond teacher beliefs and expectations, parental involvement and socioeconomic status (SES) have a significant influence on student success. Recent research and past assertions submitted by Bourdieau and Passeron (1977) strongly argued that cultural capital and SES are major factors that negatively or positively impact parental involvement. "Parents' educational capabilities, their view of the appropriate division of labor between teachers and parents, the information they had about their children's schooling, and the time, money, and other material resources available in the home all mediated parents' involvement in schooling" (Lareau, 1987).

Parents' responses to requests from middle-class schools are much higher than parents at working-class schools (Lareau, 1987). As proven throughout this review, students of color traditionally are less likely to be prepared for college. With that being understood, people of color are more likely to be in low-income positions, have constant exposure to racial discrimination, and have limited access to cultural capital leading to an ongoing cycle of social reproduction.

The cycle of social reproduction can be challenged with intentional efforts among educators to design a curriculum that creates room for multiple voices to be heard. In order to adequately meet the challenge, educators must overcome personal beliefs and low expectations, while providing thoughtful instruction that is applicable to the daily life experiences of minoritized students.

The literature related to college readiness and the related issues are well documented. For the purpose of this literature, the aforementioned themes are used to identify major issues that educators, policymakers, and parents are grappling with today. In addition, the two themes uncover a direct correlation to CRT. However, CRT supporters seek to address issues of race, racism, and power on a macro-level that hinges on the idea of challenging policies and practices that will produce long-term systemic change throughout educational research and policy.

CURRICULUM AND INSTRUCTION

Allowing space for multiple voices to be heard in an educational environment provides an extensive amount of insight regarding individual and group experiences as well as an opportunity to strengthen engagement. Research conducted by Gonzalez, Stoner, and Stovel (2003) included a qualitative study among Latina high school graduates who chose to pursue higher education. The study conducted by Gonzalez provided information regarding life experiences that can be used to identify strategies that will enhance student success.

Listening to the voice of others creates an opportunity for validation and challenges others to view events and life experiences from various angles. Lareau (1987) conducted a study that offered powerful insight and illuminated the differences between parents of low-income status as opposed to those of middle and upper-class status through the use of "voice," and allowed parents to share their understanding of the role of schooling. To demonstrate the power of voice, I submit the following testimonials:

> I see the school as being a very strong instructional force, more so than we are here at home. I guess that I am comfortable with that, from what I have seen. It is a three-to-one ratio or something, where out of a possible four, he is getting three quarters of what he needs from the school, and then a quarter of it from here. Maybe it would be better if our influence was stronger, but I am afraid that in this day and age it is not possible to do any more than that even if you wanted to (Lareau, 1987, p. 80).

A middle/upper-class father responded to the same question,

> I don't think of teachers as more educated than me or in a higher position than me. I don't have any sense of hierarchy. I am not higher than them, and they are not higher than me. We are equals. We are reciprocals. So if I have a problem, I will talk to them. I have a sense of decorum. I wouldn't go busting into a classroom and say something... They are not working for me, but they also aren't doing something I couldn't do. It is more a question of a division of labor (Lareau, 1987, p. 80).

Despite the insight offered through such qualitative examination, very little literature exists that allow for an opportunity to examine parental voices and experiences specifically from various classes that can inform educational policies and practices.

As parents and students lived experiences are included in the learning process, I argue that students will find their "voice" at an earlier age. Thus, students will be more engaged in the learning process and mentally capable of connecting pre-existing knowledge and relating it to new knowledge. If students are able to find their "voice," it will improve academic achievement and social engagement.

Students pre-existing knowledge, cultures, and histories, as argued among CRT supporters, should be part of the curriculum. How a student makes meaning out of new knowledge and engages in dialogue with instructors are reflections of his or her class background. According to Knaus (2009), having a voice supports the overall development of skills which ultimately deepens student engagement and demonstrates to students their connection to schooling (p. 134). In order to maximize on a students learning, teachers must be able to identify diverse learning needs. For example, working-class students learn "restricted" linguistic codes while middle-class children use "elaborated" codes. Critical theorists argue that schools generally affirm and reward students who exhibit the elaborately coded "middle-class" speech, while disconfirming and devaluing students who use restricted "working-class" coded speech (Darder, Baltodano, & Torres, 2003).

Utilizing a restricted "working-class" code of speech lessens the cultural capital of low income students within a school system. Cultural capital represents ways of talking and language practices, among other characteristics such as acting, modes of style, socialization and values (Wink, 1996; Darder et al., 2003) which must be considered when examining college readiness through a CRT lens. It is important to note that cultural capital refers to the general background, knowledge, disposition, and skills that are passed on from one generation to another (Bourdieu & Passeron, 1977). Therefore, these are skills that are entrenched within cultures and part of a student's daily socialization. Schools systematically devalue the cultural capital of low income working-class students while rewarding those who exhibit middle-class characteristics (Darder et al., 2003). Teachers are challenged to validate the relationship between culture and class within the classroom environment by refusing to adopt practices promoted and perceived "correct" by dominant culture in order to improve academic success among low income racially marginalized students (Darder et al., 2003).

Wink (1996) asserted that thoughtful consciousness means that we have a voice and the courage to question ourselves and the role we are playing in maintaining an educational process that we do not value (p. 26). As our consciousness is raised, we develop an understanding and use for CRT and we are equipped to act in a way that takes responsibility for a curriculum and type of instruction that values all races, cultures, and classes of students which can inform practice and policy development.

Critical Race scholars and activists support pragmatic changes within the classroom but focus greater attention on policy changes that advance the legitimizing of all races, classes, and cultures to enhance learning outcomes for students. Many supporters of CRT have argued that the current state of the school curriculum and instructional practices are to maintain White power and privilege while dismantling the experiences and knowledge of minoritized communities (Knaus, 2009), and leading with an ideology that racial minorities are deficient and inferior to White students. Changes in the overarching curriculum will induce modifications of instructional practices such as the use of storytelling and giving voice to marginalized populations as well as how we assess student learning and readiness for college.

ASSESSMENT

KnowledgeWorks Foundation (2007) proved that a large percentage of minoritized students are three years behind in reading and math by the end of 8th grade, and four years behind *if* they reach 12th grade. Subsequently, minoritized students who are traditionally low-income and African American, Latino, or Native American are less likely to score well on standardized tests, less likely to engage in classroom learning activities, and more likely to drop out of school. However, this does not concretely discount a student's "readiness" for college. What does it mean to be ready and how to assess one's readiness for college?

Failing to complete a rigorous secondary curriculum and attending resource-poor schools, minoritized students commonly score lower on standardized tests than their White counterparts (Green, 2006). Due to a poor curriculum, limited school resources, which impact standardized tests scores, minoritized populations are less likely to be admitted to four-year institutions. Jencks (1998) affirmed that people of color, particularly African American and Latino students who speak English as a second language, score lower on standardized tests than White students (p. 107). "Increasingly, decisions about college readiness are made by standardized assessments. Standardized-test-based admissions may overlook nontraditional students' historical and cultural background that might identify strengths related to readiness for college" (Byrd & Macdonald, 2005; Yosso, 2005).

The lack of congruency between academic performance and test scores, establishes a legitimate argument that standardized tests are culturally biased (Zamudio, 2011), have a negative impact on minoritized students, and are not the best predictor of academic ability or success (Osequera, 2004). Several studies have revealed that "African American and Latino students have lower scores on standardized tests because of cultural bias inherent in the tests" (Hacker, 1992; Jencks, 1998).

Bollinger (2002) declared that "admission to the top universities has magnified the importance of scoring well, resulting in heightened student and parent anxiety, growing media coverage of college admissions, and new products and product advertising" (p. B11). The issue of heightened anxiety can have a negative impact on the test scores among minoritized populations, having a negative consequence for college admission.

Standardized tests are commonly used as a determining factor in gaining admission to a credit-bearing postsecondary institution. The demand for high test scores is fueled as competition for admission to selective colleges (Walpole et al., 2005). However, the literature reveals that a rigorous K-12 curriculum and grade point average are higher predictors of student success than standardized tests such as the SAT or American College Test (ACT) (Adelman, 1999). The argument presented by Adelman challenges one to question the purpose of admissions assessment instruments. I submit that the admissions standards such as the SAT support an institutions rankings and competitive environment providing an opportunity for marketing and greater exposure and limiting access to minoritized groups. Regrettably minoritized populations are denied admission and systemic forms of oppression are retained for selfish motives upheld by institutional politics and bureaucracy.

Scholars, researchers, and activists debate the cultural biases embedded in the SAT. Due to the bias nature of the SAT one must asks a number of questions: Who designed the SAT? What was the initial motivation and purpose of the SAT? In order to adequately address the abovementioned questions, a historical review of intelligence tests leading to the development of the SAT must be considered.

According to Weissglass (1998), intelligence tests were established to determine who should be allowed to attend private institutions during the early 1900s (p. 2). The introduction of intelligence testing during the 1900s, around the time of World War I, led to additional forms of testing not only for access to private schooling, but to measure competency among newly enlisted soldiers. The use of intelligence testing continued to expand leading to research conducted by Princeton University professor Carl Brigham.

Zamudio et al. (2011) concluded that Brigham posited that African Americans, Jews, Irish, and immigrants were intellectually inferior to western and northern Europeans (p. 66). Brigham's research and position led to an appointment with the College Board and putting into practice the Scholastic Aptitude Test, known today as the SAT, the following year in 1926 (Zamudio et al., 2011). Acknowledging that the SAT was developed by someone who openly demonstrated racist ideologies and behaviors, correlates with the critique presented by CRT activists and scholars who argue that the SAT was designed to promote dominant culture and dismiss the knowledge and experiences of non-White students. However, in addition to the related challenges and hidden motives of the SAT, studies prove that funding of schools has a profound effect on student learning and preparation for standardized tests.

SCHOOL FUNDING

A large and growing body of literature has investigated unequal schooling and unequal resources as a factor in the dropout rate, lack of college readiness, and the overarching systemic forms of oppression that are threaded throughout the educational system. According to Ladson-Billings (1998), Critical Race Theory scholars argued that "school funding is a function of institutional and structural racism" (p. 20), intentionally creating and supporting unequal schooling in the US. Wong and Casing (2010) supported this notion through an examination of the state funding process by arguing that state funding has failed to be the great "equalizer" between property-wealthy schools and property-poor schools, because a larger percentage of school funding comes from community property taxes and not state or federal funds (p. 29).

Resource disparities between urban and suburban schools are prevalent today just as they were in the 1950s and warrant greater attention among scholars regarding college readiness. Bell (1980) argued, in the context of the interest-convergence dilemma, that African American students are more likely to attend isolated and inferior schools because of a failure within the legal system to inform equitable change and social reform. Still today, more than 30 years later, we know that students of color are more likely to attend urban schools with limited resources. "African American and Latino students are more likely to attend urban schools that are resource poor, to be taught by less qualified teachers, to have teachers with lower expectations, and to be tracked away from higher achieving groups" (Gonzalez et al., 2003). In order to change this pattern among minoritized students attending low resource schools, the funding policies must change in order to balance the amount of power and resources among schools despite community property taxes and external funding sources.

Although schooling practices from state to state differ, funding based on property taxes are a shared practice (Ladson-Billings, 1998). As a result, a greater percentage of racial minorities are less-likely to complete high school, and less likely to be qualified for postsecondary education. Wong and Casing (2010) framed it as such; "Money affects purchase power, and purchase power in turn affects the provision for education. The money and power relationship assumes that the wealthier the school, the more it is able to successfully educate students" (p. 18). Knaus (2009) described his experience as a teacher in California as such:

> I was unable to order books, and students finally received their required journals three weeks after the year began. There was no overhead machine, no internet access, no dry-erase pens, and no way for students to type up their papers at school unless they skipped another class (p. 136).

Essed (1991) argued that race and racism shapes the daily experiences and interaction of minoritized communities very differently than Whites (p. 52) and, as such, race is used to make meaning of each experience permeating the daily lives of racial minorities.

Minimal research is available addressing the use of cultural capital among African Americans to survive segregation and severe racial discrimination. However, Franklin (2002) defined cultural capital as "the sense of group consciousness and collective identity" that serves as a resource "aimed at the advancement of an entire group" (p. 177). Without a commitment to redesign funding formulas and modify policies that support ongoing inequities, schooling will remain in place as is; children will suffer, and virtually guarantee the reproduction of the status quo (Ladson-Billings, 1998; Morse, 2007).

CONCLUSION

To adequately achieve equality, more research regarding the issues related to college readiness through a critical lens is needed. Educational polices, practices, and promises must be reexamined in order to experience educational reform leading to closure of the achievement gap between races, and the disparity among minoritized populations that are not equally prepared for college. Therefore, educators and policymakers alike must become socially conscious and willing to challenge the status quo in order to gain different results and alleviate structural and systemic barriers that reinforce educational disparities in college readiness.

One of the overarching themes of CRT which guides multiple tenets is the belief that race and racism permeates every part of society requiring significant changes to policies and practice. Specific to this study, the application of CRT as proposed by scholars and activists strongly encourages the implementation of new policies that center on race and racism. The changes can be applied using an intentional method of deconstruction, reconstruction, and construction of educational research and policies. Deconstruction involves a critical analysis of US history using interdisciplinary methods to alleviate an inferior paradigm defined as a belief that people of color are inferior to Whites (Carter & Goodwin, 1994; Gould, 1981; Selden, 1994; Solórzano, 1998). Reconstruction involves the identification of practices, policies, and frameworks such as an inferior paradigm and challenges the proven inaccuracies. In doing so, theorists and scholars are able to inform practice and policies through the construction of new knowledge and understanding of racially diverse experiences.

The process of thoughtful analysis of policies and practices provides a framework to understand and approach the issue of college readiness among minoritized populations through a CRT lens. As a result of the literature review issues of college readiness clearly align with the tenets of CRT; modifying practices associated with curriculum and instruction, challenging the assessment procedures to determine college readiness, and correcting school funding practices to create equal schooling. It is evident that through the application of CRT we can experience positive educational outcomes specifically preparing minoritized populations for college.

Beyond uncovering the relationship between CRT and college readiness, the larger goal for this literature review is to identify a method of countering the rising number of students who are not college ready following graduation from high school. More importantly, the number of unprepared students is much higher among minoritized populations which highlights the natural need for a theoretical approach using concepts of race and racism such as CRT. As a result, the literature review answers the question among educators and policymakers, "What can be done to support student learning and improve preparation for college?" However, CRT scholars and activists promote the idea of influencing the individual, the larger motive is to change policies and practices on the local and government level that will infuse long-term change for generations and advance closure of the achievement gap and economic divide.

The relationship between Critical Race Theory and college readiness validates an immediate need for a critical pedagogy. Zamudio et al., (2011) argued that, "pedagogy is understood as the study of how teachers teach and students learn, and CRT as a framework helps us to analyze the specific educational practices that contribute to educational inequality which may transform teaching practices" (p. 91). Such practices, as addressed throughout the review of the literature, include but are not limited to curriculum design and instruction, assessment practices, and school funding. Through the use of CRT as a framework, the percentage of students who are not prepared for college may begin to decline giving rise to underrepresented populations on college campuses, enriching classroom experiences, closing the economic divide between non-Whites and Whites, and creating significant changes within American society.

What are the implications for educational policy, practice, and social justice? Apparently, there are significant and valid arguments supporting CRT. Much of the support is motivated by the obvious systemic structures that limit college readiness and college access to college among minoritized populations. Critical Race Theory offers a guided and thoughtful critique of racism and classism in the United States. However, it is important to note that CRT is not without critique. But, for this literature, I sought to uncover the relationship between CRT and college readiness that may produce change in educational research and policy development.

Many studies have investigated college readiness from various angles and perspectives. However, this becomes less when investigating the experiences of specific populations such as students of color or low-income students who are disproportionately less likely to be prepared for postsecondary education. Also, the literature becomes scarce if searching for research absent of deficit thinking, especially when using a critical lens such as CRT.

Of greater importance, is the emerging need to have a bachelor's degree in order to acquire capital and earning power in the United States. Zamudio et al., (2011) argued that success in America is tied to a university degree. She further stated that the earning power of those with a high school diploma declined by $5600.00, while those with a bachelor's degree increased by $2700.00 in 2007 (p. 63). It can be strongly assumed that this trend will continue, indicating that those without a bachelor's degree or higher will continue to lose earning power over time validating the cliché, "the poor get poorer and the rich get richer." Consequently, the importance of high school completion and the value of the university degree become ever more important. Thus, it is equally important to acknowledge the influence of race and racism on educational equality, and to critically examine how schools adequately equip *all* students to be ready for postsecondary education. The application of CRT to guide educational reform can lead to significant changes among those who are college ready, gaining college access, and ostensibly closing the economic gap between non-Whites and Whites.

REFERENCES

Adelman, C. (1999). Answers in the Toolbox: Academic intensity, attendance patterns, and bachelor's degree attainment. Washington, D.C.: U.S. Department of Education, Office of Educational Research and Improvement.

Barnes, R. (1990). Race consciousness: The thematic content of racial distinctiveness in critical race scholarship. *Harvard Law Review, 103*, 1864–1871.

Bell, D. (1980). Brown v. board of education and the interest-convergence dilemma. *Harvard Law Review, 93*(3), 518–533.

Bell, D. (1987). *And we are not saved: The elusive quest for racial justice.* New York: Basis Books.

Bollinger, L. (2002). Debate over the SAT masks perilous trends in college admission. *Chronicle of Higher Education*, pp. B11–B12.

Bourdieu, P., & Passeron, J. (1977). *Reproduction in education, society and culture.* Beverly Hills: Sage Publications.

Byrd, K., & Macdonald, G. (2005). Defining college readiness from the inside out: First-generation college student perspectives. *Community College Review, 33*, 22–37.

Carter, R. T., & Goodwin, A. L. (1994). Racial identity and education. In L. Darling-Hammond (Ed.), *Review of research in education.* Washington, DC: American Educational Research Association.

Conley, D. T. (2008). Rethinking college readiness. *New Directions for Higher Education, 144*, DOI: 10.1002/he.321, pp. 3–13.

Conley, D. T., McGaughy, C., & Gray, E. (2008). *College readiness performance assessment system.* Eugene, OR: Educational Policy Improvement Center.

Crenshaw, K. (1988). Race, reform, and retrenchment: Transformation and legitimation in antidiscrimation law. *Harvard Law Review, 101*(7), 1331–1387.

Delgado, R. (Ed.). (1995). *Critical race theory: The cutting edge.* Philadelphia: Temple University Press.

Delgado, R., & Stefancic, J. (2001). *Critical race theory. An introduction.* New York: New York University Press.

Darder, A., Baltodano, M., & Torres, R. (2003). *The critical pedagogy reader.* New York: RoutledgeFalmer.

Essed, P. (1991). *Understanding everyday racism: An interdisciplinary theory.* Newbury Park: Sage Publications.

Franklin, V. P. (2002) Introduction: cultural capital and African–American education. *The Journal of African–American History, 87*, 175–181.

Gonzalez, K., Stoner, C., & Jovel, J. (2003). Examining the role of social capital in access to college for Latinas: toward a college opportunity framework. *Journal of Hispanic Higher Education*, 2, 146–170.

Gould, S. J. (1981). *The mismeasure of man.* New York: Norton.

Green, D. (2006). Historically minoritized students: What we know, what we still need to know. *New Directions for Community Colleges*, DOI: 10.1002/cc.244, pp. 21–28.

Hacker, A. (1992). *Two nations: Black and white, separate, hostile, unequal.* New York: Ballantine Books.

hooks, b. (1994). *Teaching to transgress: Education as the practice of freedom.* New York: Routledge.

Jencks, C. (1998). Racial bias in testing. In C. Jencks & M. Phillips (Eds.), *The Black White test score gap* (pp. 55–85). Washington, DC: Brookings Institution.

Knaus, C. (2009). Shut up and listen: Applied critical race theory in the classroom. *Race Ethnicity and Education*, 12(2), 133–154.

KnowledgeWorks Foundation. (2007). High school initiatives: The Ohio high school transformation initiative: Why you should care. Retrieved April 12, 2007, from http://www.kwfdn.org/high_schools/ohsti/why

Ladson-Billings, G. (1998). Just what is critical race theory and what's it doing in a nice field like education? *International Journal of Qualitative Studies in Education, 11*(1), 7–24.

Lareau, A. (1987). Social class differences in family–school relationships: The importance of cultural capital. *American Sociological Association*, 60, 73–85.

Martinez, M., & Klopott, S. (2003). Improving college access for minority, low-income, and first-generation students. *Pathways to College Network*, p. 1–15.

Morrison, T. (1992). *Playing in the dark: Whiteness and the literary imagination.* Cambridge: Harvard University Press.

Morse, J. F. (2007). *A level playing field: School finance in the northeast.* Albany: State University of New York Press.

National Research Council. (2002). *Learning and understanding: Improving advanced study of mathematics and science in U.S. high schools.* Washington, D.C.: National Academy Press.

Osequera, L. (2004). Individual and institutional influences on the baccalaureate degree attainment of African American, Asian American, Caucasian, and Mexican American undergraduates (unpublished doctoral dissertation). University of California, Los Angeles.

Reid, M., & Moore III, J. (2008). College readiness and academic preparation for postsecondary education: Oral histories of first-generation urban college students. *Urban Education*, 43, 240–261.

Selden, S. (1994). Early twentieth-century biological determinism and the classification of exceptional students. *Evaluation and Research in Education*, 8(1), 21–39.

Solórzano, D. (1998). Critical race theory, racial and gender microagrgressiona, and the experiences of Chicana and Chicano scholars. *International Journal of Qualitative Studies in Education*, 11, 121–136.

Walpole, M., Mcdonough, P., Bauer, C., Gibson, C., Kanyi, K., & Toliver, R. (2005). This test is unfair: Urban African American and Latino high school students' perceptions of standardized college admission tests. *Urban Education*, 40, DOI: 10.1177/0042085905274536, pp. 321–349.

Weissglass, J. (1998). The SAT: Public-Spirited or preserving privilege? *Education Week*, 60.

Wink, J. (1996). *Critical pedagogy: Notes from the real world*. New York: Longman.

Wong, O. K., & Casing, D. M. (2010). *Prioritizing money and power: Equalize student achievement*. Lanham: Rowman and Littlefield Education.

Yosso, T. (2005). Whose culture has capital? A critical race theory discussion of community cultural wealth. *Race Ethnicity and Education*, 8, 69–91.

Zamudio, M., Russell, C., Rios, F., & Bridgeman, J. (2011). *Critical race theory matters: Education and ideology*. New York: Routledge.

CHAPTER 5

AN OVERVIEW OF THE HISTORY, RESEARCH, AND CULTURE OF HISTORICALLY BLACK GREEK LETTER ORGANIZATIONS

Andre Brown
University of Missouri

THE FRATERNITY MOVEMENT IN COLONIAL AMERICA

Before the inception of Alpha Phi Alpha Fraternity known by conventional wisdom as the first intercollegiate fraternity for Black men in 1906, the fraternal movement in North America had already begun with the establishment of honor societies at colonial colleges (Brubacher & Rudy, 2002; Crump & Wilson, 1972; Dreer, 1940; Kimbrough, 2003; McKenzie, 2005; Torbenson, 2005, 2009). These honor societies were inspired by 7,000 years of fraternal societies and organizations dating back to the early civilizations of the ancient Egyptians, Greeks, and Romans (Dreer, 1940). Evolving further from these traditional roots, the Black fraternity movement grew

Confronting Racism in Higher Education, pages 83–110
Copyright © 2013 by Information Age Publishing

from the exclusion of Black members in predominately White Greek letter organizations, which was, in turn, a symptom of the permeating racism, discrimination, and classism that plagued larger society (Fine, 2003; Jones, 2004; Kimbrough, 2003; McKenzie, 2005; Ross, 2001; Torbenson, 2005, 2009; Wilder & McKeegan, 1999).

Secret Societies in Colonial America

During the 1700s, students, almost entirely White Anglo Saxon Protestant males, matriculated into American college campuses under the doctrine of *in loco parentis* (Latin for, "in place of your parents"), in which students experienced a rather structured college life and were forced to conform to the values and principles placed upon them by their respective higher education institutions (Dreer, 1940; Egan, 1985; Wesley, 2000). This staunch campus culture served as the cause of frustrations among the student body. This resulted in the formation of secret societies on colonial campuses (Brubacher & Rudy, 2002; Kimbrough, 2003; Rudolph, 1990). During this time period, student organizations resembled Greek letter organizations, in terms of common member interests, private nature, and defiance of the status quo. Secret societies emerged on college campuses throughout the colonies as forums to discuss tensions between American colonies and Great Britain (Brubacher & Rudy, 2002; Jones, 2004; Kimbrough, 2003; Rudolph, 1990; Torbenson, 2009).

In 1750, students at the College of William and Mary formed the Flat Hat Club, a secret literary society distinguished for its effective organization (Jones, 2004). This group would remain in existence for 20 years, a significant duration for the time. This organization's term in secret society history is especially noteworthy because it holds the distinction of being the first campus group to have an organizational badge, secret, oath, and fraternal handshake (Jones, 2004; Kimbrough, 2003). Moreover, it is most often credited as the first underground college student society in America. Following the collapse of the Flat Hat Club, students formed the P.D.A Society, the first organization to identify itself with a combination of letters. This historical organization's members bore a preference for the social offerings of college life rather than scholastic achievement and organizational philosophy (Torbenson, 2005, 2009).

ESTABLISHMENT OF PHI BETA KAPPA

On December 5, 1776, in America's first months of independence, the first campus fraternity was founded at the College of William and Mary (Dreer,

1940; Jones, 2004; Kimbrough, 2003; McKenzie, 2005; Torbenson, 2005, 2009; Wesley, 2000). Phi Beta Kappa departed from preceding secret societies and held many common characteristics of the modern fraternity, such as a handshake, use of a password, oath of secrecy, rituals, official badge, motto, and use of Greek letters to represent the organization (Torbenson, 2009). Additionally, America's first Greek fraternity promoted a philosophy of organizational values and principles, and required members to interact with one another during regularly scheduled meetings (Jones, 2004; Torbenson, 2009).

Two Phi Beta Kappa founders and eight subsequent members were freemasons and, as Torbenson (2009) asserts, had influence in the fraternity's principle of organizational expansion. In adopting this aspect of Masonic tradition, Phi Beta Kappa branched out to other colonial campuses, while still maintaining unique aspects and traditions (Jones, 2004; Torbenson, 2009). In many cases, the communication between chapters was infrequent and separate from the mother chapter, resulting in the development of divergent traditions and practices within the single organization.

In 1826, operating in a climate of anti-Masonic sentiment, the fraternity evolved from a secret fraternal order to an honor society with an emphasis on high scholastic achievement (Torbenson, 2009). The anti-Masonic movement in America was prompted by the disappearance of William Morgan, who authored a book exposing the secrets of Masonry (Torbenson, 2009). Coupled with the disappearance of Morgan, public opinion reflected distrust in masons, who Americans felt exerted excessive influence in political, social, and economic arenas. By this time, Phi Beta Kappa, which was closely associated with Masonry, converted entirely into an honorary society through the act of publishing its organizational rites.

Although Phi Beta Kappa was established in 1776, it was not until the late 1820s and into the early 1830s that the fraternity movement was firmly established. From 1825 to 1827, three new undergraduate fraternities, Kappa Alpha, Sigma Phi, and Delta Phi, were established, and departed from their predecessors as they adopted progressively social agendas (Jones, 2004; Kimbrough, 2003; Torbenson, 2009). In addition to intercollegiate fraternities, local fraternities began to emerge on many campuses. Torbenson emphasizes that during this period, fraternities which emerged did so in accordance with developments of colonial student life and the role of faculty within social fraternities. The final contribution of Phi Beta Kappa to the American fraternity movement was its provision of a framework for the prototypical all-male Greek letter organization, with significant emphasis on secrecy and expansion to other college campuses. It should be emphasized that with the founding of Phi Beta Kappa in 1776, it would be 130 years until an intercollegiate fraternity for Black men would come into existence.

THE FIRST SORORITIES

Torbenson (2005, 2009) makes the distinction that sororities, or women's fraternities, emerged in response to increasingly coeducational institutions in the Midwest and South, not in the long established women's colleges of the East. Prior to the 1830s, few women attended college campuses that were dominated by men as they pursued education at female "academies" or "seminaries" (Torbenson, 2005, 2009). As the number of women seeking higher education increased, colleges that had previously been male dominated began to open their doors to women, and subsequently, the concern over female affiliation with male fraternities grew. With no clear restrictions against female membership, some fraternities accepted their new classmates; however, most did not.

In rare cases, women were allowed to join chapters of national fraternities (Torbenson, 2005, 2009). For several years, many fraternities debated the merits of allowing women to be affiliated with their organizations in any capacity, ranging from granting full membership to allowing peripheral associations such as decorating halls, or providing food and entertainment for male members. Unsatisfied with menial roles in male dominated fraternities, women eventually established their own Greek letter organizations which were formed to address the specific concerns of the growing female populations in their respective college environments.

The roots of the first organizations for college women can be traced back to Wesleyan College in 1851 and 1852 (Torbenson, 2005, 2009). Initially using classical names, the organizations would go on to adopt the Greek letters of Alpha Delta and Phi Mu and become the first American sororities. Both Alpha Delta and Phi Mu remained local until the early 1900s. It was not until 1867, at Monmouth College, that Pi Beta Phi, the first intercollegiate women's fraternity, was established (Jones, 2004; Torbenson, 2005, 2009). This distinction has been attributed to the sorority's partnership with an unnamed male fraternity, which allowed Pi Beta Phi the liberty to expand a second chapter in 1869. While this organization was the first of its kind, in 1874 Gamma Phi Beta established a sorority on the campus of Syracuse University that most closely resembles the modern sorority model. Initially deemed a "society", Gamma Phi Beta adopted the term "sorority" per the suggestion of a Latin professor at the University. Eventually the term grew in popularity to distinguish female from male Greek letter organizations.

THE DAWN OF THE TWENTIETH CENTURY

At the beginning of the Twentieth Century, higher education experienced social changes with the standardization of secondary education and increased college attendance (Brubacher & Rudy, 2002; Rudolph, 1990; Wesley, 2000). This increase in college enrollment, consisting primarily of men, positioned fraternal organizations, who judiciously recruited incoming freshmen, to multiply in number and membership and simultaneously increase their influence on campus.

As fraternities found themselves with an influx of members, during the latter part of the Nineteenth Century and into the Twentieth Century, the fact that Black students were faced with limited opportunities to pursue postsecondary education compounded with their exclusion from social organizations meant that fraternities remained a White tradition in American higher education (Crump & Wilson, 1972; Dreer, 1940; Kimbrough, 2003; Ross, 2001; Wesley, 2000). Because of their limited representation on campuses, Black students' rejections from fraternal organizations were overlooked as acts of discrimination. In the seventy years from 1826 to 1906 the number of Black students graduating from college and professional schools totaled an estimated 7,488, with the majority of degrees conferred from historically Black colleges and universities (HBCU) located predominately in the South (Williams & Ashley, 2004;Wesley, 2000).

The Foundation of Black Fraternalism

Before the establishment of Alpha Phi Alpha in 1906, there had been several attempts to form Black fraternal organizations (Kimbrough, 2003; McKenzie, 2005; Wesley, 2000). Similar to many of their White predecessors, some of the organizations were short lived because of the developmental challenges that Black students and institutions faced at the time. Contemporary members of historically Black Greek letter organizations (BGLOs) have often disputed which organization truly holds the distinction of being the first BGLO to sustain membership. However, it is unequivocal that the establishment and continued existence of the first Black Greek letter was established by freemasons, the original Black fraternal organization (Kimbrough, 2003).

FREEMASONRY

No discussion of fraternal organizations would be complete without addressing Freemasons and their influence on college Greek letter organizations (Kimbrough, 2003; Torbenson, 2005, 2009). Freemasonry was organized during the Fourteenth Century by persons working as skilled artisan laborers who built the cathedrals, bridges, palaces, and other structures of that time period (Kimbrough, 2003). To promote camaraderie among members, masons formed lodges not only as sources of shelter, but to serve the dual purpose of providing locations for private organizational meetings. The organization of Freemasons has been viewed as a form of early trade unions that used secret handshakes and passwords to screen and identify imposters. This aspect of Masonic tradition was influential to BGLOs, as members of similar contemporary organizations use similar gestures and codes to filter non-members (Kimbrough, 2003).

Originally, membership into Freemasonry was only available to skilled stone workers. However, around the 1600s, lodges began to grant honorary membership to masters of other crafts (Kimbrough, 2003). It was not until the Seventeenth and Eighteenth Centuries that Masonry accepted Black members. During the American Revolution, Prince Hall, a Black Methodist minister from Barbados, along with fourteen others were initiated into Military Lodge 441 under the jurisdiction of the Grand Lodge of Ireland.

In the late Eighteenth Century, the Grand Lodge of England granted a charter to Prince Hall to establish African Lodge 459 (Kimbrough, 2003). This single event, expanding Masonic fraternalism, led to the proliferation of what is commonly referred to as Prince Hall lodges. Black Freemasonry continued to expand with the establishment of Prince Hall lodges in states throughout New England. As Black students found themselves uniting under Freemasonry and sharing secretive organizational culture and tradition, the Black Greek letter organizational foundation was unknowingly being established (Rudolph, 1990). As Masonic organizations flourished, college fraternities with White membership looked to their rituals and traditions to emulate within their own culture. As evidence of this trend, Kappa Alpha Order and Chi Psi Fraternity, both White fraternities, adopted the term "lodge" from Masonic tradition in reference to what was other fraternities refer as "campus chapter" (Kimbrough, 2003).

Another similarity between Freemasonry and fraternities is their intent to serve as secret societies (Kimbrough, 2003). Only in recent times has Freemasonry emerged into the public forefront. For example, individuals have been known to wear paraphernalia that identify themselves as Freemasons. On some college campuses, particularly HBCUs, Masons are active student organizations that operate as openly as any other Greek letter organization (Jones, 2004). The influence of Freemason fraternal organizations on Greek letter fraternities is evident in their secretive nature and shared culture (Kimbrough, 2003).

THE DIVERSIFICATION OF THE SOCIAL FRATERNITY

By the dawn of Nineteenth Century, the American fraternal system had well established its presence and made an indelible impression on campus student life (Brubacher & Rudy, 2002; Jones, 2004; Kimbrough, 2003; McKenzie, 2005; Rudolph, 1990; Torbenson, 2005, 2009). Female students, who first emerged in fraternal organizations to fill peripheral, subservient roles, developed organizations to serve their specific needs in the ever-growing mixed gender climate of higher education. The growth of Freemason fraternal organizations and traditions coupled with the establishment of the first American Greek letter organization offered Black students a foundation on which to build their own Greek letter organizations to serve their unique needs.

Predecessors to the Black Fraternal Movement

A point of contention among contemporary members of BGLOs involves the identity of the first of these organizations. Conventional wisdom would concede that this honor would belong to Alpha Phi Alpha Fraternity which was found on December 4, 1906 on the campus of Cornell University in Ithaca, New York. But debate exists (Kimbrough, 2003; Ross, 2001; Wesley, 2000).

BLACK FRATERNALISM AT INDIANA UNIVERSITY

The evolution of the first Black Greek letter organization at Indiana University, the contested birthplace of Black fraternalism among college men, is not well documented, as there are two incongruent accounts of its development (Crump & Wilson, 1972; Kimbrough, 2003; Jones, 2005). One account suggests that in 1903, with a thirteen year presence on campus, Black students at Indiana University formed the Alpha Kappa Nu Greek society (Crump & Wilson, 1972; Kimbrough, 2003; Ross, 2001). According to Crump and Wilson, in the The Story of Kappa Alpha Psi, Alpha Kappa Nu existed for a short period (roughly fourteen months) and dissipated due to its failure to maintain membership. Then, in 1911, a new group, Kappa Alpha Nu, evolved on the univeristy campus and eventually changed its name to Kappa Alpha Psi (Crump & Wilson, 1972). Furthermore, Crump and Wilson suggest that Kappa Alpha Nu's name was a tribute to the groundwork laid by the Alpha Kappa Nu members, the Black students who preceeded them at Indiana University.

The other account of this evolution stems from an Indiana University historian who contends that it was not until 1911 that a Black Greek letter organization materialized on campus, when Alpha Kappa Nu purchased a fraternity house in October of that year (Kimbrough, 2003; McKenzie, 2005). Moreover, the historian affirms that Alpha Kappa Nu evovled into

Kappa Alpha Nu and established subsequent chapters in additional states. Eventually, Kappa Alpha Nu adopted its current name of Kappa Alpha Psi in response to racist comments by undergradutes students who referred to the fraternity as "Kappa Alpha Nig." On this matter both Crump and Indiana Univeristy historian concur.

During the contested evolution of what came to be known as Kappa Alpha Psi, Black students at Indiana University united under hostile campus conditions and formed what some would deem the first BGLO (Kimbrough, 2003). In the time when this fraternity was developing as a haven for the needs of Black students on the campus of Indiana University, opponents to the emancipation and integration of Blacks into larger American society held a public presence. Racially motivated hate crimes and oppressive policies were just some of the issues with which Black Americans publicly struggled. The aggression with which Black students were treated, as well as the presence of the Ku Klux Klan on the University campus at the time, was documented in the student newspaper. Campus reports also indicate that incidents in which Black men would be greeted as "nigger" or "Sambo" were commonplace (Crump & Wilson, 1972). Inspite of this hostile enviroment, Black students enrolled at Indiana University and successfully established Kappa Alpha Psi.

PI GAMMA OMICRON AND GAMMA PHI

On the campus of Wilberforce University in Ohio, there were reports of an organization that preexisted Kappa Alpha Psi (Kimbrough, 2003). According to the University's 1923 yearbook, Gamma Phi, an organization of Black students that may or may not have held the characteristics definitive of a Greek letter organization, was established in 1905. The University's 1924 yearbook edition reported a Gamma Phi membership of 35 men and six faculty members. However, record of their siginificance as a BGLO has not been supported by historians (Kimbrough, 2003; Wesley, 2000). No longer in existance today, Gamma Phi was able to establish three subsqeuent chapters before dissipating three decades after their emergence on the Wilberforce campus (Kimbrough, 2003).

Existing records suggest today's Alpha Phi Alpha Fraternity was the first BGLO for college men in American history. In Fall of 1905, Robert Harold Olge, one of the seven founders of Alpha Phi Alpha, investigated whether a BGLO had ever existed and learned that one had been rumored to exist at Ohio State University (Kimbrough, 2003; Ross, 2001; Wesley, 2000). In light of his findings, Ogle wrote a letter to the University registrar to inquire about the status of the fraternity, Pi Gamma Omicron, and found no record of the organization on the campus (Wesley, 2000). For Olge and his companions at Cornell, who were interested in founding their own fraternity, the news of the inexistence of any BGLO served as both a dissapointment and a source of motivation in establishing what would come to be known as Alpha Phi Alpha (Kimbrough, 2003; Ross, 2001; Wesley, 2000).

Foundational Period for the Black Fraternal Movement

The period from 1905 to 1930 is considered the foundational period for the Black fraternal movement on American college campuses (Kimbrough, 2003; Ross, 2001; Wesley, 2000). During the early Twentieth Century, the campuses of Cornell, Butler, Indiana University and Howard became the epicenters of the Black fraternal movement. In 1963, the final of the member of the Divine Nine, Iota Phi Theta, was founded at Morgan State University (Crump & Wilson, 1972; Dreer, 1940; Jones, 2004; Kimbrough, 2003; Ross, 2001; Wesley, 2000).

During the foundational period, Kimbrough (2003) notes that three of the four institutions where BGLOs were founded were predominately White and explains that this phenomenon occurred because of the social conditions Black students encountered at the time, and their need to find camaraderie and support on campus. While more predominantly White Institutions (PWIs) bred BGLOs at the time, Kimbrough refers to Howard University as the "cradle of Black Greek civilization," as it was the birthplace of five of the first eight Black Greek organizations (Kimbrough, 2003, p. 32). Moreover, the University is noteworthy because along with prompting the inception of other Black Greek fraternities and sororities on its campus, its first BGLO, Alpha Phi Alpha, was also the first to expand campuses, originating at Cornell and then emerging at Howard in 1907 (Kimbrough, 2003; Ross, 2001; Wesley, 2000).

THE DIVINE NINE

The foundation of BGLO history has been attributed to five fraternities and four sororities that currently operate today and comprise what is commonly known as The Divine Nine: Alpha Phi Alpha Fraternity, Alpha Kappa Alpha Sorority, Omega Psi Phi Fraternity, Kappa Alpha Psi Fraternity, Delta Sigma Theta Sorority, Phi Beta Sigma Fraternity, Zeta Phi Beta Sorority, Sigma Gamma Rho Sorority, and Iota Phi Theta Fraternity (Ross, 2001). All but the last of these Black Greek societies was established during the foundational period for the Black fraternal movement, from 1905 to 1930 (Kimbrough, 2003). The following section offers a chronological review of the histories of The Divine Nine.

ALPHA PHI ALPHA,
FIRST INTERCOLLEGIATE BLACK FRATERNITY

Not surprisingly, Black students represented a small minority on the campus of Cornell in the late Nineteenth and early Twentieth Centuries (Bradley, 2008). In 1880, Cornell graduated its first Black student. But, because of challenges associated with academic rigor, racial, and social isolation and the financial burdens of attending an Ivy League institution, the University lost a significant proportion of its already low Black student population to attrition.

In 1905, faced with such adverse circumstances, Black students from various colleges within the University organized a social support club (Bradley, 2008; Ross, 2001; Wesley, 2000). Under the leadership of graduate student, C.C. Poindexter, club members soon began to debate the merits of forming a Greek lettered organization (Kimbrough, 2003; Ross, 2001; Wesley, 2000). Undergraduate club members strongly favored the formation of a fraternity, while Mr. Poindexter argued against it, citing a lack of cultural foundation within the Black community. With his influence waning with the undergraduates students, Mr. Poindexter resigned from the organization, and subsequently, on December 4, 1906, Alpha Phi Alpha Fraternity was born (Wesley, 2000). The organization's founders, referred to as the Seven Jewels throughout the Black Greek community, are Henry Arthur Callis, Charles Henry Chapman, Eugene Kinckle Jones, George Biddle Kelley, Nathaniel Allison Murray, Robert Harold Olge, and Vertner Woodson Tandy (Bradley, 2008; Kimbrough, 2003; McKenzie, 2005; Wesley, 2000).

With the belief that Black men at other college campuses could benefit from the fellowship and camaraderie of college fraternity, Alpha Phi Alpha sought to expand. In the winter of 1907, Alpha Phi Alpha founded chapters at Howard, Virginia Union University and University of Toronto, making it the first international intercollegiate fraternity for Black students (Bradley, 2008; Wesley, 2000). By 1926, Alpha Phi Alpha established chapters at six of eight Ivy League universities including Cornell, Columbia, Yale, Pennsylvania, Brown, and Harvard (Wesley, 2000).

With a focus of service, the founders of Alpha Phi Alpha Fraternity pursued a mission of social, political, and economic uplift and racial equality (Bradley, 2008; Kimbrough, 2003; Wesley, 1997, 2000). To date, Alpha Phi Alpha has manifested its commitment to service with the enactment of national programs: "Go to High School; Go to College," a program to motivate Black youths to successfully graduate high school and pursue higher education, and "A Voteless People is a Hopeless People," a program developed to promote social and political involvement through voter education and registration (Bradley, 2008; Kimbrough, 2003; Ross, 2001; Wesley, 2000). In 2006, Alpha Phi Alpha celebrated its centennial anniversary. The first Black Greek organization since mobilized efforts to honor one of its most famous members, Rev. Dr. Martin Luther King, Jr. with a monument on the National Mall in Washington, D.C. (Ross, 2001).

ALPHA KAPPA ALPHA, FIRST BLACK SORORITY

With the newly established intercollegiate fraternity, Alpha Phi Alpha, Black students' interests in establishing similar organizations escalated. In the fall 1907 and into 1908, Howard University students, Ethel Hedgeman, Beulah E. and Lillie Burke, Margaret Flagg Holmes, Marjorie Hill, Lucy Diggs Slowe, Marie Woolfork Taylor, Anna Easter Brown, and Lavinia Norman came together to form a sorority (Evans, 2008; Kimbrough, 2003; Ross, 2001). With few women on Howard's campus at the time, Hedgeman and the eight other undergraduate students joined together to establish what would become the oldest Greek-letter organization established by Black college women, Alpha Kappa Alpha Sorority, on January 15, 1908 (Ross, 2001). To ensure the organization's continuity, the founders invited seven sophomores to join the sorority without initiation, bringing the total number of Alpha Kappa Alpha founders to 16 (Evans, 2008). The sophomores of 1908 included Norma Boyd, Ethel Jones Mowbray, Alice P. Murray, Sarah Meriweather Nutter, Joanna Berry Shields, Carrie Snowden and Harriet Josephine Terry.

As Alpha Kappa Alpha continued to grow and new members were initiated, a schism among members developed, leaving the organization to face to its first crisis (Evans, 2008; McKenzie, 2005; Ross, 2001). In the fall of 1912, a faction of undergraduate members of Alpha Kappa Alpha made proposals to change the name, motto, color, and symbols of the sorority, suggesting that the organization mimicked much of the traditions of Alpha Phi Alpha Fraternity and lacked individuality (Ross, 2001). In the face of growing dissent, Nellie Quander, a 1910 initiate of Alpha Kappa Alpha and graduate advisor to the mother chapter at Howard, led a plan that would ensure the permanence of the sorority and expanded the organization to charters in the Midwest. Quander along with Norma Boyd, Julia Brooks, Ethel Jones Mowbray, Nellie Pratt Russell and Minnie Smith hold the distinction with Alpha Kappa Alpha as the organization's "Incorporators" (Evans, 2008). Three distinct groups of Alpha Kappa Alpha, the nine founders, the Sophomores of 1908, and the Incorporators, hold the distinction of being the sorority's Twenty Pearls.

Alpha Kappa Alpha's founders, Sophomores of 1908, and Incorporators had diverse upbringings and hailed from such places as North Carolina, Washington, DC, Virginia, New York, Georgia, New Jersey, Missouri, and West Virginia. To add, Evans (2008) highlights that many embarked on journeys as unique and different as their roots, after graduation from Howard. Twelve of the Twenty Pearls never married, twelve pursue careers as teachers, and others became involved in Black community development, while being steadfast with the growth of their Alpha Kappa Alpha Sorority. Their diligent expansion efforts are evident in the organization's membership which includes such distinguish women as entertainers, Ella Fitzgerald, Phylicia Rashad, and Marian Anderson; world renowned poets, Maya Angelou and Toni Morrison; and trailblazers such as Coretta Scott King and Dr. Mae Jemison.

OMEGA PSI PHI FRATERNITY

In 1911, three years after the establishment of Alpha Kappa Alpha at Howard, three liberal arts students, Edgar Love, Frank Coleman, and Oscar Cooper along with their faculty advisor, Ernest Just, founded Omega Psi Phi Fraternity on November 17, 1911 (Dreer, 1940; Jeffries, 2008; Kimbrough, 2003; Ross, 2001; Wesley, 2000). With the founding of Omega Psi Phi, the fraternity holds the distinction of being the first intercollegiate fraternity for Black men to be established at a historically Black college (Jeffries, 2008; Ross, 2001).

Omega Psi Phi Fraternity's founding at Howard was unique in that the University initially opposed its formation due to their failure to secure permission from the University's administration. Initially, Omega Psi Phi was granted University recognition on the condition that the fraternity would not expand beyond Howard University (Dreer, 1940; Kimbrough, 2003; Ross, 2001). Although, Howard was already home to the first fraternity and sorority for Black students, this condition was placed on Omega Psi Phi because of Howard University administration's rising concern that the fraternity movement would lead to a division among the student body and potentially become a conduit for immoral behavior.

On the evening of November 17, 1911, during a meeting in Thirkield Hall on Howard's campus, Omega Psi Phi was born as an organization with the motto, "Friendship is essential to the soul" and anchored in four guiding principles: scholarship, manhood, perseverance, and uplift (Dreer, 1940; Jeffries, 2008; Ross, 2001). As Omega continued to grow, its founders and charter members worked to amend a fraternity constitution to be submitted to Howard University administration in order to be granted recognition by the school (Jeffries, 2008). Howard, like other colleges at time the time, discouraged the formation of fraternal campus organizations. Therefore, the university initially refused to recognize the organization as a legitimate student group. This denial subsequently led to student organized protest by Omega, in which members disseminated index cards announcing the existence of their fraternity throughout the Howard community (Ross, 2001). Such overt rebellion prompted the university president to denounce the members and refute the existence of Omega Psi Phi on Howard's campus.

Undeterred by the president's response, members of Omega began to lobby members of the Howard faculty for support (Dreer, 1940; Jeffries, 2008; Ross, 2001). Eventually, the members met with the University president and discussed the possibility of official recognition of Omega Psi Phi. The university granted Omega Psi Phi recognition under the conditions that the fraternity remain local, that the faculty and university approve the organization's constitution, and that the University retain power to dissolve the organization if it so desired (Ross, 2001). Eventually, the provisional status of the organization would be lifted, allowing the Omega Psi Phi to expand to other college campuses. In 1914, Omega Psi Phi established a second chapter at Lincoln University in Pennsylvania with further expansion slow and steady. In 1918, Omega Psi Phi had only three chapters. However, five years later, the organization would grow to 47 active chapters. The achievement of Omega Psi Phi stems from the foundation laid by the founders, Just, Love, Cooper, and Coleman. It was their efforts that set in motion the establishment of an organization which has produced leaders not only within the confines of their Black Greek organization, but as leaders in every movement in the Black community.

DELTA SIGMA THETA SORORITY

As Alpha Kappa Alpha Sorority struggled with internal friction at Howard during the early stages of the organization, the opportunity for a second Black sorority to emerge was established (Evans, 2008; Giddings, 1988; Kimbrough, 2003; Ross, 2001). A faction of Alpha Kappa Alpha felt that the sorority was simply a derivation of the Beta chapter of Alpha Phi Alpha Fraternity (Giddings, 1988). Kimbrough asserts that this conclusion is probable, considering that Ethel Hedgeman the key founder of Alpha Kappa Alpha Sorority was friends with, and would eventually marry the president of the newly established Beta chapter of Alpha Phi Alpha Fraternity, George Lyle. Moreover, members of the sorority felt that the name and organizational symbols did not reflect a new and unique identity.

From the perspective of contemporary members of Delta Sigma Theta, the contention stemming from these organizational issues was the impetus behind the formation of their own sorority. Thus, with the assistance of a faculty member, a band of Alpha Kappa Alpha members formed a group and selected the name Delta Sigma Theta in 1912 (Giddings, 1988; Kimbrough, 2003; Ross, 2001). Upon hearing the news of the rebellious faction, graduate members of Alpha Kappa Alpha posted an ultimatum to the dissenters to drop the name, Delta Sigma Theta, and return to Alpha Kappa Alpha or face condemnation. Still resolute after the call from Alpha Kappa Alpha, twenty-two former sisters officially founded Delta Sigma Theta Sorority on January 13, 1913.

Delta Sigma Theta's founders' objectives were to establish an organization that would utilize their collective strength to promote excellence and to provide assistance to persons in need (Ross, 2001). Founders of the sorority include: Osceola Macarthy Adams, Marguerite Young Alexander, Winona Cargile Alexander, Ethel Cuff Black, Bertha Pitts Campbell, Zephyr Chisom Carter, Edna Brown Coleman, Jesse McGuire Dent, Fredrica Chase Dodd, Myra Davis Hemmings, Olive C. Jones, Jimmie Bugg Middleton, Pauline Oberdorfer Minor, Vashti Turley Murphy, Naomi Sewell Richardson, Mamie Reddy Rose, Eliza Pearl Shippen, Florence Letcher Toms, Ethel Carr Waston, Wertie Blackwell Weaver, Madree Penn White, and Edith Motte Young.

The founders of Delta Sigma Theta represent the resilience of an indomitable spirit of individuals collectively coming together to support an uncompromising ideal. In doing so, they established an organization which now boast a membership of 200,000 predominately Black, college educated women representing chapters all over the world with a proud lineage of exemplary members that includes renowned poet, Nikki Giovanni, civil rights activist, Dr. Dorothy I. Height, and politicians Shirley Chisholm and Carol Moseley Braun (Evans, 2008; Ross, 2001).

PHI BETA SIGMA FRATERNITY

Prior to coming to the campus of Howard University in the summer of 1910, A. Langston Taylor, a high school student in Memphis, Tennessee, met a recent Howard graduate (Hughey, 2008b; Kimbrough, 2003; McKenzie, 2005; Ross, 2001). The recent alumnus discussed with Mr. Taylor his experiences at Howard, paying special respect to the BGLOs on campus. Excited about the concept of Greek life, Mr. Taylor arrived on campus with the plan of establishing a Greek letter organization. By the fall of 1913, Mr. Taylor, accompanied by his roommate and prominent minister, Leonard Morse, and another Howard student, Charles I. Brown, began to meet in November of 1913 to discuss the topic of establishing a new fraternity. By January of 1914, Phi Beta Sigma was born of the three friends' ideas and was officially established at a Washington, DC YMCA with the initiation of nine new members: S. P. Massie, J. A. Franklin, J. E. Jones, B. A. Matthews, W. F. Vincent, T. L. Austin, W. E. Tibbs, J. R. Howard, and I. L. Scruggs (Hughey, 2008b; Kimbrough, 2003; Ross, 2001). In April of the same year, the Board of Deans at Howard University granted official University recognition to Phi Beta Sigma.

From the genesis of Phi Beta Sigma, the founders and charter members sought a membership representing a wide spectrum of the Howard community and eventually established itself as an international organization under the motto, "culture for service and service for humanity" (Hughey, 2008b; Ross, 2001). In the innate stage of the fraternity, the founders and charter members included the captain of the Howard football team, associate editor of *The Howard University Journal*, presidents of the Howard debate society, college YMCA, political science club, university athletic association, and the university president. Hughey (2008b) points out that the collection of Phi Beta Sigma's distinguish membership within the university community was a contributing factor in the Board of Deans university approval of the fraternity, despite the already established presence of Alpha Phi Alpha and Omega Psi Phi at Howard.

Aiming to expand, Phi Beta Sigma set sight on the racially divided South and founded its Beta Chapter at Wiley College in Marshall, Texas, in 1915. During the same year, Phi Beta Sigma received a letter from Kappa Alpha Psi Fraternity Founder and Grand Polemarch Elder W. Diggs, dated December 11, 1915 (Hughey, 2008b; McKenzie, 2005; Ross, 2001). In the letter, Diggs inquires about the opportunity to merge the Midwestern Kappa Alpha Psi fraternity founded at Indiana University with the Eastern Phi Beta Sigma fraternity. After thoughtful consideration, the Phi Beta Sigma's general board respectfully declined the offer to merge with Kappa Alpha Psi.

In December of 1916, Phi Beta Sigma held its first conclave (national convention) in Washington, D.C. (Hughey, 2008b). As the fraternity entered the 1920s, they had established ten chapters and hosted the first ever interfraternity conclave with Omega Psi Phi in Washington DC in 1921. Kimbrough (2003) explains that the founding of Phi Beta Sigma bears significance because of the Sigma founders' unique abilities to work with female students. Their proficiency in communication with student, Arizona Cleaver, paid off with the foundation of Zeta Phi Beta, Phi Beta Sigma's constitutionally bound sister sorority. Phi Beta Sigma has continued to progress and grow into an organization that following the example of its founders and early members.

KAPPA ALPHA PSI FRATERNITY

Kappa Alpha Psi founders, Elder Diggs and Byron Kenneth Armstrong transferred from Howard to Indiana University in the fall of 1911 (Crump & Wilson, 1972; Kimbrough, 2003; McKenzie, 2005; Ross, 2001). With their transfer, the students immediately recognized the stark differences Black students experienced at a historically Black college compared to predominantly White college. Faced with limited opportunities due to racism, discrimination, and the adversity associated with attending a college that was actively hostile to Black students, Diggs, Armstrong, and eight other students formed Alpha Omega in search of a sense of belonging (Crump & Wilson, 1972; Kimbrough, 2003; Ross, 2001). This club served as an interest group until information could be ascertained on forming a permanent BGLO. As time progressed, the group formerly known as Alpha Omega, gained the knowledge and resources to found Kappa Alpha Nu on January 15, 1911 on the campus of Indiana University. Its founders include Elder W. Diggs, Ezra D. Alexander, Byron K. Armstrong, Henry T. Asher, Marcus P. Blakemore, Paul W. Caine, George W. Edmonds, Guy L. Grant, E. Giles Irvin, and. John M. Lee (Crump & Wilson, 1972; Jennings, 2008; Ross, 2001).

In 1914, with three new chapters established on college campuses in the Midwest and membership steadily growing, the fraternity changed its name from Kappa Alpha Nu to Kappa Alpha Psi to avoid racially charged derivations of their fraternity name (Crump & Wilson, 1972; Jennings, 2008; McKenzie, 2005; Ross, 2001). Today, the fraternity is an international organization with college and graduate chapters in the United States and abroad. The principle of Kappa Alpha Psi originates from the works of ten dedicated students on the campus of Indiana University, who were committed to leadership development and achievement in every endeavor.

ZETA PHI BETA SORORITY

By 1920, Black female students at Howard University had two established sororities on campus when Arizona Cleaver, along with four other women assisted by Phi Beta Sigma fraternity members, founded Zeta Phi Beta Sorority on January 16, 1920. Cleaver, in addition to Pearl Anna Neal, Myrtle Tyler, Viola Tyler, and Fannie Pettie hold the distinction of being the Pearls of Zeta Phi Beta (Hughey, 2008b; McKenzie, 2005; Ross, 2001). Zeta Phi Beta's reception into the BGLO community at Howard was warm, with formal welcomes from the members of Alpha Kappa Alpha and Delta Sigma Theta at Howard (Hughey, 2008b; McKenzie, 2005).

As Zeta Phi Beta continued to grow in membership and expand to other college campuses, the organization continued to develop internally with the establishment of the sorority magazine, the *Anchon* and incorporating the organization under the laws of Washington, DC (Ross, 2001). Also, established during the 1920s, was one of Zeta's long standing and nationally celebrated traditions: Finer Womanhood Week. In the 1930s, Zeta Phi Beta, under the direction of Grand Basileus Violette Anderson, began to actively partner with civic orientated organizations such as the National Association for the Advancement of Colored People and the National Negro Congress. In addition to Finer Womanhood Week, Grand Basileus Anderson's successor, Grand Basileus Lullelia Walker Harrison, led an administration that focused on numerous community service projects, such as the Zeta Housing Project of 1943 and the Prevention and Control of Juvenile Delinquency Project. Moreover, during the Harrison administration, the sorority became the first Black Greek lettered organization to form adult and youth auxiliary groups, the Amicae and Archonettes, to increase the organization's integration within the community.

Born during the Roaring 1920s, a time of racial segregation and inequality, Zeta Phi Beta continued to make progress holding its first boulé (convention) in conjunction with its brother organization, Phi Beta Sigma in 1920. It also enacted plans for expansion of the organization to campuses across the country (Hughey, 2008b; Ross, 2001). Ross (2001) points out that, in the early stages, the founders of Zeta Phi Beta focused on the principles of advancing education by promoting academic achievement among college women, promoting service within college and surroundings communities, promoting sisterly love and the ideals of finer womanhood. Zeta's commitment to community is evident in the organization's partnership with the March of Dimes, Z-Hope (Zetas Helping Other People Excel), Zeta National Education Foundation, and Zeta Organizational Leadership Program.

SIGMA GAMMA RHO SORORITY

The last member organization of The Divine Nine established during the foundational period of the Black fraternal movement from 1905 to 1930 was Sigma Gamma Rho Sorority (Kimbrough, 2003; McKenzie, 2005; Ross, 2001). It was at Butler University where seven young students studying education met to establish Sigma Gamma Rho Sorority on November 12, 1922. Kimbrough (2003) contends that, for the founders of this sorority, the need to join in a sisterly bond was paramount to their survival at the predominately White campus. Sigma Gamma Rho holds the distinction of being the only historically Black sorority not to be founded on the campus of Howard University (McKenzie, 2005; Ross, 2001).

Like Kappa Alpha Psi Fraternity, Sigma Gamma Rho Sorority was founded in the Ku Klux Klan stronghold of Indiana (Kimbrough, 2003). Similar to Indiana University, Black students at Butler University in Indianapolis encountered many challenges while attending college. The sorority was founded at a time when the lynching of Black men was at its peak in the South and 30% of Indiana's White male population were members of the Ku Klux Klan (Ross, 2001). The 1920s in Indiana was a period in which Black people faced the constant threat of violence, disproportionate unemployment, severe underemployment, and housing discrimination.

The founders of Sigma Gamma Rho Sorority relied on the organizational principle of self-determination to improve the dire circumstances that the broader Black community faced (McKenzie, 2005; Pruitt, Neumann, & Hamilton, 2008).

Coming from working class backgrounds from the Midwest and the South, Sigma Gamma Rho founders, known as the Pearls of Sigma Gamma Rho, established the sorority on November 12, 1922 (McKenzie, 2005; Pruitt et al., 2008; Ross, 2001). These students who hold the distinction of being the pearls of the sorority are: Mary Lou Allison Little, Dorothy Hanley Whiteside, Vivian White Marbury, Nannie Mae Gahn Johnson, Hattie Mae Dulin Redford, Bessie M. Downey Martin and Cubena McClure (Ross, 2001).

During the early years of the sorority, the founders of Sigma Gamma Rho focused on the internal development of the organization. In the first three years, the sorority focused on defining the organization by finalizing the ideals and symbols that came to represent Sigma Gamma Rho such as the organization's oath of allegiance, slogan, hymn, and coat of arms (McKenzie, 2005; Ross, 2001). By 1925, Sigma Gamma Rho expanded membership consideration to candidates outside the field of education, and held its first national boulé, where the organization introduced their motto "Greater Progress, Greater Service" which would later be adapted to "Greater Service, Greater Progress" (McKenzie, 2005; Pruitt et al., 2008; Ross, 2001). By the 1940s, Sigma Gamma Rho had formed 16 college chapters and four alumnae chapters in 13 states; the Black Greek sorority had also established a scholarship for its college members, and published its official organ, the *Aurora* (Pruitt et al., 2008; Ross, 2001).

IOTA PHI THETA FRATERNITY

Iota Phi Theta was founded on the campus of Morgan State University on September 19, 1963 by Albert Hicks, Lonnie Spruill, Jr., Charles Briscoe, Frank Coakley, John Slade, Barron Willis, Webster Lewis, Charles Brown, Louis Hudnell, Charles Gregory, Elias Dorsey, Jr., and Michael Williams (Kimbrough, 2003; McKenzie, 2005; Ross, 2001). With the Civil Rights Movement in full swing and the first BGLOs in existence for nearly sixty years, a progressive social trend emerged (Ross, 2001). White students were more accepting of their Black classmates as movements to secure civil rights were fully engaged on college campuses. In this progressive era, the founders of Iota Phi Theta etched a place of institutional belonging in their newly founded fraternal organization.

The founders of Iota Phi Theta Fraternity represented an emerging population within the landscape of American postsecondary education, the nontraditional student (Ross, 2001). Each of the fraternity's founders was three to five years older than their classmates at Morgan State University. Some of the founders of Iota Phi Theta had children, held full time jobs in addition to their school responsibilities, and some were veterans of military service. However, the common denominator among the founders of Iota Phi Theta was that many of them knew each other most of their lives, and they possessed the maturity and knowledge to found a fraternity that addressed their unique needs and meet their shared definition of what college fraternity should be. Moreover, the founders of Iota believed that that fraternity could be utilized to address the issues that impacted the Black community of their native Baltimore (McKenzie, 2005).

From the onset, the founders of Iota Phi Theta fraternity viewed hazing as destructive and immoral, especially during a time in which Black men were dying for fundamental rights (Ross, 2001). To the founders of Iota Phi Theta, the purpose of the organization was clear: "The development and perpetuation of scholarship, leadership, citizenship, fidelity, and brotherhood among men" and "Building on a tradition, not resting on one." During the fraternity's early years, it struggled to recruit new members because of its nontraditional student base. Another impediment to Iota Phi Theta's progress was its inability to secure membership with the National Pan-Hellenic Council, the governing body of the eight established historically Black Greek fraternities and sororities.

In 1967, Iota Phi Theta began efforts for expansion beyond its mother chapter at Morgan State University by establishing chapters along the Eastern Seaboard at Hampton Institute, Delaware State College, Norfolk State College, and Jersey City State College (McKenzie, 2005; Ross, 2001). By the next year, the fraternity was incorporated under the laws of the state of Maryland and shifted the direction of expansion from a regional to a national fraternity by founding chapters at Southern Illinois in 1974 and forming graduate chapters in Baltimore, Washington, DC, Hampton, Virginia, and Boston. Twenty years from its inception, Iota had completed a transcontinental expansion with the establishment of a college chapter at San Francisco State University and a graduate chapter in San Francisco in 1983.

In 1996, Iota Phi Theta Fraternity was unanimously admitted in the National Pan-Hellenic Council (McKenzie, 2005; Ross, 2001). While Iota Phi Theta may be the newest of BGLOs, it experienced expeditious expansion, while quickly amassing an impressive list of prominent members. The fraternity has been at the forefront of the plight against Black social oppression. Since its founding, the fraternity has partnered with the Big Brothers of America, the National Association of the Advancement of Colored People, the United Negro College Fund, the Southern Christian Leadership Conference, the National Federation of the Blind, and the National Sickle Cell Foundation in the name of social responsibility.

RESEARCH ON HISTORICALLY
BLACK GREEK LETTERED ORGANIZATIONS

Since their establishment, BGLOs have helped shape the Black college experience and provided Black men and women with social outlets. BGLOs began to appear during a period when many college campuses were segregated. Prominent in each of the nine BGLO histories is the need to cope with the challenges of a hostile campus community or the establishment of a unique identity. Scholarship revolving around historically BGLOs and their members focuses on racial identity development, leadership development, practical competence, and cognitive competence.

The literature on BGLOs and their members is largely underdeveloped and dated (Branch, 2001; Fox et al., 1987; T, 2003; McClure, 2006). The research that has been done on Greek life largely revolves around predominately White Greek organizations, or fails to make a distinction between predominantly White and historically Black Greek organizations (Harper, 2008; Harper et al., 2005; Howard-Hamilton, 1997; Jones, 2004; Kimbrough, 2003; Kimbrough & Hutcheson, 1998; Pascarella, Edison, & Whitt, 1996; Schuh, Triponey, Heim, & Nishimura, 1992; Taylor & Howard-Hamilton, 1995). The following section provides a review of the literature pertaining to the research on BGLOs and its members.

POSITIVE EFFECTS OF INVOLVEMENT IN FRATERNITIES
AND SORORITIES FOR BLACK STUDENTS

The positive effects of fraternity membership on Black undergraduates affiliated with BGLOs are well documented. Most of the research pertaining to Greek affiliations centers on how Greek membership promotes positive student outcomes such as cognitive development, awareness of diverse groups, and college grade point average with focuses primarily on the experiences of White students with mixed results. Reviewing the cognitive impact of Greek affiliation on first year college students, Pascarella, Edison, and Whitt (1996) found that fraternity membership in the first year of college had a significantly negative impact on White men, but a moderately positive influence on men of color. Fox, Hodge, and Ward (1987) found that characteristics most often associated with membership into White fraternities were not applicable, or were absent, in the Black Greek experience. Emphasizing that the existing scholarship fails to make the distinction between BGLOs and predominately White Greek organizations, Wilder and McKeegan (1999), supported by Pascarella, Flowers, and Whitt (2001) and Pascarella and Terenzini (2005) found, like Pascarella, Edison, and Whitt (1996), that joining a fraternity during the first year of college had negative impacts on all four measures of cognitive outcomes for White males, but exhibited a moderately positive influence for men of color.

Existing research fails to illustrate the difference in history and traditions of BGLOs which serve markedly distinct and different purposes than those of predominately White Greek organizations. Fox et al. (1987) assert that members of BGLOs had different values, priorities, and attitudes in comparison to members of predominately White Greek lettered organizations. These differences, in turn, create different Greek membership experiences for members affiliated in the two de facto segregated Greek communities. Specifically, Black students at PWIs gravitate to Black social organizations to develop a network of peers and cope with stressors associated with pressure to conform while attending a PWI (Taylor & Howard-Hamilton, 1995).

Research has shown that individuals affiliated with Greek lettered organizations showed similar levels of engagement as their unaffiliated counterparts, and, in some instances, individuals affiliated with Greek lettered organizations had higher levels of engagement (Hayek, Carini, O'Day, & Kuh, 2002). Additionally, students affiliated with Greek lettered organizations showed significantly higher levels of academic engagement and more frequent interactions with faculty members inside and outside the classroom. While this data was compiled by the National Survey of Student Engagement and includes both the predominately White Greek lettered organizations and BGLOs, this study provides evidence that despite the public sentiment projected in movies like *Animal House* or *School Daze*, which depict negative aspects of Greek life, Greek membership is beneficial to students' personal successes and collegiate experiences.

LEADERSHIP DEVELOPMENT

Early exposure to leadership experiences provides individuals in BGLOs with a solid foundation to succeed socially, academically, and professionally (Harper, Byars, & Jelke, 2005; Kimbrough, 1995; Kimbrough & Hutcheson, 1998; Sutton & Kimbrough, 2001). Specifically, leadership development during student's collegiate life has been found to be the best method to enhance students' leadership and communication skills (Harper, Byars, & Jelke, 2005). Pascarella and Terenzini (2005) assert that participation in activities such as student government, Greek organizational leadership, or being employed by university housing all contribute positively to students' leadership development during their collegiate experience.

Astin (1993) emphasizes that leadership development revolves around the concept of student involvement. Furthermore, Astin notes that "a highly involved student is one who, for example, devotes considerable energy to studying, spends a lot of time on campus, participates actively in student organizations, and interacts frequently with faculty members and other students" (p. 297). BGLOs provide Black students with valuable opportunities to be involved on their campuses (Bonner, 2006; Evans, 2004; Hughey, 2008a).

Kimbrough and Hutcheson (1998) provide results from a survey suggesting that BGLO members were more engaged on campus and had generally higher levels of confidence in their abilities to perform leadership related assignments compared to their unaffiliated counterparts. This finding is particularly significant because of the fact that membership in a BGLO is designed to be a lifelong commitment which is not typical of predominately White Greek organizations. Moreover, leadership development for members of BGLOs provides experiences that help mitigate the challenges of being part of underrepresented student populations at PWIs.

Examining the leadership abilities of Black students affiliated and not affiliated with BGLOs at a PWI in the Midwest, Kimbrough (1995) found that two-thirds of study participants reported that affiliation in a BGLO enhanced their leadership capabilities. Furthermore, Kimbrough asserts that students initiated in BGLOs have a greater likelihood than their unaffiliated counterparts to be actively involved in leadership, or serve in a leadership role in various organizations on campus including mainstream predominately White student organizations.

Patton and Bonner (2001) and Schuh, Triponey, Heim, and Nishimura (1992) assert that BGLOs provide Black students, especially those at PWIs, with a valuable social support network. Sutton and Terrell (1997) suggest that BGLOs provide leadership development for Black males while promoting academic excellence, which is a commonly espoused principle of BGLOs. Reiterating the findings of Kimbrough (1995) and Kimbrough and Hutcheson (1998), Harper and Harris (2006) explain that leadership opportunities provide BGLO members with greater connections to same race peers, therefore reinforcing common organizational missions of providing leadership and advocacy for the Black student communities on their campuses.

ADJUSTMENT TO COLLEGE

Matriculating into colleges and universities, students are allowed invaluable opportunities to explore their identity, develop cognitively, and cultivate autonomy and independence (Harper et al., 2005; Harper & Harris, 2006). Specifically for Blacks, transitioning to college presents a great deal of stress because of environmental changes, social and academic difficulties, and feelings of alienation, isolation and anxiety caused by familial separation (Harper et al., 2005). For students affiliated with BGLOs, it is difficult to quantify the impact of membership on adjusting to college life since most historically BGLOs have prohibited membership to first year students.

While BGLO membership is prohibited to first year college students, these groups provide valuable social and educational campus programming to the broader Black community. At their respective campuses, they offer access to the benefits of BGLO membership to new students (Harper, 2008; Harper et al., 2005; Harper & Harris, 2006; Kimbrough, 2003). At many PWIs, programming sponsored by BGLOs serves as informal campus orientations where new students become familiar with the inner workings of their institution and develop a campus social network. Kimbrough and Hutcheson (1998) found that the impact of social events targeting Black students made a lasting impression on the students who attended. At PWIs lacking BGLO sponsored programming, students of color would be afforded fewer opportunities for social interaction with same race peers.

The cornerstone to adjusting to college for any student population is their level of personal development and academic success (Harper et al., 2005). Academic stability and personal comfort are necessities to ensuring student adaptation to college environments. College adjustment relies heavily on the individual and environmental factors. Research has shown that a positive relationship exists between social integration and individual factors such as college satisfaction, persistence, and graduation rates (Kuh, Palmer, & Kish, 2003). These findings present a precarious situation for Black students at PWIs who often face the choice of having to assimilate into the mainstream White culture which may not parallel the culture of their home environment (Harper & McClure, 2002). BGLOs have been very important in enabling many Black students at PWIs to develop larger social networks and cultural integration and, in turn, Black Greek organizations positively affect Black students' college experiences from matriculation to graduation.

Despite the fact that six of the nine historic BGLOs were established at HBCUs, BGLOs have had a profound effect on Black students at PWIs in which these organizations address a substantial societal need (Ross, 2001). This gap can be observed empirically from a historical perspective of the founding of Black fraternities established at PWIs. Alpha Phi Alpha Fraternity was founded initially as a social support group for Black male undergraduate students attending Cornell at the turn of the Twentieth Century. In 1911, Kappa Alpha Psi Fraternity was founded on the campus of Indiana University in Bloomington under the threat of racial hostility. The founders of Kappa Alpha Psi established the fraternity to provide Black male students social and educational opportunities that previously were not available.

Sutton and Kimbrough (2001) present research data which illustrates that nearly half of study participants who identify as being affiliated with BGLOs demonstrated signs of successful adjustment. Moreover, Harper and Quaye (2007) report that 40% of the high achieving Black students that identified as being affiliated with a BGLO cited that membership in their organization was a valuable resource for support during their collegiate experience.

SOCIAL INTEGRATION AT PREDOMINATELY WHITE CAMPUSES

Higher education literature well documents the challenges Black students face with racism, college underprepardness, isolation, alienation, and confrontations with White students, faculty and staff (Allen, 1992; D'Augelli & Hershberger, 1993; Feagin, Vera, & Imani, 1996; Fleming, 1984). Black students also report more challenges making the transition to college environments compared to their White counterparts. This issue is made especially evident at PWIs where Black students often account for a small percentage of total enrollment and have fewer social outlets and organizations that promote and celebrate the culture and interest of the Black community.

Harper et al., (2005) asserts, "The impact of an institution on its students is mediated through the many subgroups that exist on the campus" (p. 397). At PWIs, BGLOs are an example of a subgroup that plays an integral role for Black students' development and in mitigating isolation and alienation. BGLOs provide Black students the opportunity to culturally express themselves. Throughout their histories, BGLOs have provided Black students an outlet to strike a balance between their identities as members of their respective organization and being a member of an underrepresented student population at a PWI. Sutton and Kimbrough (2001) contend that BGLOs provide Black undergraduates a sense of belonging, cultural connection and a wide array of transferable communication skills. Additionally, BGLOs provide educational and social programming on the campuses where they are active, to the benefit of the larger Black student population.

As previously mentioned, this paper is not an exhaustive review, as traditions, terms, and culture vary from location to location. The focus of this paper was to enlighten individuals outside of the Black Greek community to the relevant literature on these organizations. This chapter serves as an entry into the phenomena of BGLOs. Since their founding in early 1900s, BGLOs have been a prominent fixture in the lives and experiences of affiliated and non-affiliated Black students at both PWIs and HBCUs. These organizations came into existence when Black students had limited opportunities for social engagement outside the classroom and offered students the opportunity to unify and organize during a time when racial segregation and social inequality were facts of life.

Research suggests that BGLOs continue to enrich the lives of their members and the broader Black community. Scholars have attributed membership in BGLOs as positively influencing students in academic, social, and cognitive areas. Moreover, BGLOs have played a substantial role in improving the quality of life for Black students at PWIs through social and educational campus programming. To members of the organizations, they provide a solid foundation for leadership development, as well as advocacy for underrepresented and oppressed groups. These influences are evident with members of these groups who have been leaders in every social movement in America since their inception. The organizations of the Divine Nine each boast a proud and unique history. The founders of each group represent pioneers blazing a trail beyond the landscape of American higher education and leaving an indelible impression on the condition of society. The founders of the Divine Nine live on today, vicariously through the men and women who carry on their legacies and who are living out the noble principles they established. In exploring the history and existing research of BGLOs, the conclusion can be made that each Black Greek fraternity and sorority was established to address a need, and in turn has produced a force of strong Black men and women who promote the ideals and principles inherent to the organizations they represent.

REFERENCES

Allen, W. R. (1992). The color of success: African-American college student outcomes at predominantly White and historically Black public colleges and universities. *Harvard Educational Review, 62*(1), 26–44.

Astin, A. W. (1993). *What matters in college?: Four critical years revisited* (1st ed.). San Francisco, CA: Jossey-Bass.

Bonner, F. A. (2006). The historically Black greek Letter organization: Finding a place and making a way. *Black History Bulletin, 69*(1), 17–21.

Bradley, S. (2008). The first and finest: The founders of Alpha Phi Alpha Fraternity. In G. Parks (Ed.), *Black Greek-letter organizations in the twenty-first century: Our fight has just begun* (pp. 19–39). Lexington, KY: University Press of Kentucky.

Branch, C. D. (2001). *Steppin' through these hallowed halls: Performance in African American fraternities.* (Unpublished doctoral dissertation), University of California, Los Angeles, Los Angeles, CA.

Brubacher, J. S., & Rudy, W. (2002). *Higher education in transition: A history of American colleges and universities* (4th ed.). New Brunswick, NJ: Transaction.

Crump, W. L., & Wilson, C. R. (1972). *The story of Kappa Alpha Psi: A history of the beginning and development of a college Greek letter organization: 1911–1971* (2nd ed.). Philadelphia, PA: Kappa Alpha Psi Fraternity, Inc.

D'Augelli, A. R., & Hershberger, S. L. (1993). African American undergraduates on a predominantly White campus: Academic factors, social networks, and campus climate. *Journal of Negro Education, 62*(1), 67–81.

Dreer, H. (1940). *The history of the Omega Psi Phi Fraternity: A brotherhood of Negro college men, 1911 to 1939.* Washington, DC: Omega Psi Phi Fraternity, Inc.

Egan, R. (1985). *From here to fraternity.* New York, NY: Bantam.

Evans, S. Y. (2004). Black Greek-lettered organizations and civic responsibility. *Black Issues in Higher Education, 21*(17), 98–98.

Evans, S. Y. (2008). The vision of virtuous women: The twenty pearls of Alpha Kappa Alpha sorority. In G. Parks (Ed.), *Black Greek-letter organizations in the twenty-first century: Our fight has just begun* (pp. 41–66). Lexington, KY: University Press of Kentucky.

Feagin, J. R., Vera, H., & Imani, N. (1996). *The agony of education: Black students at white colleges and universities.* New York, NY: Routledge.

Fine, E. C. (2003). *Soulstepping : African American step shows.* Urbana, IL: University of Illinois Press.

Fleming, J. (1984). *Blacks in college.* San Francisco, CA: Jossey-Bass.

Fox, E., Hodge, C., & Ward, W. (1987). A comparison of attitudes held by Black and White fraternity members. *Journal of Negro Education, 56*(4), 521–534. doi: 10.2307/2295350

Giddings, P. (1988). *In search of sisterhood : Delta Sigma Theta and the challenge of the Black sorority movement* (1st ed.). New York, NY: William Morrow.

Harper, S. R. (2008). The effects of sorority and fraternity membership on class participation and African American student engagement in predominantly White classroom environments. *College Student Affairs Journal, 27*(1), 94–115.

Harper, S. R., Byars, L. F., & Jelke, T. B. (2005). How Black Greek-letter organizations membership affects college adjustment and undergraduate outcomes. In T. L. Brown, G. Parks, & C. M. Phillips (Eds.), *African American fraternities and sororities: The legacy and the vision* (pp. 393–416). Lexington, KY: University Press of Kentucky.

Harper, S. R., & Harris, F. (2006). The role of Black fraternities. In M. J. Cuyjet (Ed.), *African American men in college* (pp. 128–153). San Francisco, CA: Jossey-Bass.

Harper, S. R., & McClure, M. L. (2002). *Blacks students' perception of an reactions to largely White phyiscal spaces and activities at a predominately White institution.* Paper presented at the National Association of Student Personnel Administrators, Boston, MA.

Harper, S. R., & Quaye, S. J. (2007). Student organizations as venues for Black identity expression and development among African American male student leaders. *Journal of College Student Development, 48*(2), 127–144. doi: 10.1353/csd.2007.0012

Hayek, J. C., Carini, R. M., O'Day, P. T., & Kuh, G. D. (2002). Triumph or tragedy: Comparing student engagement levels of members of greek-letter organizations and other students. *Journal of College Student Development, 43*(5), 643–663.

Hughey, M. W. (2008a). Brotherhood or brothers in the 'hood'? Debunking the 'educated gang' thesis as black fraternity and sorority slander. *Race, Ethnicity, & Education, 11*(4), 443–463. doi: 10.1080/1361332080247902.

Hughey, M. W. (2008b). Constitutionally Bound: The founders of Phi Beta Sigma Fraternity and Zeta Phi Beta Sorority. In G. Parks (Ed.), *Black Greek-letter orga-*

nizations in the twenty-first century: Our fight has just begun (pp. 95–114). Lexington, KY: University Press of Kentucky.

Howard-Hamilton, M. F. (1997). Theory to Practice: Applying Developmental Theories Relevant to African American Men. *New Directions for Student Services, 1997*(80), 17–30.

Jeffries, J. L. (2008). The last shall be first: The founders of Omega Psi Fraternity. In G. Parks (Ed.), *Black Greek-letter organizations in the twenty-first century: Our fight has just begun* (pp. 67–94). Lexington, KY: University Press of Kentucky.

Jennings, M. E. (2008). The pride of all our hearts: The founders of Kappa Alpha Psi fraternity. In G. Parks (Ed.), *Black Greek-letter organizations in the twenty-first century: Our fight has just begun* (pp. 115–124). Lexington, KY: University Press of Kentucky.

Jones, R. L. (2004). *Black haze: Violence, sacrifice, and manhood in Black Greek-letter fraternities.* Albany, NY: State University of New York Press.

Kimbrough, W. M. (1995). Self-assessment, participation, and value of leadership skills, activities, and experiences for Black students relative to their membership in historically Black fraternities and sororities. *Journal of Negro Education, 64*(1), 63–74.

Kimbrough, W. M. (2003). *Black Greek 101: The culture, customs, and challenges of Black fraternities and sororities.* Madison, NJ: Fairleigh Dickinson University Press.

Kimbrough, W. M., & Hutcheson, P. A. (1998). The impact of membership in Black greek-letter organizations on Black students' involvement in collegiate activities and their development of leadership skills. *Journal of Negro Education, 67*(2), 96–105. doi: 10.2307/2668220

Kuh, G. D., Palmer, M., & Kish, K. (2003). The value of educationally purposeful out-of-class experiences. In T. L. Skipper & R. Argo (Eds.), *Involvement in campus activities and the retention of first year college students* (pp. 19–34). Columbia, SC: University of South Carolina National Resource Center for the First Year Experience and Students in Transition.

McClure, S. M. (2006). Voluntary association membership: Black Greek men on a predominantly white Campus. *Journal of Higher Education, 77*(6), 1036–1057. doi: 10.1353/jhe.2006.0053

McKenzie, A. (2005). In the Beginning: The early history of the divine nine. In T. L. Brown, G. S. Parks, & C. M. Phillips (Eds.), *Africam American fraternities and sororities: The legacy and the vision* (pp. 181–210). Lexington, KY: University Press of Kentucky.

Pascarella, E. T., Edison, M. I., & Whitt, E. J. (1996). Cognitive effects of greek affiliation during the first year of college. *NASPA Journal, 33*, 242–259.

Pascarella, E. T., Flowers, L. A., & Whitt, E. J. (2001). Cognitive effects of Greek affiliation in college: Additional evidence. *NASPA Journal, 38*(3), 280–301.

Pascarella, E. T., & Terenzini, P. T. (2005). *How college affects students : A third decade of research* (2nd ed.). San Francisco, CA: Jossey-Bass.

Patton, L. A., & Bonner, F. A., II. (2001). Advising the historically Black Greek letter organization: A reason for angst or euphoria? *National Association of Student Affairs Professionals Journal, 4*(1), 17–30.

Pruitt, B., Neumann, C. E., & Hamilton, K. (2008). Seven schoolteachers challenge the Klan: The founders of Sigma Gamma Rho sorority. In G. Parks (Ed.),

Black Greek-letter organizations in the twenty-first century: Our fight has just begun (pp. 125–140). Lexington, KY: University Press of Kentucky.

Ross, L. C. (2001). *The divine nine: The history of African American fraternities and sororities.* New York, NY: Kensington.

Rudolph, F. (1990). *The American college and university: A history.* Athens, GA: University of Georgia Press.

Schuh, J. H., Triponey, V. L., Heim, L. L., & Nishimura, K. (1992). Student involvement in historically Black greek letter organizations. *NASPA Journal, 29*(4), 274–282.

Sutton, E. M., & Kimbrough, W. M. (2001). Trends in Black student involvement. *NASPA Journal, 39*(1), 30–40.

Sutton, E. M., & Terrell, M. C. (1997). Identifying and developing leadership opportunities for African American men. In M. J. Cuyjet (Ed.), *Helping African American men succeed in college* (pp. 55–64). San Francisco, CA: Jossey Bass.

Taylor, C. M., & Howard-Hamilton, M. F. (1995). Student involvement and racial identity attitudes among African American males. *Journal of College Student Development, 36*(4), 330–336.

Torbenson, C. L. (2005). The origin and evolution of college fraternities and sororities. In T. L. Brown, G. Parks, & C. M. Phillips (Eds.), *African American fraternities and sororities: The legacy and the vision* (pp. 37–66). Lexington, KY: University Press of Kentucky.

Torbenson, C. L. (2009). From the beginning: A history of college fraternities and sororities In C. L. Torbenson & G. Parks (Eds.), *Brothers and sisters: Diversity in college fraternities and sororities* (pp. 15–45). Madison, NJ: Fairleigh Dickinson University Press.

Wesley, C. H. (1997). *Henry Arthur Callis: Life and legacy* (2nd ed.). Baltimore, MD: Foundation.

Wesley, C. H. (2000). *The history of Alpha Phi Alpha: A development in college life, 1906–1979* (18th ed.). Chicago, IL: Foundation.

Williams, J., & Ashley, D. (2004). *I'll find a way or make one: A tribute to historically Black colleges and universities* (1st ed.). New York, NY: Harper Collins.

Wilder, D., & McKeegan, H. (1999). Greek-letter social organizations in higher education: A review of research. In J. Smart (Ed.), *Higher education: Handbook of theory and research* (Vol. 14, pp. 317–366). New York, NY: Agathon.

CHAPTER 6

LEGAL AND EDUCATIONAL FOUNDATIONS IN CRITICAL RACE THEORY

Evelyn Y. Young
Boston College

Over the past half century, U.S. education has undergone substantial progress toward the elimination of the achievement gap through efforts of desegregation, Title I, Head Start, school finance reform, and affirmative action. However, much of the legal and historical precedence in addressing the topic of educational equity, opportunity, and achievement has centered around the issue of socioeconomic disparity, not racial inequality. Even today, as the Obama administration pushes for higher achievement, more rigorous standards, greater accountability, and more innovative solutions to turn around underperforming schools, what continues to be missing from the discourse is the presence of racism in educational ideologies, policies, and practices. Although education researchers and scholars have long recognized the existence of the racial achievement/opportunity gap, only since the mid1990s have we begun to use Critical Race Theory (CRT) as the lens by which we examine the systemic roots of racism in U.S. schools. This chapter provides a general overview of the literature in CRT in both

Confronting Racism in Higher Education, pages 111–138
Copyright © 2013 by Information Age Publishing

111

law and educational research. In particular, it utilizes a CRT perspective to examine the interplay of racism in the areas of curriculum and instruction, educational policy, school finance, assessment, and educational leadership.

CRITICAL RACE THEORY IN LAW

Critical Legal Studies (CLS) arose in the 1970s in the aftermath of the Civil Rights Movement. Originally comprised of largely White, liberal, male professors in legal scholarship (Dalton, 1987), the movement sought to challenge "the role of law in helping to rationalize an unjust social order" (Crenshaw et al., 1995, p. xviii). CLS scholars derived the theory of hegemony from the works of Antonio Gramsci (1971), who defined hegemony as:

1. The "spontaneous" consent given by the great masses of the population to the general direction imposed on social life by the dominant fundamental group; this consent is "historically" caused by the prestige (and consequent confidence) which the dominant group enjoys because of its position and function in the world of production.
2. The apparatus of state coercive power which "legally" enforces discipline on those groups who do not "consent" either actively or passively. This apparatus is, however, constituted for the whole of society in anticipation of moments of crisis of command and direction when spontaneous consent has failed (p. 12).

CLS scholars looked upon this concept of hegemony to explain "the continued legitimacy of American society by revealing how legal consciousness induces people to accept or consent to their own oppression" (Crenshaw, 1988, p. 1351). They argued that legal doctrine was susceptible to manipulation, and that the opinions of the Supreme Court often reflected the ideological positions of the dominant[1] group (Crenshaw et al., 1995; Matsuda, 1987). What appeared to serve the interest of the underclass, in reality, confirmed the higher status and power of the ruling party (Bell, 1980).

Although CLS scholars "condemn[ed] racism, support[ed] affirmative action, and generally adopt[ed]] the causes of oppressed people through the world" (Matsuda, 1987, p. 331), they also believed that the remedies to racial prejudice and social injustice lay in the ideals of meritocracy, integration, neutrality, and colorblindness (Bell, 1987; Crenshaw, 1988; Delgado, 1984; Gotanda, 1991; Matsuda, 1987; Peller, 1990). CRT scholars, on the other hand, veered with respect to CLS scholars' ideals of a raceless, colorblind society. From the outset, critical race theorists placed "race and racism...as central pillars of hegemonic power" (Crenshaw et al., 1995,

p. xxii). They posited that oppression was rooted in racism and that "race consciousness . . . must be taken into account in efforts to understand hegemony and the politics of racial reform" (Crenshaw, 1988, p. 1335). Critical race theorists contended that CLS was "elitist and exclusionary," "lack[ed] a program," was "cynical," and "fail[ed] to resolve conflicts of value" (Matsuda, 1987, p. 331). Thus, CRT scholars formed a movement of their own, one which centered on the analysis of law through "fiction, personal experiences, and the stories of people on the bottom [to] illustrate how race and racism continued to dominate our society" (Bell, 1992a, p. 144).

Matsuda, Lawrence, Delgado, and Crenshaw (1993) framed CRT around six central themes:

1. racism is endemic to American life
2. legal claims of neutrality, colorblindness, and meritocracy are to be viewed with skepticism
3. racism is rooted in a contextual and historical analysis of the law
4. experiential knowledge of the oppressed is fundamental in analyzing the existing legal and social structures
5. CRT is interdisciplinary and eclectic, and
6. CRT works toward eliminating racial oppression as well as ending all forms of oppression (pp. 6–7).

Each of the themes is discussed in greater depth in below.

Theme 1: Critical Race Theory Recognizes that Racism is Endemic to American Life

For the majority of Whites in America, it is difficult for them to conceptualize the meaning of Whiteness. The reason for this is because Whiteness is a taken-for-granted privilege (Frankenberg, 1993; Giroux, 1997; hooks, 1994; McIntosh, 1990; Tatum, 1992). Frankenberg (1997) argues, "Whiteness makes itself invisible precisely by asserting its normalcy, its transparency, in contrast with the marking of others on which its transparency depends" (p. 6). Harris (1993) associates Whiteness as a property right, that anyone in possession of it is guaranteed membership into society's upper caste. She writes,

> being White automatically ensure[s] higher economic returns in the short term, as well as greater economic, political and social security in the long run. . . . Becoming White increase[s] the possibility of controlling critical aspects of one's life rather than being the object of others' domination. . . . [Furthermore], Whites have come to expect and rely on these benefits, and over

time these expectations have been affirmed, legitimated, and protected by the law (1993, p. 1713).

Recognizing the privileges bestowed upon her as a result of her White-ness, McIntosh (1990) laments, "I have come to see White privilege as an invisible package of unearned assets which I can count on cashing in each day, but about which I was 'meant' to remain oblivious" (p. 10). Among these unspoken privileges are the freedom to associate with people of her own race without question or glare, the assurance of being able to feel safe in public places, and the certainty that people would not assume that her accomplishments were the result of affirmative action practices (McIntosh, 1990).

One privilege that she does not mention is the right to speak against rac-ism without sounding like someone who has blown race out of proportion. When Whites attack an image, speech, or action as defamatory and racist, others look upon them as righteous, politically correct, if not downright heroic. However, when people of color accuse Whites of employing racist speech or practices, the Whites' reaction is to scoff at the accusers for play-ing the "race card." In fact, some will turn the accusation around and claim that the real racists are those who see everything in racial terms. This places minorities in a double-bind position: to vocalize their objection is to risk being targeted as hyper-racists; to remain silent is to submit to their own op-pression. The Constitutional provision of "freedom of speech" is a privilege that is reserved for the dominant group. People in the minority groups who choose to exercise that privilege must use it at their own discretion.

Theme 2: Critical Race Theory Expresses Skepticism toward Dominant Legal Claims of Neutrality, Objectivity, Colorblindness, and Meritocracy

America in the 1970s witnessed a surge of opposition to the Civil Rights Movement, as neo-conservatives attacked race-based policies as antithetical to the fundamental values of democracy (Crenshaw, 1988). They advocated for a colorblind interpretation of Constitutional and judicial analysis, and they sought to dismantle affirmative action programs by heralding the prin-ciples of equal opportunity. As overt racist practices began to wane in the wake of the post-Civil Rights era, the majority of Americans increasingly believed that racial discrimination was no longer a problem (Bell, 1987, 1992a). As a result, it became more difficult to prove discriminatory prac-tices, as seemingly "neutral" standards masked the underlying motives for the denial of housing, employment, health care, and equal schooling (Bell, 1987, 1992a).

Sharply criticizing the viewpoint of neutrality, Gotanda (1991) argues that "[a] color blind interpretation of the Constitution legitimates, and thereby maintains, the social, economic, and political advantages that Whites hold over other Americans" (pp. 2–3). Non-recognition of race protects the property interest of Whites and denies the historical and social context of White domination (Harris, 1993). Moreover, CRT advocates also regard meritocracy as symptomatic of the persistence of racism (Bell, 1987, 1992a; Gotanda, 1991; Matsuda et al., 1993; Peller, 1990). Merit alone is incapable of earning a minority his/her position in the dominant group, nor can it overcome the deep-seated belief of White superiority. The flaws behind the idea of meritocracy are twofold: One, it assumes that everyone starts out on equal footing in life; and two, it assumes that everyone faces the same opportunities and obstacles along life's journey. Supporters of meritocracy also embrace the standpoint of equal opportunity, yet one's ability to merit success is intricately tied to one's race and one's social background. In fact, not only does the rhetoric of equal opportunity discriminate against minorities on the basis of merit, but it also works against them on the basis of "reverse discrimination" (Bell, 1992b). One such example was the landmark case, *Regents of the University of California v. Bakke*, where the Court ruled that an affirmative action policy may not unseat White candidates on the basis of their race. According to Bell (1992b), the Court's interpretation of the Fourteenth Amendment in the *Bakke* case ignored the patterns of racism throughout history and the pervasiveness of White privilege in societal standings (Bell, 1992b). It affirmed that while the law appeared to support the effort to dismantle racism, it would only go as far as it bore no harm to the dominant class.

Theme 3: Critical Race Theory Challenges a Historicism and Insists on Contextual/Historical Analysis of the Law

The rationale that the Supreme Court gave in its ruling in *Brown* was that segregation "has a detrimental effect upon the colored children ... [for] a sense of inferiority affects the motivation of children to learn" (*Brown v. Board of Education*, 1954, p. 494). Yet, for centuries prior to *Brown*, minority students had been subjected to inferior education in segregated schools, and in many instances, had been denied educational opportunities altogether (Bell, 1980; Spring, 2004). Thus, the unexpected regard for the educational welfare of minority students led scholars of color to question the sincerity of the Court's motives (Bell, 1980).

Bell (1980) argued that the historical context of the day rendered it impossible for the Supreme Court to rule against school desegregation. He posited three suppositions for the Court's decision:

1. to gain international approval for America's struggle against communism,
2. to assure Blacks fighting in WWII that their sacrifice for freedom and liberty was as true at home as it was abroad, and
3. to increase economic productivity by transitioning the South from a rural, plantation society to a capitalistic enterprise.

Thus, it could be argued that the decision in *Brown* was not made on the grounds of equality and morality, but on the basis of "interest-convergence." As he aptly put it, "the interest of Blacks in achieving racial equality will be accommodated only when it converges with the interests of Whites" (1980, p. 523).

An example of the "interest-convergence" argument was the busing phenomenon that occurred as a result of court-ordered desegregation (Apple & Pedroni, 2005). To achieve the goal of integrated schools, thousands of Black children were bused out of their neighborhoods over long distances into White suburban schools. Instead of mandating that an equal number of White students be bused into Black neighborhoods and vice versa, the burden to attain racial balance fell upon the shoulders of minority children. At times, the extent of the travel adversely affected the health and educational welfare of the children (Apple & Pedroni, 2005). Busing continued despite the fact that research showed that "court orders mandating racial balance may be educationally advantageous, irrelevant, or even *disadvantageous*" to colored children (Bell, 1976, p. 480). bell hooks (1994) personally recounted the dismay of entering a desegregated school as a young child. To her, White teachers in integrated schools taught obedience and reinforced domination. Black students learned quickly that they did not belong there, and that as much as they resented being bused to White majority schools, the Whites resented the Black students' presence even more.

Theme 4: Critical Race Theory Insists on Recognition of the Experiential Knowledge of People of Color and Our Communities of Origin in Analyzing Law and Society

As Matsuda reminds us, "Every person . . . has an accent. Your accent carries the story of who you are" (1991, p. 3129). Storytelling from the perspective of those "on the bottom" is a technique that is heralded by CRT scholars (Matsuda, 1987). It is set in contrast to the formal, legalistic discourse of members of the dominant class. It avers that "members of marginalized groups, by virtue of their marginal status, are able to tell stories different from the ones legal scholars usually hear" (Delgado, 1990, p. 95).

The use of personal experiences shed light on the varied perspectives of individuals, and their purpose is to counter the voices of the oppressors.

Dalton (1987) articulates three mechanisms employed by CLS scholars to silence the voices of minority scholars. One, legal scholarship prides itself on rhetoric that is structurally complex, inundated with archaic Latin phrases, and mired in facts, details, and intricate analyses. It is scholarship that is intended to bar commoners from participating in intellectualized legal discourse, and it scorns literature that displays less sophisticated techniques. CRT scholars regard CLS scholars' writing as impersonal and removed from reality, entrenched in interpretation of the law apart from race and gender concerns. Yet, the "critics" tend to dismiss CRT writing as lacking in academic quality, thus giving CRT scholars the sense that "if you don't talk th[e] talk, you won't be heard" (Dalton, 1987, p. 441).

Another silencing method is what Dalton (1987) refers to as the, "I don't want to be made to feel like a guilty White male" syndrome (p. 442). That CRT writing focuses on the hegemonic nature of White dominance is uncontestable; its purpose is to emancipate the invisibles of society through discourse with its oppressors. When those of the dominant class refuse to see themselves as complicitous to the subjugation of those on the bottom, the voice of the oppressed is muted with a simple statement of absolution: "I'm not a racist." The underlying message of that statement is, "Don't blame me for what happened in the past. I'm sorry for what happened to your people, but I'm not at fault for your present situation."

A third method of silencing is to bar people of color from speaking for themselves. Whites speak on behalf of the minorities, advocating for "their" causes and arguing amongst themselves about how to remedy "their" problems. Minorities' points of view are assumed, not confirmed by their own testimonies. In such instances, minority scholars feel talked for and talked about, but not talked to (Dalton, 1987). They plead to be heard, to have an opportunity to articulate their thoughts. As Henry Louis Gates (1987) contests, "Blacks lay veiled in a shroud of silence, invisible not because they had no face, but rather because they had no voice. . . . Without a voice, the African is absent, or defaced, from history" (p. 104).

Theme 5: Critical Race Theory is Interdisciplinary and Eclectic

CRT is derived from a number of disciplines, including "liberalism, law and society, feminism, Marxism, post-structuralism, critical legal theory, pragmatism, and nationalism" (Matsuda et al., 1993, p. 6). From these disciplines, critical race theorists have learned to view race and racism as historically and socially constructed, to empower the lives of the marginalized by engaging them in emancipatory discourse, to constantly search for answers and not accept the inevitability of the present situation, and to challenge the status quo so as to resist conforming to the ideologies of the dominant class.

CRT is interdisciplinary not only because of the sources that it has drawn from, but also because of the sources that it has contributed to. Stemming from CRT are FemCrit, LatCrit, AsianCrit, TribalCrit, and WhiteCrit (Yosso, 2006). Each of these look critically at how the legal system represses groups of people based on gender, sexual preference, ethnicity, culture, and social status. As a critique of its own dominant position, critical Whiteness studies arose to challenge the illegitimacy of its subjugation of others. Critical White theorists seek to overthrow their own power in an attempt to counter the regimes of racism, sexism, and classism (Leonardo, 2002; Roediger, 1991, 1994). They argue that, "what oppressed people of color need from Whites is not sympathy as much as a self- and collective-reflection on their own White privilege in a system of White racism, a system that will remain permanent without a revolutionary transformation of White consciousness" (Allen, 2002, p. 32).

Crenshaw (1989) also warns of the need to look at race, gender, and class theories not in isolation from one another but as an intersection of the multiple layers of oppression. She contends that legal interpretations and critical discourse often adopt a single-axis framework, examining discrimination on the basis of race or gender, but not as a combination of both. Such observation fails to account for the compounded effects of the oppression felt by people marginalized on multiple fronts. Crenshaw (1989) notes, "the intersectional experience is greater than the sum of racism and sexism, (thus) any analysis that does not take intersectionality into account cannot sufficiently address the particular manner in which Black women are subordinated" (p. 140). Thus, CRT alone is an insufficient lens by which to analyze the discriminations faced by individuals bearing multiple markers. An interdisciplinary understanding of race, gender, and sociocultural theories is necessary to encapsulate the experiences of those living in intersectional dimensions.

Theme 6: Critical Race Theory Works toward the End of Eliminating Racial Oppression as Part of the Broader Goal of Ending All Forms of Oppression

Critical race theorists recognize that race is only one of many elements that are subject to discrimination. People of color commiserate with other oppressed groups who fall under the umbrella: "other." The marginalized understand that as long as a group of people has the power to exert control over the legal, political, social, and economic aspects of society, no other person who falls outside of the circle of the dominant group is safe from oppression. Erick Fromm (1966) describes the oppressors' pleasure in subordinating others as such:

> The pleasure in complete domination over another . . . is the very essence of the sadistic drive. Another way of formulating the same thought is to say that the aim of sadism is to transform a man into a being, something animate into something inanimate, since by complete and absolute control the living loses one essential quality of life—freedom (p. 32).

Thus, Blacks, Jews, women, and homosexuals are all susceptible to being reduced to nonexistent objects. As it is, their silenced voices have transformed them into invisible creatures, beings that are to be talked about and referred to, but not associated with. Ellison (1947/1995) reminds his readers of his disassociation from society with the powerful words, "I am an invisible man" (p. 3). Those are words that can be muttered from every member of the subordinate class.

CRT scholars are ever conscious of the fact that the fate that awaits them—the absolute loss of life, liberty and the pursuit of happiness—is the same fate that awaits all marginalized groups if they do not fight against hegemony in a concerted effort. Despite the seeming hopelessness in the fate of the oppressed, critical race theorists adamantly place their faith in the hope that circumstances are not written in stone and that change is possible. In this seemingly contradictory duality of fatalism and optimism, Fanon describes, on the one hand, the inevitable assimilation of the Blacks, yet on the other the belief in the alterability of the human condition. He writes, with an air of concession, "For the Black man there is only one destiny. And it is White" (Fanon, 1967, p. 10). Yet, a few paragraphs later, he makes this argument, "But society, unlike biochemical processes, cannot escape human influences. Man is what brings society into being. The prognosis is in the hands of those who are willing to get rid of the worm-eaten roots of the structure" (p. 11). In other words, as long as there are those who are willing to resist the oppressive structure that the dominant class has created, there is hope for a counterrevolution.

Freire (1970/2005) asserts that a pedagogy of the oppressed is a "pedagogy [that] must be forged *with*, not *for*, the oppressed in the incessant struggle to regain their humanity" (p. 48). The struggle for freedom requires awaking the underclass from their state of oppression as well as conjoining the efforts of the oppressors in "true solidarity" with the oppressed. By true solidarity, Freire means to "enter into the situation of the (oppressed)" and to "fight at their side to transform the objective reality which has made them 'beings for the other'" (p. 49). Through emancipatory discourse, both the oppressed and the oppressors can become liberated from the strongholds of hegemony. Both parties need to name the world together, to critique the forces that contribute to the oppression, and to construct a world that is founded upon hope (Freire, 1970/2005, 1994).

CRITICAL RACE THEORY IN EDUCATION

The centrality of race in CRT scholars' examination of legal issues led a similar movement among education scholars a decade later. Dissatisfied with how schools served to perpetuate class differences in society, education scholars employed the ideologies established by critical theory and critical pedagogy to condemn the hegemonic nature of academic institutions. But because critical theory and critical pedagogy failed to stress the prevalence of racism in educational practices, scholars of color began to adopt the ideas of CRT into their analysis of racism in schooling.

In a paper Ladson-Billings and Tate presented at the American Educational Research Association meeting in 1994 entitled, "Toward a Critical Race Theory in Education," the authors linked the six tenets of CRT in law to issues of race and equity in academic situations. Since then, many education scholars have utilized the concepts of racial hegemony, counternarratives, Whiteness as property, and interest convergence to analyze the racial inequities that persist in education (Chapman, 2005; Dixson & Rousseau, 2006; Ladson-Billings, 1998; Ladson-Billings & Tate, 1995; Lopez, 2003; Solórzano, 1998; Solórzano & Yosso, 2002; Yosso, 2005). Furthermore, Ladson-Billings (1998) urges school leaders and educators to critically examine how race is played out in the areas of curriculum, instruction, assessment, and school funding, in particular as they relate to the suppression of "intellectual rights" of minority children.

In recent years, a proliferation of CRT scholarship has surfaced in educational research. The majority of the studies have focused on the application of CRT in the areas of *curriculum and instruction, education policy, counternarratives,* and *educational leadership.* Each of these areas will be examined in detail below.

CRT in Curriculum and Instruction

Despite the recent proliferation of studies using CRT to examine the role of racism in educational settings, the use of the theory as a pedagogical tool is still in its infancy. Much like McLaren's (2007) contention with critical theory, where he argues that although much is written about the theoretical underpinnings of critical pedagogy, little is offered in terms of guidance to educators on how to implement the ideas into practice. CRT runs a similar risk, and Ladson-Billings warned of the possibility of such occurrence when the theory began to gain momentum in educational research in the 1990s. She wrote,

> What, then, might happen to CRT in the hands of educational researchers and school personnel?...I doubt if it will go very far into the mainstream. Rather, CRT in education is likely to become the "darling" of the radical left, continue to generate scholarly papers and debate, and never penetrate the classrooms and daily experiences of students of color (1998, p. 22).

To date, there are but only a few studies that have attempted to integrate CRT as a theoretical framework into an evaluation or a construction of classroom pedagogy (DeCuir-Gunby, 2007; Iseke-Barnes, 2000; Knaus, 2009; Rogers & Mosley, 2006; Stovall, 2005; Young, 2010). All of these studies used the CRT lens to challenge the students and teachers to wrestle with the presence of White dominance and institutional racism in the classroom curriculum. Moreover, the studies heavily stressed the importance of attending to the students' voices, and utilizing their counterstories as starting points to critique and resist the Eurocentric policies and curriculum that bear little to no relevance to the students' daily lives.

For example, in Knaus's (2009) work with 20 students in an urban continuation high school, many of whom had been in juvenile halls or probation previously, he noted with irony how meaningless the idea of having to meet proficiency on standardized tests was when his students were often victims of hunger, sexual and physical abuse, and street violence. Through the use of journaling and discourse, Kraus provided the students a forum to

1. develop and express voice,
2. demonstrate the overwhelming nature of racism, poverty, and violence that shapes everyday life; and
3. develop the tools to survive" (p. 145).

Thus, while No Child Left Behind (NCLB) sought to normalize the students' knowledge to reflect the Western canon, Knaus used the minority students' stories to render such a narrow curricular focus as undemocratic and oppressive.

Moreover, Rogers and Mosley (2006) introduced the concept of racial literacy (Guinier, 2004) to challenge a group of second graders to recognize Whiteness and to critique the practice of colorblindness. Using literature such as *The Bus Ride* (Miller, 1998) and *Martin Luther King, Jr. and the March on Washington* (Ruffin, 2001), the authors led the children in a critical analysis of how the narratives and illustrations in the texts portrayed stereotypical assumptions of Whiteness and Blackness. They also pushed the children to confront their own Whiteness and to recognize that racism is as prevalent today as it was in the days of the Civil Rights Movement. The authors noted that curriculum of silence only serves to reinforce the "practice of colorblindness, denial of racism, and the uncritical reproduction of White privilege" (p. 484). Moreover, they argued that if educators were to disrupt this silence in the elementary school setting, White children would more likely be attentive to the presence of privilege and power, the counternarratives of racial minorities, and the efforts of White allies in their resistance to racial oppression throughout their upbringing.

CRT in Education Policy

Over the last decade, a preponderance of literature has arisen utilizing CRT as the epistemological lens to examine the racial overtones that preside over matters of education policy. In particular, CRT scholars have used the tenet of interest-convergence to focus their analysis of legal and policy issues with regards to desegregation, assessment, and school finance.

Desegregation

2005 marked the 50th anniversary of *Brown v. Board of Education*, and with it came an outpouring of anger from education scholars who lamented over the unfulfilled promises for racial integration and educational equity that *Brown* had proffered to procure. Due to practices of White flight, tracking, busing, and the voucher system, schools today are arguably more segregated on the basis of race than in the pre*Brown* era (Kozol, 2006; Saddler, 2005). As a result, Saddler argues that "African American youth are not only mis-educated but actually 'de-educated'" (p. 44), in that they are being "systemically excluded from the education system and/or being systematically destroyed within that system" (p. 44).

Many scholars support Saddler's claim, citing evidence of ability grouping throughout K-12 schooling as a way to maintain the racial imbalance of students in college preparatory versus vocational programs (Oakes, 2008). Solórzano and Ornelas (2004) argue that the common practice of "schools within schools" fulfills the districts' responsibility to meet *Brown's* mandate for racial integration while continuing the practice of racial re-segregation within schools. More notably, they highlight how Latinas/os and/or Hispanics and African American students are disproportionally excluded from Advanced Placement (AP) courses, and how such practices preclude their opportunities to colleges that weigh AP courses in the admissions process.

Furthermore, Beratan (2008) contends that continued overrepresentation of minority students in special education programs is enhanced by an intersectionality of institutional ableism and racism. One of the stipulations under the Individuals with Disabilities Education Improvement Act (IDEA) is to provide students who qualify for special education services to be placed in the "least restrictive environment." Using the theory of interest-convergence, he argues:

> [t]he institutional abl[e]ism built into IDEA's LRE clause serves to legali[z]e the discrimination that it was intended to alleviate. With this legal and accessible discrimination at its disposal, the special education system offers the general education system a means of maintaining the discrimination that *Brown v. the Board of Education* made illegal. The disproportionate identification of minority students as disabled becomes the means of transposing disability discrimination in place of racist discrimination. Understanding this makes it easier for us to recognize the explicit connection between the development of special education and White America's interest in recouping its losses from the *Brown* decision (pp. 348–349).

As these practices show, while *Brown* provided the rhetoric of equal opportunities and racial reform in education, its outcomes have remained more or less the same. *De facto* segregation continues to dominate all facets of public schooling. As these scholars argue, unless there is an interest for Whites to mobilize toward desegregation inside and outside of schools, it is unlikely that full racial integration will be achieved.

Assessment

Since its enactment in 2002, NCLB has been much scrutinized for its poor implementation, putative measures, lack of funding, and unscientifically based methods of remediating failing schools (Borkowski & Sneed, 2006; Gay, 2007; Hursh, 2005). More specifically, it has been argued that in its attempt to promote educational equity for all students, the statute has had the effect of privatizing education for majority gains (Emery, 2007), un-democratizing education (Sleeter, 2008), and widening the gap between minority and nonminority students (Gay, 2007; Darling-Hammond, 2007).

Gillborn (2008) argues that the "assessment game" is a conspiracy set up by the dominant group to legitimize their status as the social and intellectual elites while psychologically manipulating the oppressed to believe that their lack of educational attainment is due to their own laziness, familial dysfunctionalism, or lack of intellectual ability. It is set up such that the only measure of the students' scholastic aptitude is determined by a single paper-and-pencil test while failing to account for the numerous factors leading to the outcome, including the lack of opportunity to learn (Starratt, 2003), poor teacher preparation (Darling-Hammond, 2006), inadequate funding (Alemán, 2006; Vaught, 2009), and deficit thinking on the part of the entire educational system (Anyon, 1997; Feagin, 2006). Ladson-Billings puts it this way:

In the classroom, a poor-quality curriculum, couple with poor-quality instruction, a poorly prepared teacher, and limited resources add up to poor performance on the so-called objective tests. CRT theorists point out that the assessment game is merely a validation of the dominant culture's superiority (2004, p. 60).

The "game" is not lost upon students either. One of the students in the urban continuation high school in Knaus's (2009) study said,

Listen, if I fail a test that asks me questions I have never seen, that judges me based on courses I did not take, is that my fault? Is it my responsibility to learn what a teacher don't teach?...then don't test me on things I don't know. I can tell you what I don't know without having to sit through your test (p. 38).

The rhetoric of NCLB purports to eliminate the racial and economic achievement gap, but its putative measures for failing schools have merely served to sustain, if not widen the gap (Gay, 2007). Simply because initial reports have indicated an increase in the performance of racial and social minorities, the gap has not been eliminated, and neither is it ever likely to be. Systemic oppression will see to it that the status quo is maintained, even while giving a false pretence of care on the part of the dominant group. Gillborn (2008) goes as far as to argue that if in the unlikely event that Black students begin to master and outperform Whites on the standardized tests, it is probable that another strategy will be concocted to "reengineer" Black students' failure. We have seen this done time and again with the ever-changing laws to ensure that escaped slaves are properly returned to their owners[2] the enactment of literacy requirements to disenfranchise Blacks[3], and the establishment of a tracked system to recreate a "separate but equal" educational policy in the face of desegregation laws (Kozol, 2006; Oakes, 2005). Is it, therefore, so impossible to conceive of a conspiracy plot to maintain the racial stratification with the development of assessment tests that are intended to *fail* minority students?

School Funding

Ladson-Billings (1998) contends that "no area of schooling underscores inequity and racism better than school funding" (p. 12). In *Savage inequalities: Children in America's Schools*, Kozol (1991) shocked the nation when he exposed the deplorable conditions in which some of the nation's poorest schools operated. In the largely underfunded urban schools that he examined, the schools lacked updated textbooks, functional laboratory facilities and bathrooms, and qualified teachers who set rigorous curriculum and high expectations for the students. Although many legal battles have been fought over the issue of disparate school funding (e.g., *McDuffy v. Secretary of the Executive Office of Education*, 1993; *San Antonio Independent School District v. Rodriguez,* 1973), Darling-Hammond (2007) argues that "schools serving large number of low-income students and students of color [continue to] have larger class sizes, fewer teachers and counselors, fewer and lower-quality academic courses, extracurricular activities, books, materials, supplies and computers, libraries and special services" (p. 247).

Alemán (2006) uses a CRT framework to examine the racially discriminatory practices built into the Texas school finance policy. Since the 1960s, school finance policy in Texas has been challenged in the courts and legislature. After decades of lawsuits filed against the state for its failure to provide equitable funding to poor districts that were made up mostly of minority students, a more equalized system was finally established in 1995 under Robin Hood. Robin Hood aimed to take all of the property taxes collected by the state and redistribute them equitably across all districts, thereby "robbing" wealthier school districts the funds that they could have collected through local property taxes. Within a few years of the law being in effect, however, the largely wealthy, White, male-dominated legislature in both major political parties fought to eliminate the bill, claiming that the system was inherently unfair and un-American (Alemán, 2006). More disconcertingly, when Alemán interviewed eight Mexican American superintendents in mostly poor districts regarding their perception of the racial implications of the unequal funding system, the majority of the superintendents did not see Robin Hood as a race issue, but rather as a class issue. Many even regarded the bill as being *unfair* to the wealthier school districts, which supported Harris's (1993) contention that Whiteness as a property right is legitimated and reinforced through color bind discourse.

Vaught (2009) also used CRT to study the racially discriminatory financial system practiced at one large, urban school. Using a practice called "differential student funding," the district sought to provide school choice to students by attaching different amounts of money to different kids. Schools with a higher number of English Language Learners, Title I students, and students with special needs, therefore, would have the benefit of receiving more funds than schools with students in regular education. However, as Vaught found out,

> [T]he money attached to each child stopped following him or her at the front door of the school. All monies were put into one pot, divided evenly across the number of students enrolled at each school, and reported as the per-pupil dollars" (p. 552).

Thus, the money that had been rightfully entitled to predominantly racial minorities was often taken by vocal White parents who demanded enrichment and accelerated programs for their children. According to these parents, each child was entitled to his/her "per-pupil expenditure," regardless of where the money had come from and to whom it actually belonged. In this sense, Vaught argues, "Black children were objectified as currency" who were "owned" by middle-class Whites (2009, p. 559).

Furthermore, NCLB is designed such that the schools serving the neediest students are at the greatest risk of losing federal funds. Rather than providing more financial support to failing schools, the putative measures under the statute remove the much-needed funding by way of vouchers and extra tutoring services provided by outside educational agencies. Darling-Hammond warns, "[i]f left unchanged, the Act will deflect needed resources for teaching and learning to ever more intensive testing of students, ranking of schools, bussing of students and lawyers' fees for litigating the many unintended consequences of the legislation" (2007, p. 247). If the concept of "robbing from the rich" in the Robin Hood bill is unsettling for politicians, what could explain their condoning the practice of "robbing from the poor"? No one would find such practice legal or ethical, unless of course, one views the "poor" as inherently undeserving of the services rendered to them in the first place. As Vaught (2009) argues, intellectual property is a right reserved for the Whites. In the eyes of a White dominant society, the "robbing" is nothing more than rightly cashing in on what naturally belonged to them.

CRT in Counternarratives

Perhaps the most commonly used strategy in the work of critical race theorists is the telling of counternarratives. In naming one's own reality and attending to the voices of the oppressed, those who are traditionally marginalized in the dominant discourse use storytelling so as to challenge the stereotypical images placed on them. Delgado (1989) argues that counternarratives serve a threefold purpose:

1. to debunk the validity of the "rational" and "formulaic" discourse commonly used by Anglo-American scholarship, and the illegitimacy of the "personal" and "experiential" knowledge of racial minorities,
2. to heal the nihilistic wounds of minorities whose perceptions of self and their own culture has been denigrated by the dominant group, and
3. to make the oppressors become aware of their power and their role in perpetuating the oppression of others.

Solórzano and Yosso (2002) conceptualized "critical race methodology" as a strategy that focuses on the stories and experiences of students of color. For example, Solórzano, Ceja, and Yosso (2000) used CRT and LatCrit to study the microaggressions experienced by African American students on college campuses, and found that the students often felt invisible, isolated, and racially discriminated by peers and professors in classroom settings. Delgado Bernal (2002) argued that "the histories, experiences, cultures, and languages of students of color have been devalued, misinterpreted, or omitted within formal educational settings," and that counternarratives provide a venue for students of color to be recognized as "holders and creators of knowledge" (p. 105). Meanwhile, Howard and Reynolds (2008) used the strategy to engage middle-class African American parents in focus group discussions on their and their children's experiences in schools. The authors found that many of the parents felt that their voices were excluded from the decisions that really mattered, such as the hiring of more teachers and administrators of color, budget issues, disciplinary practices, and the need for more cultural and ethnic diversity in the curriculum.

Counternarratives come in a variety of genre and are used in fictional and nonfictional forms. As nonfictions, they represent a personal account of the stories told by people of color. As fictions, they depict a different reality as seen or imagined by the oppressed. These altered realities are based on actual historical precedents, and they represent the fears and concerns of minorities in present and futuristic terms. For example, through the use of counternarratives, Yosso (2006) illustrates a fictional, yet probable, account of a group of Chicana mothers actively involved in critical discourse regarding the educational inequities of the school. Unlike typical PTA meetings where parents are merely assigned duties to serve the interests of the school, *Madres Por la Educación* fought to change the ways in which knowledge is constructed, challenged a curriculum that centered on Whiteness, and opposed the uneven distribution of resources across the district. The parents in this story were leaders for change and revolutionists against unjust educational practices. In short, Yosso told this story to envision the potential for engaging minority parents' in a vastly different manner than has been traditionally done. Rather than relegating them to the inconsequential roles of planning multicultural nights and sharing ethnic foods, critical race educators place the voices of minority parents and students at the center of schools' decision-making power, especially when the make-up of the school consists primarily of students of color.

In essence, the underlying question that all those who employ the strategy of counterstories is "whose voices are heard and whose voices are left out?" (Delgado Bernal, 2002; Yosso, 2005). The efforts of CRT scholars are, therefore, to deconstruct the traditional line of insider/outsider knowledge and to make minority voices count in the larger discourse.

CRT in Educational Leadership

Research using CRT in the work of school leadership began to surface nearly a decade after the introduction of CRT into the field of education (Alémán, 2006; Lopez, 2003; Parker & Villalpando, 2007). The volume of work included in this book represents the latest scholarship on the integration of CRT into school administration research and brings a wealth of resources in guiding leadership training and policy changes. Until recently, however, much of the work done in the area of race and leadership has been centered on the framework of critical theory and antiracist education. Race-oriented scholars in the field contend that school leadership programs often avoid the discussion of race and do not adequately prepare students to become antiracist educators (Lopez, 2003; Parker & Shapiro, 1992; Young & Laible, 2000). For example, in a study of graduate students' experiences in three educational administration programs across the country, Parker and Shapiro (1992) found that the students were frustrated with the dearth of attention paid to diversity issues, in particular topics dealing with race, urban education, disabilities, sexual orientation, and class differences. Instead, the students reported learning far more about these topics through informal discussions with one another outside of class. Because of this lack of preparation, many White leaders fail to recognize racism as the root of educational, social, and structural inequalities in school settings, or worse, their own complicity in the perpetuation of White dominance (Lopez, 2003; Young & Laible, 2000).

Even though education leaders are well aware of the "racial achievement gap," the proposed solutions have tended to come in the forms of tacking on additional services. Among these commonly used strategies include the offering of in-school Title I services and remedial afterschool tutoring to underachieving students, collaborating with community agencies that provide comprehensive social services, and referring parents to programs that offer early intervention services. In these situations, the students and parents are deemed as helpless individuals who need the assistance of kind-hearted benefactors to raise them out of their oppressed state. Instead of regarding minority parents and students as collaborators of school reform and allies in the effort to uproot racism, administrators and teachers often see them as problems to solve.

For those reasons, Lopez argues that it is essential for students in educational administration preparation programs to engage in "critical dialogue about the role of racism in society" (2003, p. 76). Since racism occurs on the basis of action *and* inaction, Young and Laible (2000) argue that it is imperative that administrators actively promote antiracism in their school environment. Ladson-Billings and Grant (1997) describe antiracist education as a practice that "challenges the total school environment to understand the ways in which racism is manifested in schools and society. It encourages educators to integrate antiracist concepts into all subject areas . . . [and it] attempts to reveal the adverse effects of racism on student learning and development" (p. 20).

Educational leaders who are committed to antiracism cannot stop short at simply discussing the students' state of oppression or change the curriculum to incorporate a more multicultural dimension. Instead, they need to engage in self-reflective practices that seek to reject "ideologies and practices steeped in blatantly biased or color blind traditions [in efforts] to transform schools" (Cooper, 2009, p. 695). Dantley (2005) argues that a "spiritual" transformation is in order in urban educational leadership. He means this less so in a religious sense, but more in an overtone of critical consciousness, moral resolve, and hopeful idealism. He writes,

> [R]ace-transcending leaders . . . critically reflec[t] on the context within which schools are established and contend with the issues of power that are at work there. They facilitate a learning environment that is not put off by the systemic realities of racist, sexist, and classist behavior. They see it . . . as an opportunity to use the academic and intellectual prowess of the learning community to attack and redirect these practices of inequality and social injustice (p. 670).

The positionality of school leaders wields decision-making power that can adversely or beneficially affect the educational experiences and outcomes of minority students. To construct schools as sites of liberation requires administrators who are committed to continuous self-reflection, and who are willing to stand firmly on the principles of anti-discrimination in the face of opposition from the teachers, the parents, and the community.

FROM THE "DARLING OF THE RADICAL LEFT" TO THE HEART OF TEACHER EDUCATION

To date, much research has been done in the field of teacher education to challenge preservice and inservice teachers to confront their own White racism (Cochran-Smith, 2000; Gay & Kirkland, 2003; Gillespie, Ashbaugh, & DeFiore, 2002; Marx, 2004; Sleeter, 1994; Tatum, 1992). Much also has been done in the area of critical Whiteness studies to render Whiteness visible and to centralize Whites in the position of domination and exploitation (Fine, Weis, Powell, & Mun Wong, 1997; Frankenberg, 1997; Giroux, 1997; Leonardo, 2002; Roediger, 1991, 1994; Scheurich, 1993). The volume of studies on the power and privilege of Whiteness has been instrumental in forwarding the field of education to address the deep-seated social and racial inequalities present in American schooling. At the same time, however, the preponderance of literature written on this topic has also posed several problems.

One is that the unsystematic, highly individualized approaches to raising the race consciousness of educators in teacher preparation programs or professional developments have engendered a smorgasbord of ideas as to how to engage educators in difficult conversations about race and racism. Aside from the two underlying premises of making Whiteness visible and unpacking White privilege, there seems to be little consensus as to how to begin such a politically, emotionally, and racially sensitive conversation, how to handle resistance from the participants, and how to link this new-found awareness (if that should come to pass) to social activism. The vagueness associated with this type of training has led scholars to caution the adverse effects that poorly constructed and ill-prepared programs can have on the participants' psychology (Henze, Lucas, & Scott, 1998; Tatum, 1992). It may lead to guilt, shame, anger, resentment, and greater resistance (Gillespie et al., 2002; Tatum, 1992). It may even embitter Whites toward being victims of "reverse discrimination" or grow fed up with all of the "White bashing" (Gillespie et al., 2002). To avoid such a spectrum of reactions, it would behoove scholars in this area to conglomerate their wealth of experiences to approach the task of raising educators' race consciousness in a more cohesive, methodical fashion.

This leads to a second problem with the current effort to address White racism: that racism is considered as an individual pathology (Vaught, 2008). Discourse on racism typically centers on efforts to push Whites to come to grips with their own prejudiced nature. It fails to recognize that racism is a *systemic* problem, and that the roots are much deeper and more pervasive than getting individuals to become aware of their own racist ideologies. Although present studies situate the need for race consciousness within a context of structural inequalities and White supremacy, the researcher is wholly satisfied when the participants demonstrate an inkling of recognition of their own White privilege. There is little analysis of how their privilege is situated in the legal, social, and historical oppression of racial minorities, or how a purposeful dismantling of their privilege is necessary in order to effect systemic change. It is, after all, easy to engage in intellectual, circuitous discourse about race and racism if one's lifestyle is more or less unaffected by one's awareness of *others'* oppression. It is infinitely harder to bear others' oppression as one's own, which would inevitably lead one to desire change not merely on an individual level, but on a larger, systemic scale.

A third problem is that these studies are predominantly conducted by White researchers, whose primary objective is to raise the race consciousness of White educators. However, White scholars' conceptualization of racism is vastly different from scholars of color's experience with racism, and White participants' understanding of White privilege is incomparable to minority participants' familiarity with racial oppression and ostracization. To engage in discourse about *White* racism when either the researchers or the participants is non-White may raise issues of power and positionality. Would students of color in teacher preparation programs amplify their racialized experiences so as to give White instructors what they would like to hear in order to receive a higher grade? Would White teachers in professional development sessions trivialize minority scholars' experiences with discrimination on account of their being overly sensitive to race issues? Even in the most ideal of circumstances where all participants reflected upon their racial experience with utmost candor, where power and positionality did not influence the dynamics of the discussion, one would still have to acknowledge that a discourse that is centered on "blind racism" or "White privilege" among Whites would still be radically different from a discourse that is centered on "systemic racism" and "oppression" between people of color. This is perhaps why scholars of color find the dominant discourse on racism somewhat unsatisfactory. It continues to leave out the voices of the marginalized while glorifying the progress made by Whites.

The use of CRT in raising the race consciousness of educators alleviates the problems noted above. First, the thematic nature of CRT readily lends itself to addressing the historical, social, and political context of race and racism in a methodical manner. A critique on the "endemic nature of racism" and the "myth of meritocracy" is rooted in legal and historical precedents, not merely on theoretical hypotheses or circumstantial interpretations. Rather than challenging the existence of White privilege as an amorphous entity, CRT provides concrete examples of how Whiteness has garnered unmerited benefits throughout U.S. history. Second, CRT emphatically rejects the viewpoint that racism is symptomatic of individual pathology; instead, it unwaveringly positions racism as a systemic condition. CRT scholars seek not only to raise educators' consciousness to their own blind prejudices, but more importantly to the pervasiveness and persistence of racism in society. Third, CRT was a movement created by students of color who felt a need to center their understanding of legal analysis from a racialized perspective. Their refusal to be taught Constitutional Law from White, distinguished professors was indicative of their desire to have their marginalized experiences be heard and validated, not to be dismissed or objectified by the traditional interpretation of the law. CRT was and is intended to bring a "colored" perspective to the dominant discourse, not to be sidetracked by discourse on Whiteness. While dismantling the invisibility of Whiteness is undoubtedly a goal of CRT scholars, the more pressing objective is affirming the lived experiences of minorities in the enduring presence of racial discrimination and oppression.

CONCLUSION

CRT is by no means the anathema to all of the multifaceted problems related to urban education. However, an appreciation and understanding of the tenets that underlie the theory is paramount if policy and pedagogical changes in education are to occur at a structural, rather than a surface level. Over the last decade, as state commissioners, superintendents, school administrators, and teachers scrambled to fall into compliance with the NCLB, just as they continue to do so with the Race to the Top initiative (RttT) and the common core curricular standards, one cannot help but wonder what hegemonic forces must be at play to have a league of educators so readily accede to the demands of the federal government. In retrospect, we could perhaps say that the goals behind NCLB were never intended to meet the educational needs of low-achieving children in the nation's highest-poverty schools or to close the achievement gap. If they were, assessment data would have been used to direct money and teacher training to underperforming schools rather than transferring the much needed funds out of the schools through vouchers and outside supplemental educational agencies. Instead, NCLB was created with the purposeful intention of giving the federal government legal access to the design of a national curriculum and accountability system, along with greater control in managing the teachers' union, teacher preparation programs, and teacher credentialing pathways.

From a CRT perspective, we can only begin to surmise why such widesweeping reforms are suddenly necessary when U.S. education has long been plagued by the problem of the racial achievement gap. Whether the real reasons lie in the United States's fear of losing its economic and political dominance in the international sphere in the soon coming decades, or in its interest to move education toward a market-based enterprise, one thing we do know is this: With every effort to standardize curriculum, assessment, and accountability, our nation's educational system also moves increasingly toward centralization (understood as the concentration of power in the hands of a group of individuals). Already, we have witnessed what NCLB can do to compel millions of free-thinking educators into servile obedience, whether willingly or unwillingly. We can only imagine how many millions more of the educators', teachers', and students' voices will be silenced under the rhetoric of innovation and reform.

NOTES

1. The term "dominant" is used in reference to the status of being in a position of power in a legal, historical, and social sense, not in terms of the majority.

2. The Fugitive Slave Act of 1793 gave slave owners the right to pursue runaway slaves in any state or territory, and made the assistance of runaways a punishable crime. In *Prigg v. Pennsylavnia* (1842), the U.S. Supreme Court held the Fugitive Slave Act of 1793 constitutionally binding, but included the clause, "*unless prohibited by state legislation*" (emphasis in original) in its final verdict. This clause opened the door for Northern states to pass laws prohibiting state officials from capturing runaway slaves and left the enforcement of the Fugitive Slave Act to federal agents. In 1850, in an effort to secure the joining of California into the Union as a free state, the Fugitive Slave Act was revised as part of the Compromise of 1850 to make the Act enforceable in all U.S. states. This required all government officials—state or federal—to assist slave catchers in capturing runaway slaves within the state borders (Murrin et al., 1996).

3. Literacy tests were used throughout the late 1800s to the mid1900s to disfranchise Blacks as a way to circumvent the 15th Amendment, which gave all citizens the right to vote. To ensure the continued voting rights of illiterate Whites, a "grandfather clause" was passed, which stipulated that anyone who could vote before 1870, along with their descendants, did not need to meet the requirements of the literacy test. This practice was eventually overturned with the passage of the Voting Rights Act of 1965 (Murrin et al., 1996).

REFERENCES

Alemán, E. (2006). Is Robin Hood the "Prince of Thieves," or a pathway to equity?: Applying critical race theory to school finance political discourse. *Educational Policy, 20*(1), 113–142.

Allen, R. L. (2002). *Whiteness as territoriality: An analysis of white identity politics in society, education, and theory.* Unpublished doctoral dissertation, University of California, Los Angeles.

Anyon, J. (1997). *Ghetto schooling: A political economy of urban educational reform.* New York: Teachers College Press.

Apple, M. W., & Pedroni, T. C. (2005). Conservative alliance building and African American support of vouchers: The end of *Brown's* promise or a new beginning. *Teachers College Record, 107*(9), 2068–2105.

Bell, D. (1976). Serving two masters: Integration ideals and client interests in school desegregation litigation. *Yale Law Journal, 85*(4), 470–517.

Bell, D. (1980). *Brown v. Board of Education* and the interest-convergence dilemma. *Harvard Law Review, 93*(3), 518–533.

Bell, D. (1987). *And we are not saved: The elusive quest for racial justice.* New York: Basic Books.

Bell, D. (1992a). *Faces at the bottom of the well: The permanence of racism.* New York: Basic Books.

Bell, D. (1992b). Racial realism. *Connecticut Law Review, 24*(2), 363–379.

Beratan, G. D. (2008). The song remains the same: Transposition and the disproportionate representation of minority students in special education. *Race, Ethnicity, and Education, 11*(4), 337–354.

Borkowski, J. W., & Sneed, M. (2006). Will NCLB improve or harm public education? *Harvard Educational Review, 76*(4), 503–525.

Brown v. Board of Education. (1954). 347 U.S. 483.

Chapman, T. K. (2005). Pedaling backward: Reflections of *Plessy* and *Brown* in Rockford Public School's de jure desegregtion efforts. *Race, Ethnicity, and Education, 8*(1), 29–44.

Cochran-Smith, M. (2000). Blind vision: Unlearning racism in teacher education. *Harvard Educational Review, 70*(2), 157–190.

Cooper, C. W. (2009). Performing cultural work in demographically changing schools: Implications for expanding transformative leadership frameworks. *Educational Administration Quarterly, 45*(5), 694–724.

Crenshaw, K. (1988). Race, reform, and retrenchment: Transformation and legitimation in antidiscrimination law. *Harvard Law Review, 101*(7), 1331–1397.

Crenshaw, K. (1989). Demarginalizating the intersection of race and sex: A black feminist critique of antidiscrimination doctrine, feminist theory and antiracist politics. *University of Chicago legal Forum, 1989,* 139–167.

Crenshaw, K., Gotanda, N., Peller, G., & Thomas, K. (Eds.). (1995). *Critical race theory: The key writings that formed the movement.* New York: The New Press.

Dalton, H. L. (1987). The clouded prism. *Harvard Civil Rights-Civil Liberties Law Review, 22*(2), 435–448.

Dantley, M. E. (2005). African American spirituality and Cornel West's notions of prophetic pragmatism: Restructuring educational leadership in American urban schools. *Educational Administration Quarterly, 41*(4), 651–674.

Darling-Hammond, L. (2006). Highly qualified teachers for all. *Educational Leadership, 64*(3), 14–20.

Darling-Hammond, L. (2007). Race, inequality, and educational accountability: The irony of "No Child Left Behind". *Ethnicity & Education, 10*(3), 245–260.

DeCuir-Gunby, J. (2007). Negotiating identity in a bubble: A critical race analysis of African American high school students' experiences in an elite, independent school. *Equity & Excellence in Education, 40*(1)26–35.

Delgado, R. (1984). The imperial scholar: Reflections on a review of civil rights literature. *University of Pennsylvania Law Review, 132*(3), 561–578.

Delgado, R. (1989). Storytelling for oppositionists and others: A plea for narrative. *Michigan Law Review, 87*(8), 2411–2441.

Delgado, R. (1990). When a story is just a story: Does voice really matter? *Virginia Law Review, 76*(1), 95–111.

Delgado Bernal, D. (2002). Critical race theory, Latino critical theory, and critical raced-gendered epistemologies: Recognizing students of color as holders and creators of knowledge. *Qualitative Inquiry, 8*(1), 105–126.

Dixson, A. D., & Rousseau, C. K. (2006). *Critical race theory in education: All God's children got a song.* New York: Routledge.

Ellison, R. (1947/1995). *Invisible Man.* New York: Vintage Books.

Emery, K. (2007). Corporate control of public school goals: High-stakes testing in its historical perspective. *Teacher Education Quarterly, 34*(2), 25–44.

Fanon, F. (1967). *Black skin, white masks.* New York: Grove Press.

Feagin, J. R. (2006). *Systemic racism: A theory of oppression.* New York: Routledge.

Fine, M., Weis, L., Powell, L. C., & Mun Wong, L. (Eds.) (1997). *Off white: Readings on race, power and society.* New York: Routledge.

Frankenberg, R. (1993). *Shades of black: Diversity in African-American identity.* Philadelphia: Temple University Press.

Frankenberg, R. (Ed.) (1997). *Displacing whiteness.* Durham, NC: Duke University Press.

Freire, P. (1970/2005). *Pedagogy of the oppressed.* New York: Continuum.

Freire, P. (1994). *Pedagogy of hope: Reliving pedagogy of the oppressed.* New York: Continuum.

Fromm, E. (1966). *The heart of man: Its genius for good and evil.* New York: Harper & Row.

Gates, H. L. (1987). *Figures in black: Words, signs, and the "racial" self.* New York: Oxford University Press.

Gay, G. (2007). The rhetoric and reality of NCLB. *Race, Ethnicity, and Education, 10*(3), 279–293.

Gay, G., & Kirkland, K. (2003). Developing cultural critical consciousness and self-reflection in preservice teacher education. *Theory Into Practice, 42*(3), 181–186.

Gillborn, D. (2008). *Racism and education: Coincidence or conspiracy?* New York: Routledge.

Gillespie, D. Ashbaugh, L., & DeFiore, J. (2002). White women teaching white women about white privilege, race cognizance and social action: Toward a pedagogical pragmatics. *Race, Ethnicity, and Education, 5*(3), 237–252.

Giroux, H. A. (1997). Rewriting the discourse of racial identity: Towards a pedagogy and politics of whiteness. *Harvard Educational Review, 67*(2), 285–320.

Gotanda, N. (1991). A critique of "Our Constitution is color-blind". *Stanford Law Review, 44*(1), 1–68.

Gramsci, A. (1971). *Selections from the prison notebooks.* New York: International Publishers.

Guinier, L. (2004). From racial liberalism to racial literacy: Brown v. Board of Education and the interest-convergence dilemma, *Journal of American History, 91*(1), 92–118.

Harris, C. I. (1993). Whiteness as property. *Harvard Law Review, 106*(8), 1707–1791.

Henze, R., Lucas, T., & Scott, B. (1998). Dancing with the monster: Teachers discussing racism, power, and white privilege in education. *The Urban Review, 30*(3), 187–210.

hooks, b. (1994). *Teaching to transgress: Education as the practice of freedom.* New York: Routledge.

Howard, T., & Reynolds, R. (2008). Examining parent involvement in reversing the underachievement of African American students in middle-class schools. *Educational Foundations, 22*(1/2), 79–98.

Hursh, D. (2005). The growth of high-stakes testing in the USA: Accountability, markets and the decline in educational quality. *British Educational Research Journal, 31*(5), 605–622.

Iseke-Barnes, J. M. (2000). Ethnomathematics and language in decolonizing mathematics. *Race, Gender & Class in Education, 7*(3), 133–149.

Knaus, C. B. (2009). Shut up and listen: Applied critical race theory in the classroom. *Race, Ethnicity, and Education, 12*(2), 133–154.

Kozol, J. (1991). *Savage inequalities: Children in America's schools.* New York: Crown Publishing.

Kozol, J. (2006). *The shame of the nation: The restoration of apartheid schooling in America.* New York: Crown Publishing.

Ladson-Billings, G. (1998). Just what is critical race theory and what's it doing in a *nice* field like education? *Qualitative Studies in Education, 11*(1), 7–24.

Ladson-Billings, G. (2004). New directions in multicultural education: Complexities, boundaries, and critical race theory. In J. A. Banks & C. M. Banks (Eds.), *Handbook of research on multicultural education* (2nd ed., pp. 50–65). San Francisco, CA: Jossey-Bass.

Ladson-Billings, G., & Grant, C. A. (1997). *Dictionary of multicultural education.* Phoenix: Oryx Press.

Ladson-Billings, G., & Tate, W. F. (1995). Toward a critical race theory of education. *Teachers College Record, 97*(1), 47–68.

Leonardo, Z. (2002). The soul of white folk: Critical pedagogy, whiteness studies, and globalization discourse. *Race, Ethnicity, and Education, 5*(1), 29–50.

Lopez, G. R. (2003). The (racially neutral) politics of education: A critical race theory perspective. *Educational Administration Quarterly, 39*(1), 68–94.

Marx, S. (2004). Regarding whiteness: Exploring and intervening in the effects of white racism in teacher education. *Equity & Excellence in Education, 37*(1), 31–43.

Matsuda, M. J. (1987). Looking to the bottom: Critical legal studies and reparations. *Harvard Civil Rights-Civil Liberties Law Review, 22*(2), 323–399.

Matsuda, M. J. (1991). Voices of America: Accent, antidiscrimination law, and a jurisprudence for the last reconstruction. *Yale Law Journal, 100*(5), 1329–1408.

Matsuda, M. J., Lawrence, C. R., Delgado, R., & Crenshaw, K. (1993). *Words that wound: Critical race theory, assaultive speech, and the First Amendment.* Boulder, CO: Westview Press, Inc.

McDuffy v. Secretary of the Executive Office of Education (1993). 415 Mass. 545

McIntosh, P. (1990). White privilege: Unpacking the invisible knapsack. *Independent School, 49*(2), 31–35.

McLaren, P. (2007). *Life in schools: An introduction to critical pedagogy in the foundations of education* (5th ed.). Boston: Pearson Education, Inc.

Miller, W. (1998). *The bus ride.* New York: Lee & Low Books.

Murrin, J. M., Johnson, P. E., McPherson, J. M., Gerstle, G, Rosenberg, E. S., & Rosenberg, N. L. (1996). *Liberty, equality, power: A history of the American people.* Fort Worth, TX: Harcourt Brace & Company.

Oakes, J. (2005). Keeping track: How schools structure inequality (2nd ed.). Hartford: Yale University Press.

Oakes, J. (2008). Keeping track: Structuring equality and inequality in an era of accountability. *Teachers College Record, 100*(3), 700–712.

Parker, L., & Shapiro, J. P. (1992). Where is the discussion of diversity in educational administration programs? Graduate students' voices addressing an omission in their preparation. *Journal of School Leadership, 2*(1), 7–33.

Parker, L., & Villalpando, O. (2007). A race(cialized) perspective on education leadership: Critical race theory in educational administration. *Educational Administration Quarterly, 43*(5), 519–524.

Peller, G. (1990). Race consciousness. *Duke Law Journal, 1990*(4), 758–847.

Roediger, D. (1991). *The wages of whiteness.* London: Verso.

Roediger, D. (1994). *Toward the abolition of whiteness.* London: Verso.

Rogers, R., & Mosley, M. (2006). Racial literacy in a second-grade classroom: Critical race theory, whiteness studies, and literacy research. *International Reading Association, 41*(4), 462–295.

Ruffin, F. E. (2001). *Martin Luther King, Jr. and the march on Washington.* New York: Grosset & Dunlap.

Saddler, C. A. (2005). The impact of *Brown* on African American students: A critical race theoretical perspective. *Educational Studies, 37*(1), 41–55.

San Antonio Independent School District v. Rodriguez (1973). 411 U.S. 1

Scheurich, J. J. (1993). Toward a white discourse on white racism. *Educational Research, 22*(8), 5–10.

Sleeter, C. E. (1994). White racism. *Multicultural Education, 1*(4), 5–8, 39.

Sleeter, C. E. (2008). Teaching for democracy in an age of corporatocracy. *Teachers College Record, 110*(1), 139–159.

Solórzano, D. G. (1998). Critical race theory, race and gender microaggressions, and the experience of Chicana and Chicano scholars. *Qualitative studies in education, 11*(1), 121–136.

Solórzano, D. G., Ceja, M., & Yosso, T. J. 2000). Critical race theory, racial microaggressions, and campus racial climate: The experiences of African American college students. *The Journal of Negro Education, 69*(1/2), 60–73.

Solórzano, D. G., & Ornelas, A. (2004). A critical race analysis of Latina/o and African American Advanced Placement enrollment in public high schools. *The High School Journal, 87*(3), 15–26.

Solórzano, D. G., & Yosso, T. J. (2002). Critical race methodology: Counter-storytelling as an analytical framework for education research. *Qualitative Inquiry, 8*(1), 23–44.

Spring, J. (2004). *Deculturalization and the struggle for equality.* New York: McGraw Hill.

Starratt, R. J. (2003). Opportunity to learn and the accountability agenda. *Phi Delta Kapan, 85*(4), 298–303.

Stovall, D. (2005). Where the rubber hits the road: CRT goes to high school. In A. D. Dixson & C. K. Rousseau (Eds.), *Critical race theory in education: All God's children got a song* (pp. 231–240). New York: Routledge

Tatum, B. D. (1992). Talking about race, learning about racism: The application of racial identity development theory in the classroom. *Harvard Educational Review, 62*(1), 1–24.

Vaught, S. E. (2009). The color of money: School funding and the commodification of black children. *Urban Education, 44*(5) 545–570.

Vaught, S. E., & Castagno, A. E. (2008). "I don't think I'm a racist": Critical race theory, teacher attitudes, and structural racism. *Race, Ethnicity, and Education, 11*(2), 95–113.

Yosso, T. J. (2005). Whose culture has capital? A critical race theory discussion of community cultural wealth. *Race, Ethnicity, and Education, 8*(1), 69–92.

Yosso, T. J. (2006). *Critical race counterstories along the Chicana/Chicano educational pipeline.* New York: Routledge.

Young, E. Y. (2010). Challenges to conceptualizing and actualizing culturally relevant pedagogy: How viable is the theory in classroom practice? *Journal of Teacher Education, 61*(3), 248–260.

Young, M. D., & Laible, J. (2000). White racism, antiracism, and school leadership preparation. *Journal of School Leadership, 10,* 374–413.

CHAPTER 7

CRITICAL RACE THEORY AND AFRICAN AMERICAN WOMEN'S THEORETICAL LEADERSHIP CONSTRUCTIONS

Changing Frameworks for Changing Times

Collette Madeleine Bloom
Texas Southern University

INTRODUCTION

This chapter examines how the double bind of race and gender influences the leadership practice of three African American women (AAW) principals in urban schools. Research questions from a study based on themes from Murtadha and Larson's (1999) work—anti-institutionalism, rational resistance, a sense of urgency and deep spirituality—sought a more inclusive view of the realities of leadership from an Afrocentric feminist epis-

Confronting Racism in Higher Education, pages 139–159
Copyright © 2013 by Information Age Publishing
All rights of reproduction in any form reserved.

temological standpoint. Using shared constructions, interviews were completed to illuminate cultural and interpersonal understandings about how educational and political institutions' discriminatory practices based on sex and race exacerbate inequities in society.

Additionally, an attempt is made to describe how the use of antithetical knowledge and Critical Race Theory (CRT) is being used to build new scaffolding from the current one-dimensional paradigm of leadership preparation in schools using three distinct vantage points:

1. CRT and African American Women's leadership theories,
2. African American women's leadership access and opportunities,
3. Informing theory through storytelling and other oral histories, and
4. keeping the vision alive.

Based on previous interviews with three former principals in urban schools, this chapter highlights both thoughts and findings from these multiple meetings. Over time, I have had the opportunity to rethink and re-conceptualize the forces influencing leadership construction for African American women. To this end, I continue my research with adaptations for this technologically dynamic era.

WOMEN AND LEADERSHIP THEORIES

When discussing leadership and leadership styles, across the board in the most current studies, women possess the most useful and used traits, habits, and skills in leading organizations (Eagly, 2007; Eagly, Johannesen-Schmidt, & Van Engen, 2003; Irby & Brown, 1995b). They also possess the feminine dimension of caring, with the added expectation that women socialize communally. Men, on the other hand, carry with them the expectation that they are agentic, displaying the characteristics of confidence, self-direction and aggressiveness (e.g., Newport, 2001; Shakeshaft, 1987; Williams & Best, 1990).

Rost (1991) defined leadership as "an influence relationship among leaders and followers who intend real changes that reflect their mutual purposes" (p. 102). This 'influence relationship' is based on the leader's ability to use power resources to persuade others. These may include,... "expertise, position, reasoned argument, reputation, prestige, personality, purpose, status, content of the message, interpersonal and group skills, give and take behaviors, authority or lack of it, symbolic interaction, perception, motivation, gender, race, religion, and choices" (Rost, 1991, p. 105). Most principals will use these resources that best match their own personal selves, which include their interpretation of their own racial and gender identity and self-efficacy about the limits of their power in a leadership position, as well as the constraints evident within a particular working environment.

'Influencing relationships' and the use of power has long been the bastion of the male-leadership style. On the other hand, as more and more women are entering the schools as principals, a more caring and nurturing environment has become the hallmark of women leadership. Winning through masculine-style competiveness continues to weaken as more women enter the work world. Newly prepared women leaders are enjoying better paying jobs with more authority and responsibilities, thus adding to their ability to influence direct reports and to change the culture of the organization. One study by Aburdene and Naisbitt (1992) found that women, in etching out new pathways and reaching new horizons, are building new theoretical constructions about leadership and ways of leading. These new paradigms change long-held cultural mores about women in leadership positions.

As cracks appear in the male-controlled educational leadership establishment, theorists are now able to begin the task of understanding how new ways of leading and new theoretical constructions will support the preparation women in leadership for the future. Eagly (2007, p. 1) suggests that "Given that leaders' effectiveness depends on context, it is reasonable to think that stereotypically feminine qualities of cooperation, mentoring, and collaboration are important to leadership, certainly in some contexts, and perhaps increasingly in contemporary organizations... these issues are critical to understanding women's participation and success as leaders".

But how do these new theories for women in leadership impact African American women (AAW)? White women are not burdened with the bind of race within the larger hegemonic American society, and they carry with them White privilege and White access, which women who are Black do not. Several questions arise from this—do AAW have the same issues and burdens as White women in American society? How does the double bind of race and gender impact the leadership practice? A brief review of the development of new theories for AAW offers a positive outlook for the future.

CRITICAL RACE THEORY
AND AAW LEADERSHIP THEORIES

Deal and Peterson (1994) argue that leadership in schools is both a complex and ambiguous process. Building effective capacity on performance outcomes requires that we use the best ideas from existing models, building new theories and empirically testing them, and employing this new knowledge to create intensive professional development programs advancing the possibility of producing leaders with more depth and capacity. As different voices and different experiences expand within the community of leaders in our nation, members within these various communities must establish their own distinctive voices in public school systems, institutions of higher learning, and government agencies. This variety of voices and experiences must compete with the undeclared American standard of what "normal" looks and sounds like. The mythic norm of what constitutes the standard of leadership in American society remains "White, male, young, thin, heterosexual, Christian, and financially secure" (Lorde, 1984). Research confirms that despite more than thirty years of data to the contrary, the myth remains that the ideal manager conforms to a masculine stereotype. Organizational and leadership theory has permitted such an image to remain essentially undisturbed (Hill-Collins, 1991; Etter-Lewis, 1993; hooks, 1994; Lorde, 1995).

The accumulated knowledge over the last forty years has produced significant and substantial insights about leadership styles, traits, and skills (Burns, 1978; Hoy & Miskel, 2008; Hunt, 1999). However, these studies have left scholars with the feeling that the applications and usefulness of these theories were static, overly rigorous and not congruent with today's fast-paced information systems and growing diverse society (Brookfield, 1992). It was the introduction of 'new leadership' models described as wide-ranging and highly influential models for use in social organizations (Bass, 1985; Burns, 1978; Hunt, 1999) that began to appear in scholarly journals. Descriptions such as Laissez-faire, transactional and transformational arose as the new sorts of leadership styles. The style that seems to have gained the most traction over the last ten years is transformational. Eagly (2007, p. 4) writes that transformational "[l]eadership researchers responded to this changing environment by defining good leadership as future-oriented rather than present-oriented and as fostering followers' commitment and ability to contribute creatively to organizations." This matches the shifting paradigms inherent in the formation of leadership trends for the future.

Concomitant with the introduction of new theories about leadership emerged non-traditional perspectives (Devault, 1993; Olesen, 1994). These new theories increased the popularity of subjective perspectives and more demand for the use of qualitative methodologies (Butler, 2011; Denzin & Lincoln, 1994, Fendler, 2011; Lunenburg, 2003; Olesen, 1994). Of particular note is the perspective of feminist research which originated shortly after the beginning of the women's movement in the United States (1960 onward). Subsumed in feminist research came the study of other women from all backgrounds and ethnicities. White women's studies (considered by Fee [1983] to be liberal, radical and Marxist) soon became a mixture of multiple and complex positionalities: male-oriented, female-oriented, Western-feminist oriented; religious-oriented; African, Asian, and Latino-oriented. Olesen (1994) contends that most male-oriented research methodologies were contained in the phrase "...add women and stir..." (p. 159). Any group could, of course, be replaced with the word women, and it would accurately reflect the condition of all leadership studies. One major outlier of the feminist model (which is inclusive of ALL women) denies one truth of American life: White women retain White privilege; women of color do not. This privilege bears on the style and theoretical constructions of leadership of African American women.

The 1970s began to give voice to women of color. In the Black community, the works of authors such as Toni Cade Bambara, Ntosake Shange, Angela Davis, Toni Morrison, Alice Walker, and Audre Lorde presented ideas hailing from a platform of proud identity. African American women of the 1990s and beyond are circumscribing the limits of a more clearly defined collective African American woman's standpoint about womanhood (Hill-Collins, 1991). The ability of African American women in general, and African American women in educational administration in particular, to voice their own personal experiences through conversations and storytelling presents a new set of ideas through lived experiences that adds depth and richness to the larger picture of leadership in urban schools.

New strategies to achieve racial justice, strategies informed by critical theory, feminism, postmodernism, and other intellectual theories, have appeared as the gains of the civil rights era slowly erode (Bell & Nkomo, 2001; Capper, 1992; Crenshaw, 1995; DiStephano, 1990; Hill-Collins, 1991; Lather, 1991;Weedon, 1997). The development of Critical Race Theory (CRT) has expanded from outside its field of origin (law) into such areas as education (Ladson-Billings, 1998) and women's studies (Crenshaw, 1995). Critical Race Theory offers a venue for finding a deeper understanding of why educational reforms, inadequate feminist, minority leadership theory, and abysmal African American student achievement scores continue to plague the American educational system. CRT does not offer excuses; it offers a legitimately chronicled explanation for how we as a nation have arrived at a crossroads in education (Dixon & Rousseau, 2006). Ladson-Billings (1998) asserts that Critical Race Theory is a form of oppositional scholarship, not an abstract set of rules or ideas. Delgado (1995a) describes the critical elements of the CRT:

1. racism in America is a normal fact of daily life and should not be considered aberrant or rare, and
2. the assumptions of White superiority are so pervasive in our political and legal systems as to be unrecognizable.

NORMATIVE MODEL OF LEADERSHIP UNMASKED

A Western, Eurocentric male epistemology remains the normative model in educational administration research. The incorporation of viewpoints about the world of work for minority women leaders in urban schools is not a part of mainstream theory. This absence of minority women's ways of knowing in research perpetuates their continued marginalization, creating a gap in the literature. The failure of African American women to build theoretical knowledge construction in academe allows other groups to further stereotype and marginalizes their educational contributions. This is why by understanding what theories can do—and by extension, cannot do—we are better able to develop those theories that inform practice.

The most useful description of organizational theory as posited through the lens of educational administration is "a set of interrelated concepts, definitions, and generalizations that systematically describes and explains patterns of regularities in organizational life" (Hoy & Miskel, 2008, p. 3). Theories have a practical role in organizations, just as they do in our everyday lives—they provide general explanations and guide research. In the organizational context, theories inform the phenomenon of leadership. According to Lynham and Chernak (2006), the study of theory is undertaken to produce new knowledge about the world. Theories help leaders "to understand, explain, anticipate, know, and act in the world in better and more informed ways and to better ends and outcomes" (p. 82). Torraco (1997) identified several ways that theory is useful in developing an organization's human resources. Among these are: (a) responding to new problems which have no previously identified solution, (b) reinterpreting old data and giving it new meaning, (c) identifying new issues and research questions that need to be answered, and (d) guiding and informing research and improving professional practice.

By nature, theories are general and abstract and thus are useful or not useful, not true or false. They are useful in that they "generate accurate predictions about events and help us to understand and influence behavior" (Hoy & Miskel, 2008, p. 3). Applying traditional leadership theory to AAW leaders in educational administration positions may open the door to the re-evaluation of traditional leadership theory. Continual and ongoing refinement of a theory ensures that it continues to hold relevancy in the workplace. As mentioned earlier, if the theory is no longer useful for the leader, or the leader finds that constructing new ways of carving out workable, utilitarian answers to the current problems of leading, then we have the prototype for a new theoretical construction of leadership. This is particularly relevant for African American women who do not usually have grounded theory that reflects their lives or lived realities. As leaders in urban schools, African American female principals' ways of leading may differ from their White, female counterparts, and may be drastically different from traditional male leadership paradigms. Austin (1995) calls for an African American feminist research agenda that would be grounded in the life circumstances of African American women.

Simply questioning the applicability of leadership theory to the race, gender, and social class of the leader undermines the assumption that universal organization and management theories exist (Bell and Nkomo, 2001; Gioia & Pitre, 1990). Yukl (2002) also cautions not to interpret the results of early leadership studies as universal theories of effective leader behavior. Superimposing the same style across all situations is not warranted. By bringing to the conversation new and previously silenced voices, we can move beyond questioning and begin to challenge orthodox theories of this social phenomena, shifting leadership knowledge from a deterministic-individualistic paradigm to a more reflexive, non-deterministic and collective one, pushing the notion of leadership to new heights of understanding and bringing us closer to an alternative worldview of leadership (Hill-Collins, 1991; Crenshaw, 1995; Ladson-Billings, 1998).

Capper (1992) charges that the study of leadership from an African American woman's perspective is both inadequate and incomplete. As the numbers of African American women principals continue to grow, it is becoming increasingly evident that little is known about African American women's theoretical constructions of leadership (Montenegro, 1993), thereby limiting their knowledge base within the leadership field. "Without our [African American] voices in written works and oral presentations, there will be no articulation of our concerns" (hooks, 1989, p. 105).

For over four hundred years in this country, "the dominant conceptual imagination . . . has overlooked the material reality of racism and cultural annihilation in their theoretical formulations" (Murtadha & Larson, 1999, p. 3). Failure to recognize the contributions of marginalized and oppressed groups continues to hamper the conversations necessary to conceptualize different realities and experiences. The unheard voices of African American men and women only make a whisper when competing with the dominant theoretical discourse in American colleges and universities. Without those theoretical frameworks and conceptualizations, leadership institutions and universities cannot adequately prepare future leaders to best serve the needs of other Americans who do not match the mythic norm (Bell, 1997; Montenegro, 1993). Marginalization in academe is known as "institutional silencing" (Gitlin, 1994, p. 4). This silencing heightens the absence of more enlightened discourses regarding leadership for those other than White males.

AFRICAN AMERICAN WOMEN'S LEADERSHIP ACCESS AND OPPORTUNITY

Irby and Brown (1999) have identified variances in the way that women perceive barriers to attaining administrative positions from men. These gendered expectations about the "right way to lead" are challenged by feminist images of leadership. Although welcomed for their refreshingly alternative perspective of how women lead, the model is far too global in its scope. The leadership style and practices of African American women principals have not been adequately described or included in the literature.

Historically, because African American women have been portrayed as a single entity, existing along one continuum with few differences among them, longstanding differences structured along the axes of race, color, class, nationality, religion, and region have begun to surface (Banks, 1995; Crenshaw, 1995; Hill-Collins, 1991). The incorporation of viewpoints about the world of work for African American women is not part of mainstream leadership theory. The viewpoints of African American women are alternative ways of knowing that differ significantly from Western, Eurocentric, male-dominated epistemologies (Willis, 2001).

Leadership definitions abound. The definition used for this chapter is one associated with a person being in a position of authority and holding a certain degree of power and influence on a school campus. For African American women (AAW), the double-bind of race and gender can constrain their pathway to successful leadership practice (Bell & Nkomo, 2001; Hine & Thompson, 1998). As such, history offers little hope that equity of opportunity and positions of authority will ever be achieved without the federal mandates and legislation in place to keep people from lapsing into familiar patterns of behavior and biased ways of thinking (Bloom & Erlandson, 2003). CRT suggests that the pervasiveness of racial and gender discrimination permeates and reorders the employment opportunities offered to minority women.

Peitchinis (1989) submits that "Employment discrimination refers to access to employment opportunities, and to the assignment of responsibilities upon securing of employment" (p. 24). This statement is significant in its simplicity. Although, the numbers of women administrators in education are greater now than ever before, AAW remain underrepresented as a gender and race, especially when considering the entire profession of education which is comprised of more than 70% women. Several older studies mirror outmoded explanations for the paucity of numbers of women in educational administration:

1. lack of aspiration for administrative positions,
2. inadequate preparation, and
3. lack of natural leadership ability (Foschi, 2000; Gupton & Slick, 1996; Yeakley, Johnston, & Adkison, 1986; Shakeshaft, Brown, Irby, Grogan & Ballenger., 2007).

Over time, these conclusions have faded and have little ongoing support. African American women's representation in educational administration has continued to expand as numbers grow. The circumstances that originally supported the explanations for reduced numbers have shifted significantly and new explanations have emerged. In acknowledging these shifts, researchers and schools of education may be better able to offer new paradigmatic frameworks for the construction of more appropriate leadership theoretical constructions. Furthermore, AAW's marginalized status may limit access to social connections in predominantly White organizations. Access to power as well as the freedom to exercise one's own power and authority often lies in informal social networking systems (Gostnell, 1996). Lack of access to these systems may disadvantage the AAW leader's ability to influence organizational processes and actions (Byrd, 2008).

INFORMING THEORY THROUGH STORYTELLING AND OTHER ORAL HISTORIES

The African American woman professional is a fundamentally unrecognized source of local community strength in American society. The stories of these women are uniquely American in their scope. The names of these heroes are known only within their own communities, rarely receiving prominence in the mainstream saga of the nation's heroes. Each woman possesses the ability to cope with the ongoing demons of racism and sexism for the benefit of their communities.

As the faces of urban public school students in America become more African American and brown, the face of leadership in America's urban schools should reflect those demographic changes. Murtadha and Larson (1999) contend, "...principals of color, especially African American women, typically emerge as the leaders of urban schools that are undersupported and economically depleted." Moreover, these researchers assert, "they [women of color] are expected to establish and carry out educational agendas that clash with what they and the community see as vital to the education of African American children (p. 7)."

The findings of the interviews support and extend the work of Murtadha and Watts (2005), suggesting that the principals survive and thrive through a committed dependence on family, community, spirituality, and the arts, especially Black literature. Using self-affirming words and listening to stories of the success of others, each participant proudly accepts her cultural and ethnic heritage. The participants construct theoretical perspectives and successful leadership practices based on their own knowledge construction about equity, access, and opportunity, thereby enabling disenfranchised youth to advance academically.

Recommendations advocate that universities train future African American women principals in skill-based knowledge for urban school leadership. Further, creating strong mentorship networks and encouraging pro-equity discourse can support preparation programs for future minority administrators. Despite the noteworthy advances present in curricula addressing multicultural awareness, most students are isolated in their independent knowledge about other races. These differences become apparent when open discussions about attitudes, patterns of behavior occur.

Over the last two decades, African American women have achieved increased visibility and recognition in dominant academic discourses (hooks, 1989). However, Hill-Collins (1996) warns that we

> ...must be attentive to the seductive absorption of Black women's voices in classrooms of higher education where Black women's texts are still much more welcomed than Black women ourselves. Giving the illusion of change, this strategy of symbolic inclusion masks how the everyday institutional policies and arrangements that suppress and exclude African Americans as a collectivity remain virtually untouched.

The teller can share what is and what ought to be. Storytelling, narrative, autobiography, and personal history are appropriate venues for engaging and contesting negative stereotyping (Delgado, 1995b; Ladson-Billings, 1998). The advantage of this theoretical framework for oppressed people is that it challenges the White standard of normalcy as it grounds its conceptual framework in the distinctive experiences of people of color (Calmore, 1995; Banks, 1995). Blackness is not a condition from which one needs liberation or redemption; rather African Blackness is a cultural way of perceiving and knowing. As the researcher, it influences who I am and what I will write about as I live in the White world of educational administration.

KEEPERS OF THE VISION

African Americans as a community, forbidden an education during slavery, historically have a strong belief in the power of education to lift the forgotten and downtrodden out of the clutches of poverty and hopelessness. The African American community believes that inequities in the distribution of resources and opportunities can be ameliorated through education. Higginbotham and Cannon (1992) observe:

> Lacking wealth, the greatest gift an African American family has been able to give to its children has been the motivation and skills to succeed in school. Aspirations for college attendance and professional positions are stressed as family goals, and the entire family may make sacrifices and provide support. African American women have long seen the activist potential of education and have sought it as a cornerstone of community development—a means of uplifting the race (p. 332).

Although African American women differ in style and methods, they share an approach to leading that is lacking in unsuccessful urban schools. Providing a culturally relevant environment is a necessity to the success and future promise of African American children. African American women principals become pivotal conduits as the "keepers of the vision" for parents and the African American community. These principals, who are leaders of marginalized and oppressed communities, must engage in transformational leadership that focuses on survival strategies as a central tenet to daily practice (Murtadha & Larson, 1999).

Murtadha and Larson (1999) have identified four specific ways in which African American women lead differently from their White female colleagues, using a womanist (African American feminist) leadership perspective. These leadership narratives of African American women all were rooted in "anti-institutionalism, rational resistance, a sense of urgency and deep spirituality" (p. 4). Additionally, success or failure in leadership for African American women often rests on the mutual understanding of other African American women mentors who are willing to share and guide principals, especially during the first year as leaders in a school setting.

Although a growing number of works have addressed this issue in recent years, there is still a need for additional narrative to enrich the common heritage that binds African American women principals together as leaders. Here are a few of the new constructions on what African American women have learned from their work. These themes emerged after extensive interviews, document reviews, and on-site visits with three former urban school leaders in successful schools. Collecting data for this work occurred over two years. The women, known as Claire, Grace and Rose shared their lived experiences with me over this time period. These findings are abbreviated here for this chapter. From the field, six main themes emerged seamlessly.

LESSONS FROM THE FIELD: NEW CONSTRUCTIONS ON LEADERSHIP THEORY

Beating the Odds

Claire, Grace, and Rose succeeded when the odds suggested they should have failed. The acceptance of personal triumphs and tragedies explained the foundation of their spirituality. Each woman attributed their leadership success and inner confidence to strong roots in the Black church. They considered the community to be an extended family on which they could lean and seek support and comfort. Both celebration and sorrow could be brought to the Church. A longstanding personal relationship with God empowered their work, allowing each to know that the path to effective leadership begins with a strong belief in God's righteousness. Claire Broussard shared an aspect of her early lessons in trusting in God. "My parents instilled in me at a young age that without God I cannot succeed at anything. Every morning, I go to my knees and pray for His support and guidance as I go about my work. And He has blessed with every day for the trust that I give to Him only."

Identity Formation

Claire, Grace, and Rose reject the notion that they are deficient, or less than because of race or sex. Each is 'whole' without Whiteness or maleness as part of their being. None inferred that they would have better or fuller lives if White or male. Rose Atwell, who proved that a woman could lead a secondary school, tensed up at the thought of male superiority in the workplace. "Most men became principals by default. Women were treated as servants to male principals in schools. I was determined to become a principal and to change a school using what I knew as an African American and a woman. And I did—my way."

The Power of Language

The women used words as a vehicle to shape and control their lives. In all of the interviews, each repeated words and phrases from their parents, identifying each as a 'truth' about reality. They recited poetry and phrases from Black artists and displayed Black paintings, pictures, and literature in their homes and at work. In the words of Grace Cleveland, "I am nothing if not what my parents said I was. I have a tradition to uphold. It was a driving force in my life to live up to what my parents expected of me."

Sexism

Although each woman understood how racist practices functioned to constrain advancement and maintain the status quo in the workplace, they were not so sophisticated about how sexist discriminatory practices operated in the workplace, even within the Black community. Sexist practices were prevalent within segregated communities. Only Rose understood that being overlooked for promotion could occur because of sex. She explained, "Black men were just as chauvinistic as any other man, Black or White." These women never used or alluded to negative stereotypes of Black women, such as mammy, Jezebel, or Aunt Jemima, either formally or informally. Their identity formation was clear and firmly etched within their psyches.

Racism

Claire, Grace, and Rose accepted their own ethnic and cultural heritages completely. Racism was a problem caused and invented by White people; it was not their battle. And although they could not deny the impact of racism on all African Americans, they used their positions as leaders to start discussions about change. They rejected the idea of living like a victim because of racist ideology. Each believed that she survived and thrived based on her own efforts and internal locus of control.

New Perspectives

With age, each woman took on more risks in her career. Changing career sites and challenging male dominated work environments became a part of their world's work. The women reconciled old memories, and integrated them into new perspectives for the present and future. By drawing connections between memories and new experiences, they have become more centered as leaders. Leadership decisions are based on what they have defined as truth for African Americans in this country.

IMPLICATIONS FOR RESEARCH

Little knowledge in the literature exists about how race and gender affect leadership practice for African American women. Educational administrative research can build capacity within the field of minority leaders by encouraging African American women to contribute to the knowledge base about Black women by researching their own culture.

Universities can begin to include more pro-equity discourse as a means to reduce institutional silencing. Include narratives in coursework as a way to individual empowerment, community building, and cultural transmission for future African American Women principals. This discourse will also expand the knowledge base of others outside of the African American community on how leadership practice is constructed in the minds of women who have historically been left out of leadership paradigms.

Encourage storytelling as a way to understand the content and epistemology of Black women's ideas, and teach skills-based strategies for leadership in

America's most difficult schools: Crisis management, working with the juvenile justice system, lack of parental involvement, and generational poverty.

WRITING AND THINKING ABOUT RACE IN SCHOOLS

The American Civil Rights Movement, which began in the early 1950s, ushered in an unprecedented period of cultural awareness regarding the extensive and significant achievements of African Americans to the capitalistic success of the United States. Their previously unheralded presence in the landscape of life in the United States positioned Negroes on the forefront of change during the nation's turbulent challenges in the social re-ordering of its people. These paradigmatic shifts in national attitude and behavior toward the African American minority population began to appear in textbooks and eventually as new and more dynamic teaching methodologies. Culturally relevant pedagogy (Ladson-Billings, 1998) and more inclusive leadership constructions (i.e., postmodern theories and critical theories) signaled the beginning of a leadership training era that appreciates the culture and knowledge base present within each community. Using naturalistic inquiry and other postmodern qualitative methodologies adds new dimensions and value to the empirically numbered facts (Erlandson, Harris, Skipper, & Allen, 1993). Universities acknowledged the necessity for materials that were more representative of the diversity of future leaders by building programs that addressed issues of women and minority women in leadership. Not a given, many university professors have continued to address the scarcity of multicultural materials by creating their own, a glaring absence of culturally relevant resources remains an issue for many educators (Gay, 2000; Banks, 1995; Yoder, Schleicher, McDonald, 1998).

The adequacy of educational leadership programs in addressing the needs, expectations, and interests of all future women leaders has been challenged (Irby & Brown, 1999). Furthermore, Mertz and McNeely (1998) contend that a multidimensional approach, which examines context, ethnicity, and other factors, is required when conducting research on the issue of leadership style. African American women's leadership practices have not been adequately included in the development of leadership theory, creating a gap in the literature. Ongoing research continues to sustain those theories that reflect longstanding and current ontologies (hooks, 1994).

Ladson-Billings (1998) and Lawrence (1995) assert that voice shapes the contextual contours of reality by interpreting life's experiences. The words used by the teller can articulate and validate common experiences. American women of African descent in the 1990s began to develop a "voice," a self-defined, collective African American woman's standpoint about African American womanhood (Hill-Collins, 1991). This paper hopes to offer a more expansive portrait of leadership viewed from the window of the African American woman principal. It expects to explain a construction of leadership that does not match the mythic norm, but represents effective leadership in schools that are filled with the destitute and the marginalized. The voices heard through narratives will reflect the lived experiences of African American women principals.

Educational institutions are powerful mechanisms for perpetuating the race, class, and gender inequities in society. Who controls them, who benefits from institutional resources, and who is best able to negotiate their way through institutional structures all reveal patterns of race, class, and gender inequity (Bloom & Erlandson, 2003). Still, it is important to realize that power does not operate only in a "top-down" fashion. Challenges to institutions come in many ways, but change begins with analysis.

IMPLICATIONS FOR LEADERSHIP PREPARATION PROGRAMS

Young and Laible (1999) bemoaned the failure of most of the educational administration departments in the United States to significantly or adequately address issues of racism and sexism and its consequences on leadership practice. Consequently, educational programs "continue to produce primarily White middle class administrators with little understanding of, or interest in, the institutionalized system of White privilege, oppression, and racism" (p. 11).

The issues of underrepresentation of women and racial-ethnic minorities lead us to question our present understanding of culture and diversity and to examine the role of scholars of color with university systems. The era of developing diversity refers to the critical role of the universities, which must be pacesetters for multicultural identity. Universities and colleges must prepare for differences, for the distinct, for the dissimilar, the various, and the alternative with the next generation of scholars—and in doing so, must find advantages and value in diversity. Universities must be at the forefront of these shifting views, providing the higher education necessary to confront a changing world. Often, we possess power of which we are not even aware (referent, delegated, legitimate); therefore, we are unable to share our power with others.

Having said this, presented here are four short points for consideration of university preparation program developers as we begin to develop them into critical thinkers doing action research about their own work as leaders in school administration. We have a moral imperative to teach our preservice African American women administrators how to think about their presence in the university and in the public schools:

1. Scholars of color are just recently (within the last fifteen years) learning that their power is increased through mentoring (and being mentored), networking, intuition, and by providing leadership. Power is a tool used to obtain a desired outcome and those scholars of color need to identify that outcome. Women of color see the world through a different lens concurrently, and, as a result, respond to situations on both the thinking and the feeling levels. African American women must discern where their power lies within the university and meld it to the self-efficacy within themselves. Women of color must be able to answer the question: What is it that we, as female scholars of color, want to achieve as our legacy though our research at the university and leading in our schools?

2. Maintain your authenticity and identity. It is easy for the "outsider" to become something that she perceives the university and the school district administrators want her to be. But, staunchly maintaining who we are at our core is critical for continued professional development and success and for those students of color who look to you, (sometimes unknowingly) for clarity of purpose and modeling. We must teach our women of color to never relinquish their ethnicity, history, or place in the world because living it and being proud of who you are may make others who are unlike you uncomfortable.

3. It is our duty as university professors to raise the level of African American female consciousness of those colleagues and other members around us who refuse to admit our presence or value the growth of scholarly endeavors within their institutions. Unknowingly, the elation of acceptance into the hallowed halls of doctoral programs and leadership tracts, the silent erosion of our "personal self", is subsumed in order to maintain our likeability factor. Doing so becomes a tragic mistake.

4. Encourage African American female students to write about those issues in leadership that are a part of their communities and underrepresented families, ensuring that their voices are heard. Knowledge production through oral communication remains a powerful and clearly alternate means of liberatory inclusiveness. The use of portraiture as done by Sarah Lawrence Lightfoot (1994) is one way of sharing intuitive and connective stories of successful lives of African Americans.

CRT—THE THEORETICAL POSSIBILITIES
FOR A POSTMODERN ERA

For members of marginalized groups, CRT offers the opportunity to share life experiences while openly acknowledging that perceptions of truth, fairness, and justice reflect the mindset, status, and experience of the knower (Delgado, 1995b). Edward Said (1994, p. 135) has called these kinds of writings "antithetical knowledge," or the counter-accounts of social reality by subversion, subaltern elements of the reigning order. CRT suggests that one powerful way of dispelling and challenging the mythic norm of society is by telling stories. Additionally, new ways of mentoring minorities that use their own schema to advance their careers will be included.

As our culture becomes more and more global, diverse, and complex, images of what a leader "looks like" and expectations of leaders are quickly adjusting to what the new world order needs in a leader (Lynham & Chermak, 2006). Technology has transformed the landscape of schools and schooling; so much so, that women are leaping into leadership positions more rapidly within the last ten years than in the previous fifty years of public education. This does not mean that barriers have been removed; it means that barriers to women's access to leadership positions have been reduced. Technological transparencies to leadership opportunities allow women to access more and different levels within educational administration. More important is the numbers of AAW who attempt and succeed in educational administration, defying the odds, and annihilating out-dated and archaic ways of thinking about all women and leadership positions.

Universities are the think-tanks of America, and it is from these places that we should unmask the phantom that provides research which is counterintuitive and destructive to the survival of African Americans as a people. Reading what is being written in our areas of interest requires that we build on it, or challenge it openly and publicly if it does not ring true to our lived experiences.

NOTE

Negro was not considered a pejorative term during the days of Jim Crow laws. It was the legal reference given to all Americans of African descent to separate them from other people of color. Negroes were primarily those who held ancestry from Africa and who were subject to the laws of segregation. Attribution to this class of people was noted particularly by skin color.

REFERENCES

Aburdene, P., & Naisbitt, J. (1992). *Megatrends for women.* New York: Villard.

Austin, R. (1995). The intersection of race and gender. Sapphire bound. In K. Crenshaw, N. Gotanda, G. Peller & K. Thomas (Eds.), *Critical race theory: The key writings that formed the movement* (pp. 426–437). New York: The New York Press.

Banks, T. (1995). The search for an oppositional voice. Two life stories: Reflections of one African American woman law professor. In K. Crenshaw, N. Gotanda, G. Peller, & K. Thomas (Eds.), *Critical race theory: The key writings that formed the movement* (pp. 329–336). New York: The New York Press.

Bass (1985). *Leadership and performance beyond expectation.* New York: Free Press.

Bell, D. (1997). White superiority in America: Its legal legacy, its economic costs. In R. Delgado & J. Stefancic (Eds.), *Critical white studies: Looking behind the mirror* (pp. 596–600). Philadelphia, PA: Temple University Press.

Bell, E. L., & Nkomo, S. (2001). *Our separate ways: Black and White women and the struggle for professional identity.* Boston, MA: Harvard Business School Press.

Bloom, C., & Erlandson, D. (2003). African American women principals in urban schools: (Re)alities, (re) constructions, and (re)solutions. *Educational Administration Quarterly, 39*(3) 339–369.

Brookfield, S. (1992). Developing criteria for formal theory building in adult education. *Adult Education Quarterly, 42*(2), 79–93.

Burns (1978). *Leadership.* New York: Harper & Row.

Butler, C. (2011) *Postmodernism.* New York: Sterling.

Byrd, M. (2008). *To enter and lead: Re-negotiating meanings of leadership and examining leadership theory of social power from the perspectives of African American women leaders in predominantly White organizations.* Unpublished doctoral dissertation, Texas A & M University, College

Calmore, J.O. (1995). The search for an oppositional voice. Critical race theory, Archie Shepp, and fire music: Securing an authentic intellectual life in a multicultural world. In K. Crenshaw, N. Gotanda, G. Peller & K. Thomas (Eds.), *Critical race theory: The key writings that formed the movement* (pp. 315–329). New York: The New York Press.

Capper, C. (1992). A feminist poststructural analysis of non-traditional approaches in educational administration. *Educational Administration Quarterly, 28,* 103–124.

Crenshaw, K.W. (1995). The intersection of race and gender. Mapping the margins: Intersectionality, identity, politics and violence against women of color. In K. Crenshaw, N. Gotanda, G. Peller, & K. Thomas (Eds.), *Critical race theory: The key writings that formed the movement* (pp. 357–383). New York: The New York Press.

Deal, T. E., & Peterson, K. D. (1994). *The principal's role in shaping school culture.* Washington, DC: U. S. Government Printing Office.

Delgado, R. (1995a). *Critical race theory: The cutting edge.* Philadelphia, PA: Temple University Press.

Delgado, R. (1995b). Legal storytelling: Storytelling for oppositionists and others. In R. Delgado (Ed.), *Critical race theory: The cutting edge* (pp. 267–277). Philadelphia: Temple University.

Denzin, N., & Lincoln, Y. (1994). *Handbook of naturalistic inquiry.* Thousand Oaks, CA: Sage.

Devault, M. (1993). Different voices: Feminists' methods of social research. *Qualitative Sociology, 16*, 77–83.

DiStephano, C. (1990). Dilemmas of difference: Feminism, modernity, and postmodernism. In L. Nicholson (Ed.), *Feminism/postmodernism* (pp. 63–82). New York: Routledge.

Dixson, A. D., & Rousseau, C. K. (2006). *Critical race theory in education: All God's children got a song.* New York: Routledge.

Eagly, A. H. (2007). Female leadership advantage and disadvantage: Resolving the contradictions. *Psychology of Women Quarterly, 31*, 1–12 doi:10.1111/j.1471-6402.2007.00326.x

Eagly, A. H., Johannesen-Schmidt, M. C., & Van Engen, M. L. (2003). Transformational, transactional, and laissez-faire leadership styles: A meta-analysis comparing women and men. *Psychological Bulletin, 129*, 569–591.

Erlandson, D., Harris, E., Skipper, B., & Allen, S. (1993). *Doing naturalistic inquiry: A guide to methods.* Newbury Park, CA: Sage.

Etter-Lewis, G. (1993). *My soul is my own: African American women in the professions.* New York: Routledge.

Fee, E. (1983). Women and health care: A comparison of theories. In E. Fee (Ed.). *Women and health: the politics of sex in medicine* (pp.17–34). Englewood Cliffs, NJ: Baywood.

Fendler, L. (2011). *Michel Foucault.* London: Continuum International Publishing Group, Ltd.

Foschi, M. (2000). Double standards for competence: Theory and research. *Annual Review of Sociology, 26*, 21–42.

Gay, G. (2000). Culturally responsive teaching: Theory, research, and practice. *Multicultural Education Series.* New York: Teachers College Press.

Gioia, D. A., & Pitre, E. (1990). Multi-paradigm perspectives in theory building. *Academy of Management Review, 15*(4), 584–602.

Gitlin, A. (Ed.). (1994). *Power and method: Political activism and educational research.* New York: Routledge.

Gostnell, G. M. (1996). *The leadership of African American women: Constructing realities, shifting paradigms.* ProQuest Dissertations. UMI No. 9701103.

Gupton, S.L., & Slick, G.A. (1996). *Highly successful women administrators: The inside stories of how they got there.* Thousand Oaks, CA: Corwin Press.

Higginbotham, E., & Cannon, L. (1992*). Rethinking mobility: Towards a race and gender inclusive theory* (Research Paper no. 8). Memphis, TN: Center for Research on Women, Memphis State University.

Hill-Collins, P. (1991). *Black feminist thought: Knowledge, consciousness, and the politics of empowerment.* New York: Routledge.

Hine, D., & Thompson, K. (1998). *A shining thread of hope: The history of Black women in America.* New York: Broadway Books.

hooks, b. (1989). *Talking back; thinking feminist; thinking African American.* Boston, MA: South End Press.

hooks, b. (1994). *Teaching to transgress.* New York: Routledge.

Hoy, W., & Miskel, C. (2008). *Educational administration: Theory, research, and practice* (8th ed). New York: McGraw-Hill.

Hunt, J. G. (1999). Transformational/charismatic leadership's transformation of the field: An historical essay. *Leadership Quarterly, 10*(2),129-144.

Irby, B., & Brown, G. (1999, February). *Exemplary practices in women's leadership development and gender equity.* Paper presented at the meeting of the American Association of Colleges for Teacher Education, Washington, DC.

Irby, B., & Brown, G. (1995b, April). *Constructing a feminist inclusive theory of leadership.* Paper presented at the Annual Meeting of the American Educational Research Association, San Francisco, CA.

Irby, B. J., Brown, G., Duffy, J., & Trautman, D. (2002). The synergistic leadership theory. *Journal of Educational Administration, 40*(4), 304–322.

Ladson-Billings, G. (1998). Just what is critical race theory and what is it doing in a nice field like education? *Qualitative Studies in Education, 2*(1), 7–23.

Lather, P. (1991). *Getting smart: Feminist research and pedagogy within the postmodern.* New York: Routledge.

Lawrence III, C. R. (1995). The word and the river: Pedagogy as scholarship as struggle. In K. Crenshaw, N. Gotanda, G. Peller, & K. Thomas (Eds.), *Critical race theory: The key writings that formed the movement* (pp. 336–351). New York: The New York Press.

Lightfoot, S. (1994). *I've known rivers: Lives of loss and liberation.* New York: Viking Penguin.

Lorde, A. (1984). *Sister outsider.* Trumansburg, NY: The Crossing Press.

Lorde, A. (1995). Age, race, class, and sex: Women redefining difference. In M. Anderson & P. Hill-Collins (Eds.), *Race, class and gender: An anthology* (pp. 532–540). Belmont, CA: Wadsworth Publishing Company.

Lunenburg, F. C. (2003). The post-behavioral science era: Excellence, community, and justice. In F. C. Lunenburg & Carolyn S. Carr (Eds.), *Shaping the future: Policy, Partnerships, and emerging perspectives* (pp. 31–55). Lanham, MD: Rownam & Littlefield.

Lynham, S. A., & Chermak, T. J. (2006). Responsible leadership for performance: A theoretical model and hypotheses. *Journal of Leadership and Organizational Studies, 12*(4), 73–88.

Mertz, N. & McNeely, S.R. (1998). Women on the job: A study of female high school principals. *Educational Administration Quarterly, 34*(2), 196–222.

Montenegro, X. (1993). *Women and racial minority representation in school administration.* Arlington. VA: American Association of Administration.

Murtadha, K., & Larson, C. (1999, April). *Toward a socially critical, womanist, theory of leadership in urban schools.* Paper presented at the annual meeting of the American Educational Research Association, Montreal, Canada.

Murtadha, K., & Watts D.M. (2005). Linking the struggle for education and social justice: Historical perspectives of African American leadership in schools. *Educational Administration Quarterly, 41*(4), pp. 591–608.

Newport, F. (2001, February 21). *Americans see women as emotional and affectionate, men as more aggressive: Gender specific stereotypes persist in recent Gallup poll.* Retrieved from on August 15, 2011 from http://brain.gallup.com

Olesen, V. (1994). Feminism and models in qualitative research. In Y. S. Lincoln. & N. K. Denzin, *Handbook of qualitative research* (pp. 158–174). Thousand Oaks, CA: Sage.

Peitchinis, S. G. (1989). *Women at work: Discrimination and response.* Toronto, CA: McClelland & Stewart.

Rost, J. C. (1991). *Leadership for the twenty-first century.* New York: Praeger.

Said, E. W. (1994). *Culture and imperialism.* New York: Knopf.

Shakeshaft, C. (1987). *Women in educational administration.* Newbury Park, CA: Sage.

Shakeshaft, C., Brown, G., Irby, B. J., Grogan, M., & Ballenger, J. (2007). Increasing gender equity in educational leadership. In S. Klein (Ed.) *Handbook of gender equity in schools* (pp. 103–129). Mahwah, NJ: Laurence Erlbaum Associates.

Torraco, R. J. (1997). Theory-building research methods. In R. A. Swanson & E. F. Holton III (Eds.*), Human resource development handbook* (pp. 114–137), San Francisco: Berrett-Koehler.

Weedon, C. (1997). *Feminist practice and poststructuralist theory* (2nd ed.). New York: Basil Blackwell.

Williams, J. E., & Best, D. L. (1990). *Measuring sex stereotypes: A multinational study.* Newbury Park, CA: Sage.

Willis, A. (2001). An African American female research journey: Epistemological, conceptual and methodological concerns. In B. M. Merchant & A. I. Willis (Eds.), *Multiple and intersecting identities in qualitative research* (pp. 43–59). Mahwah, NJ: Erlbaum.

Yeakley, C C., Johnston, G. S., & Adkison, J. A. (1986). In pursuit of equity: A review of research on minorities and women in educational administration. *Educational Administration Quarterly, 22*(3), 110–149.

Yoder, J. D., Schleicher, T. L., & McDonald, T. W. (1998). Empowering token women leaders: The importance of organizationally legitimated credibility. *Psychology of Women Quarterly, 22,* 209–222.

Young, M.D., & Laible, J. (1999, April). *Developing anti-racist school leaders.* Paper presented at the annual meeting of the American Educational Research Association, Montreal, Canada.

Yukl, G. A. (2002). *Leadership in organizations.* (5th ed.). Upper "Saddle River, NJ: Prentice Hall.

CHAPTER 8

RE(THINKING) RACE

Positioning Multiracial Representations within Critical Pedagogy

Claire Peinado Fraczek
University of Washington

... critical pedagogy is not simply concerned with offering students new ways to think critically and act with authority as agents in the classroom; it is also concerned with providing students with the skills and knowledge necessary for them to expand their capacities both to question deep-seated assumptions and myths that legitimate the most archaic and disempowering social practices that structure every aspect of society and to take responsibility for intervening in the world they inhabit

—Giroux, 2007, p. 2

Given the historical legacy of de jure and contemporary de facto segregation in the U.S., scholars have taken up the call toward more democratic education through analyses in which race and racism become focused lenses for studying oppression (Bell, 1992; Solórzano & Yosso, 2002; Ladson-Billings & Tate, 1995). Two significant bodies of literature have simultaneously developed as methods for studying (and combating) race and racism. This chapter centralizes Critical Race Theory (CRT) and Critical Whiteness Studies (CWS) as two complementary yet distinctive bodies of

Confronting Racism in Higher Education, pages 161–180
Copyright © 2013 by Information Age Publishing

literature that have emerged to address racialized systems of oppression. I centralize these two bodies as the consideration of both provides important implications for how racial pedagogy is taught and articulated in ways that inform social justice leadership. Building on the work of some of the key foundational texts of CRT and CWS scholars (Ladson-Billings & Tate, 1995; Crenshaw, 1995; Solórzano, 1998; Gillborn, 2005; Leonardo, 2009; Wise, 2005; Thompson, 2003), my intention is to provide critique as a form of further engagement, as I claim that neither literature base has effectively problematized the monolithic categories of race that it seeks to represent. Because the foundational texts are often initial sites of entry for students learning about critical theory and racialized topics, I will show that this essentializing phenomenon is not surprising as it is symptomatic of the larger racial system of White supremacy; yet, without deeper critiques of monolithic narratives, a racist system persists and thrives.

While CRT and CWS offer important interventions for theorizing race and racism, both, in different ways, fail to interrogate the monoracial foundations of their own theories. In this chapter I will demonstrate the ways in which monoracial foundations are imbedded in these two approaches and argue that, through a mixed-race analytic, theorists working in the field of CRT and CWS will be better able to trace out and analyze the dynamic interplay of race and racial categorizations as a tool for addressing racism. This chapter offers insights for educational leaders who seek to sharpen their engagement with racialized subjects in ways that account for the contemporary platform on which race and racism operate. In particular, as we enter an era in which multiracial representations of people are increasingly claimed and recognized via discourse, media, and policies, this chapter offers an analytical framework to amplify and extend CRT and CWS literature and pedagogy in ways that acknowledge and respond to multiracial representations. I will compare and contrast the tenets, merits, and strategies of each theoretical framework while considering the strengths and limitations of each for higher education contexts. Through these exercises, I develop an argument for the productive possibilities of engaging and utilizing a mixed analytic in racial pedagogy, and conclude with a discussion of implications for higher education leadership more broadly.

THE ROOTS OF CRITICAL RACE THEORIES

Beginning in the 1970s, various cultural and feminist theorists such as Omi, Winant, and the Combahee River Collective provided groundbreaking, collaborative work to help clarify the meaning and deployment of race and racism in social contexts (Combahee River Collective, 1994; Omi & Winant, 1994). While not necessarily housed within CRT or CWS frameworks per se, these scholars have both contributed to and enhanced the work of anti-oppressive theories, and deserve mention as examples of powerful backdrops on which these theoretical methods operate. For instance, Omi and Winant suggest that, "we should think of race as an element of social structure rather than as an irregularity within it; we should see race as a dimension of human representation rather than an illusion" (1994, p. 55). In short, they assert that race is socially constructed (as opposed to biological), yet they also maintain that this socially structured reality manifests itself via material and behavioral interactions, and thus cannot be conceptualized or treated as mere illusion. In addition, the work of Black feminists such as the Combahee River Collective takes a holistic view of multiple oppressive structures as interlocking, yet they use their positions as Black feminists (i.e., racialized women) to begin unpacking these interlocking oppressions. In, "A Black Feminist Statement" they write:

> We are actively committed to struggling against racial, sexual, heterosexual, and class oppression and see as our particular task the development of integrated analysis and practice based upon the fact that major systems of oppression are interlocking. The synthesis of these oppressions creates the conditions of our lives. As Black women we see Black feminism as the logical political movement to combat the manifold and simultaneous oppressions that all women of color face" (1994, p. 177).

I highlight these particular examples from cultural and feminist studies because the interdisciplinary nature of CRT and CWS are informed by such work, and contain elements of the very strategies that CRT and CWS employ.

EARLY CONCEPTIONS OF CRITICAL RACE THEORY

Beginning in the late 1970s, Derrick Bell, Richard Delgado, Mari Matsuda, and Kimberlé Crenshaw, among other legal scholars, began critiquing the philosophy and application of neo-liberal individualism that was reflected so strongly in legal discourse. By centralizing race in their critiques, an early movement formed within the Critical Legal Studies (CLS) community, led by scholars of color, to question notions of objectivity and judicial incrementalism in American law (Crenshaw, 2002). Crenshaw summarizes the early iterations of CRT by noting, "we described this engagement as constituting a distinctively progressive intervention within liberal race theory and a race intervention within CLS" (p. 1343). Importantly, CRT's legal roots were born out of a need for racial realism in the law. Through explicit attendance to racial categories, critical legal scholars accounted for the ways in which various racialized populations were disproportionately impacted by judicial decisions, and exposed how the law served to maintain a system of White supremacy despite liberal discourse to the contrary. In the ensuing decade, additional scholars began to flesh out a stronger articulation of these ideas, including the endemic nature and centrality of racism, and the role of property within this system (Bell, 1992; Harris, 1993; Dixson & Rousseau, 2005). With Harris' (1993) publication of *Whiteness as Property*, she traced how power and privilege (such as the right to and deployment of property) continued to be reified along racial lines of Whiteness, and that the law served to uphold and maintain such a system.

EXTENSIONS OF CRT INTO EDUCATION

Over time, CRT gained traction not just within Critical Legal Studies, but also across a variety of disciplines, including education. Ladson-Billings and Tate (1995) first introduced CRT into educational discourse as a way to problematize the "multicultural paradigm" that often failed to critique the structural deficiencies of the educational system. As multicultural education scholars, they acknowledged and contributed to progressive strides within the field, with a particular emphasis on the importance of culturally relevant pedagogy (Ladson-Billings, 1992). Yet, these authors also criticized multicultural and diversity movements within education as rooted in similar strategies as civil rights reform, which, due to philosophies of liberal individualism and incrementalism, had unfortunately not changed the basic structures of racism and inequality (Ladson-Billings & Tate, 1995). For instance, they argued:

> Less often discussed are the growing tensions that exist between and among various groups that gather under the umbrella of multiculturalism—that is, the interests of groups can be competing or their perspectives can be at odds. We assert that the ever-expanding multicultural paradigm follows the traditions of liberalism—allowing a proliferation of difference. Unfortunately, the tensions between and among these differences is rarely interrogated, presuming a 'unity of difference'—that is, that all difference is both analogous and equivalent (Ladson-Billings & Tate, 1995, pp. 61–62).

Their primary concern was that pedagogy within multicultural education needed to not just recognize differences, but to recognize how and why these differences mattered in education, pedagogy, resource distribution, and policies. Instead of aligning within the multiculturalist framework, they introduced three CRT propositions for understanding social (and school) inequities more thoroughly:

1. Race continues to be a significant factor in determining inequity in the United States.

2. U.S. society is based on property rights.
3. The intersection of race and property create an analytic tool through which we can understand the social (and consequently, school) inequity (Ladson-Billings & Tate, 1995, p. 48).

In their discussion on property, Ladson-Billings and Tate (1995) assert that property is not only shrouded within individualist notions of democracy (and in this country, capitalism), but that property rights, access, and benefits extend to factors such as curriculum, or "intellectual property" (p. 54). The primary CRT argument is that such access to various properties are disproportionately limited for people of color, primarily because of the endemic nature of racism and White hegemony.

Since Ladson-Billings and Tate's (1995) introduction of CRT into education, a number of scholars have used CRT analyses in educational research, policy and pedagogy. As CRT continued to evolve in the last decade, Yosso, Parker, Solórzano, and Lynn (2004) developed a further articulation of CRT's tenets within education. They claim that CRT analyses within education contain the following:

1. Intercentricity of race and racism with other forms of subordination.
2. Challenge to dominant ideology.
3. Commitment to social justice.
4. Centrality of experiential knowledge.
5. Transdisciplinary perspective (pp. 3–4).

The authors point out that "these five themes are not new, but collectively they challenge the existing modes of scholarship in education" (Yosso, et. Al., 2004, p. 4). In particular, CRT scholars challenge claims of neutrality, objectivity, meritocracy, and colorblindness, and insist on the privileging of marginalized voices of color through narratives and experiential knowledge (Delgado, 1989; Ladson-Billings & Tate, 1995; Dixson & Rouseau, 2005, Solórzano, 1998; Harper, Patton & Wooden, 2009). CRT also "challenges ahistoricism and insists on a contextual/historical analysis of the law" (Dixson & Rousseau, 2005).

In the context of higher education, CRT has captured the most attention through analyses and critiques of affirmative action policies (Yosso et al., 2004; Taylor, 2000). For instance, Yosso et al., (2004) claim that there are three central arguments operating within affirmative action discourse. The first is a colorblind rhetoric that de-historicizes racist legacies and assumes an equal playing field for all participants. Therefore, the argument goes, affirmative action policies should be abolished as they unfairly provide benefits to "less qualified" people of color. The more liberal arguments in favor of affirmative action include:

1. diversity arguments such as, the admission of underrepresented minority students enhances campus diversity, and
2. remediation arguments, which consider past and current discriminatory practices as a rationale for remedy, such as, university admission (Yosso et al., 2004).

In the context of affirmative action court cases and legislation such as *Bakke v. Regents of the University of California, Grutter v. Bollinger*, and Washington State's Initiative 200, various scholars point out that a remediation argument has not garnered majority support to date (Taylor, 2000; Yosso et al., 2004). Instead, the two dominant paradigms of colorblindness or diversity gain the most traction in legal decisions, and each of these primarily uphold a system of Whiteness as property, with subsequent benefits to White students. While "diversity" arguments may appear to correct past discrimination in university admission, this rationale, in fact, operates through "interest convergence," in which minority populations only benefit *in tandem* with White populations (Taylor, 2000; Bell, 1992). In other words, legislation will only incrementally change to benefit non-White populations if Whites also gain something, and a system of Whiteness is maintained (in this case, access to diverse learning environments in which to better "socialize" White graduates for diverse workforce environments). CRT analyses such as these are useful for unpacking and highlighting the structural nature of policies, and the disparate material effects between people of color versus Whites.

INTRODUCTION AND EVOLUTION
OF CRITICAL WHITENESS STUDIES

Just as CRT notes the endemic nature of racism, CWS may be conceptualized as a sub-category within CRT in which to deepen an analysis on institutional and systemic racism. Yancy (2004) describes Whiteness as "a multitude of individual, collective, intentional, unintentional, isolated, systemic actions that synergistically work to sustain and constantly regenerate relationships of unequal power between Whites and non-Whites" (pp. 14–15). Whereas CRT and CWS are related and interconnected—both are interested in exposing the systemic nature of racist practices—CWS has evolved in a slightly different manner. While non-White scholars such as W.E.B. DuBois, James Baldwin, Toni Morrisson, bell hooks, and Richard Wright, have written from a critical Whiteness orientation for decades, CWS has also more recently engaged White scholars who are interested in naming and confronting the power that benefits them, and thus, is an attempt to confront oppressive systems (Bush, 2004; Roediger, 1998; McIntosh, 2001; Gillborn, 2005; Wise, 2005). CWS emphasizes the role of Whiteness in racial inequality and works to develop antiracist practices. Ruth Frankenberg (1993) is one such White scholar who further articulated the social construction of Whiteness. In *White Women, Race Matters*, she explains some key tenets of CWS:

> Naming "Whiteness" displaces it from the unmarked, unnamed status that is itself an effect of its dominance. Among the effects on White people both of race privilege and of the dominance of Whiteness, are their seeming normativity, their structured invisibility.... To speak of Whiteness is, I think, to assign *everyone* a place in the relations of racism. It is to emphasize that dealing with racism is not merely an option for White people—that, rather, racism shapes White people's lives and identities in a way that is inseparable from other facets of daily life (Frankenberg, 1993, p. 6).

Not only does Frankenberg name the invisibility and normativity of a White identity, she also notes a general lack of awareness of White privilege as a function of Whiteness. Whereas racism has generally been conceptualized and interpreted in mainstream discourse and practice as a personal or individual action (i.e., someone with a racist "identity" or action), theorists from CRT and CWS centralize the systemic nature of racism and place all identities within the system.

EXTENSIONS OF CRITICAL WHITENESS STUDIES INTO EDUCATION

Similar to critical race theorists, critical Whiteness scholars began publishing material with the goal of interrupting traditional methods of multiculturalist training that often de-centered racist systems. Authors such as Clark & O'Donnell (1999) and Lea & Sims (2008) seek to name and identify White identities to encourage deeper reflection and an active positioning of the role of Whiteness in education, particularly for pre-service teachers who are predominantly White women. In the end, this strategy aims to *deconstruct* the oppressive nature of Whiteness. Clark & O'Donnell write:

> ...antiracist White consciousness must be characterized by a willingness to interrupt, actively resist, at the level of thought and practice, enjoyment of White race privilege [Jackson, 1976a; Hardiman, 1979]. Thus, the process of transformation in our racial identity development as White Americans ultimately forces us to embrace ourselves as both racist and antiracist (Clark & O'Donnell, p. 2).

For critical White scholars and activists, antiracist performances must always be measured alongside an acknowledgement of a pre-existing and replicating racist reality that continues to benefit Whiteness.

One significant and ongoing critique of CWS is that the re-centering of Whiteness in pedagogy perpetuates the ongoing marginalization of people of color (Ringrose, 2007). That is, White identities are *always* otherwise centralized in the academy, and critical pedagogy is one place that has worked to centralize marginalized voices. An introduction of CWS into critical pedagogy simply repositions Whiteness—in all its power and incarnations—in the classroom (Thompson, 2003). For instance, Thompson notes that some critical Whiteness pedagogy actually serves to ameliorate "White guilt," which in effect, reinforces White privilege. She writes:

> Despite their commitment to decentering and denormalizing Whiteness, White identity theories keep Whiteness at the center of antiracism. Although they call upon Whites to challenge racism and privilege, their central preoccupation is with White identity development: antiracism is organized around White students' personal growth (Thompson, 2003, p. 15).

However, while the concern about Whiteness being re-centered is certainly valid, a number of scholars have responded with the suggestion that critical Whiteness pedagogy be introduced "in conjunction with texts that decenter Whiteness" (Clark & O'Donnell, 1999; DiAngelo, 2004; Sleeter & Bernal, 2004). Or, further, that a presumed "end point" of antiracist White stage-development models be problematized (Thompson, 2003). In addition, CWS invites White students to engage in the dialectic that Freire (1970) names as crucial for uncovering and unlocking systematic oppression. In other words, CWS has a responsibility component for White students and scholars that requires White engagement with racist systems in ways that most other disciplines ignore.

THE TRAP OF BINARY DISCOURSE

One of the greatest strengths of both CRT and CWS lies in the ability to counter "colorblind" and "post-racial" narratives in mainstream discourse through an attendance to empirical data that illuminates racialized disparities. Because these pedagogical methods centralize race and racism—through racialized White and non-White narratives and attention to historicization—individuals are more equipped to understand their role(s) within oppressive institutional and systemic structures. Unfortunately however, each method operates within the monoracial frameworks that this country upholds. As far as pedagogical practice in which narratives and dialogues are employed, most strategies draw upon monoracial White and non-White narratives to illustrate various positions and experiences within racist structures (Derman-Sparks & Phillips, 1997; Clark & O'Donnell, 1999; Lea & Sims, 2008). For instance, Clark & O'Donnell acknowledge the binary-driven tropes that contextualize a classroom, yet they still draw upon them to teach about racism. In suggesting a classroom activity they write:

> ...an important piece of the classroom discussion of this text might include having White students who have had experiences with the class, comparing and contrasting their narratives with ours. Especially, Students of Color, but generally every student, should also be strongly encouraged to contest all of these narratives, ours and those shared by White classmates, for the continued racist bias they are able to discern in them (Clark & O'Donnell, 1999, p. 8).

While these authors conscientiously invite critique of all narratives, the exercise is still positioned as an either/or dichotomy. Monoracial White students typically encounter guilt, frustration, distancing, disengagement, and despair as they "come to grips" or realize their own complicity in Whiteness. In contrast, non-White students of color often experience frustration, impatience with White people "getting it," and pain as racialized realities become spotlighted in classroom discourse (Derman-Sparks & Phillips, 1997).

So where does this leave mixed race students in the context of classroom conversations about race? These dichotomous exercises can position multiracial students who may claim both White and non-White, or multiple non-White racial representations into binary-driven critiques, thereby forcing a singular racial posture and engagement with class material. In practice, most monoracial people simply *assign* multiracial people to a non-White status, and assume that non-White narratives will suffice for multiracial students. That is, a multiracial student either adopts a non-White identity or "passes" as White. This practice is highly problematic in that it forces students to conceptually fragment their racialized selves into essentialist identity-politics discourses. A requirement to "choose" which fragmented self to name or claim, thereby furthers essentialist narratives of race for all students in the class, as any complexity of a racialized self gets reduced in both representation and individual performance for the classroom community.

THE TRAP OF HISTORY VERSUS EXPERIENCE

Historicizing practices in CRT utilize historical methods of analysis to describe how contemporary circumstances (such as material inequities) may be explained in reference to a longer historical policy record. However, methodological implications of CRT's tenets of historicization and counter-stories should also be pushed. For instance, historicizing practices in CRT generally focus on systemic policy implications, which stand separate from, though relevant to, *personal* narratives and counter-stories (Taylor, 1999; Harper, Patton & Wooden, 2009). In contrast, the counter-stories that are published within CRT tend to emphasize how racism is operationalized in everyday *contemporary* life, without drawing upon historicized narratives that help open up the complexity of racial identity and experiences (Harris' (1993) work on Whiteness as Property is one significant exception). While systemic analyses of historical oppression are necessary, the specificity that comes from textured analyses in personal narratives tend to get lost or bifurcated in CRT praxis. That is, CRT does great work in both historicizing systemic inequalities and invoking personal counter-narratives as a site of knowledge production, yet CRT does not typically invoke both *together*. The ability to pedagogically weave both together is particularly useful for multiracial students who seek to articulate how multiracial experiences are not just an additive process of two singular racialized identities, but distinctive experiences altogether, and representations that push CRT in its move toward praxis.

THE TRAP OF "FIXED" IDENTITY REPRESENTATIONS

An additional limitation of critical Whiteness pedagogy can be the stasis or perceived stasis of "White resistance" among students (Ringrose, 2007). Ringrose argues that the positioning of White students in critical Whiteness pedagogy as "static resisters of change" not only reifies and essentializes Whiteness, it prevents intellectual and psychological growth for both White and non-White learners in a classroom. She critiques the pedagogy and "turns the gaze back" by asking, "how does framing of others' ideological or discursive wrong-headedness secure our own 'White exceptionalism" (Ringrose, 2007, p. 327)? Instead, she calls for a deeper investigation within CWS of, "how racially marginalized students engage with discourses of anti-racism and Whiteness," and to "study...the complex intersubjective dynamics and difficult psychical effects of these engagements across a range of students" (Ringrose, 2007, pp. 332-333). Here, the author doesn't explicitly include multiracial students in this call, yet there is clearly room to investigate multiple racialized representations—including mixed race students—within the field. The absence of explicitly naming multiracial representations as valuable sites of knowledge production is symptomatic of critical pedagogy's lack of engagement with a growing mixed race student population.

Similar to Ringrose's analysis above, critical race pedagogy continues to rely on a reconstruction of a strict theoretical binary regarding who counts as White or non-White. For instance, Leonardo (2009), a critical Whiteness scholar argues:

> Moreover, a "critical race pedagogy" [Lynn, 1999] cannot be guided by a White perspective, which is not to say that it cannot include White experienc-

es as points of departure. Although experiences do not speak for themselves, interpretation always begins with their lived dimensions (p. 186).

In each of the above examples, Ringrose and Leonardo hint at potential complexities among White and non-White racialized representations, yet they still reinscribe the Black/White binary to make their respective points. Such practices tend to reduce positionality discourses into "fixed" identity categories rather than fluid representations of race as sites of agency.

In Leonardo's (2009) analysis, he draws on the critical dimensions from both CRT and CWS regarding the meaning and salience of experiential knowledge. Whereas both CRT and CWS emphasize an opening up of previously silenced experiences, CRT focuses on silencing that occurs from oppressed racial positions, while CWS names silence from the racialized position(s) of oppressor. However, following these authors' logic, what then is the "lived dimension" of a multiracial person who might claim White and non-White experiences, or can "pass" as White? Should one be satisfied with the traditional heuristics of White and non-White racial assignments based on phenotype? What lessons regarding the social construction of race get lost when one relies on these heuristics?

For example, Thompson (2003), a CWS scholar, offers a consistent analysis with both Ringrose (2007) and Leonardo (2009), and further implicates the dangerous traps of White, antiracist "good intentions" for students who are learning about race. She writes:

> Other White students may invoke narratives that attempt to invalidate charges of racism by proving that the speaker has always been connected to people of color and has had any number of near-color experiences—perhaps a former African-American boyfriend, a Korean-American school friend in first grade, or a memorable teaching experience involving foreigners. In such narratives, the White student may not seek entirely to escape responsibility; she may recognize, for example, that her near-color experiences have not stopped her from enjoying White privilege. Her concern is less to avoid blame than to demonstrate friendship and solidarity with people of color—to show that she *gets* racism in ways that other Whites do not (pp. 9–10).

In Thompson's example, what should one make of multiracial students who might "pass" (either intentionally or not) as White? What counts as a "colored" experience and who gets to decide? Thompson's static framing of Whiteness in this example erases the (social) construction of Whiteness itself. Here, Thompson's analysis risks positioning melanin and the operation of racism through visible forms "of color" as a singular mechanism by which to measure White versus colored experiences. This measurement—ironically a function of White supremacy itself—erases the historical genealogies of multiracial "passers" who still often experience the negative material and psychological consequences of a racialized state, in ways that monoracially identified White students would/do not. Particularly in higher education when racialized representations can become more salient for students, educators should exercise caution in how they invite and position students in conversations about race. Drawing on the *multiple* dimensions of lived experience through race—including material (economic), historical, and contemporary dimensions—provides more complex opportunities to recognize students' whole, racialized selves, particularly for those who bring multiple racialized experiences to the conversation.

Multiracial "passers" live in a context with different, and more nuanced material consequences for Whiteness and Blackness than those who could pass prior to civil rights legislation, for instance. Precisely because of postracial rhetoric, many multiracial students feel increasingly pulled to claim their multiple racial and ethnic histories. For some, these claims serve as a reminder of the danger and flexibility of racialized constructions. That is, claiming a mixed identity is a political act—with opportunities to dismantle or problematize social constructions of race. On the other hand, the political act of claiming mixed-ness can also distance one from people of color, particularly if mixed race categories materialize via identity politics in which resources are redistributed from one disenfranchised population to another—without disrupting larger hegemonic conditions of White supremacy.

Another limitation within CRT and CWS movements is the relative dearth of multiracial role models from which to draw support. Both CRT and CWS include monoracial role models (both White and non-White) as sources of support and scholarly mentorship during students' critical engagement and reflection. For instance, in developing an antiracist position, Thompson (1999), a White scholar, writes:

> I also realized I needed antiracist White people in my daily life with whom I could share stories, talk about complex "racialized" interactions (in the classroom, for example), and brainstorm about strategies. Most importantly, I needed White friends whom I could trust to give me honest feedback (p. 68).

Similarly, in a culture of heightened racial identity consciousness and deployment, non-White critical race scholars have galvanized (although under recognizably different and oppressive circumstances) to create safe(r) spaces in which to discuss oppressive systems. However, mixed race scholars who produce and teach CRT and CWS usually position themselves along the racial binary axis. Whereas scholars such as Renn (2004) have suggested that multiracial educators "out themselves" in ways that provide mentorship to multiracial students, there are still few scholars within academia who do so. And while one should avoid essentializing multiracial students and scholars as another tacked-on identity group, the critical dimensions of CRT and CWS scholarship could be enhanced by recognizing and including multiracial voices—and importantly, not just the voices from students who are already positioned less powerfully than faculty within the academy.

THEORIZING A MIXED ANALYTIC

An unanswered question regarding CRT and antiracist literature concerns the nature of interlocking oppressions that were highlighted near the beginning of this essay with the Combahee River Collective. Both CRT and CWS have been influenced and enhanced by feminist scholars and methodology, which employ a textured framework for understanding, evaluating and combating oppression. Typically, race, class, and gender are among the many lenses through which scholars produce deeper, more holistic analyses from which to deconstruct oppressive conditions (Crenshaw, 1995; Sandoval, 2003; Crenshaw, 1995). In this way, one can gain clarity on how privilege and oppression interact in complicated webs of experience. However, in both CRT and CWS, these various oppressions operate along different, and usually intersecting axes. One might conceptualize this strategy as a two-dimensional snapshot in which various vectors of race, class, gender, et cetera intersect, and the intersection point(s) are supposed to "explain" a particular lived experience. Yet, because a multiracial identity is along the *same* axis, racial theory and pedagogy demand a more textured analysis and strategy.

Overwhelmingly, CRT and CWS centralize singular racial positions as locations from which to analyze *other* axes of privilege and oppression. Too often, however, theory and praxis falsely assume that one can "know" race at any given moment, including what constitutes Blackness, Whiteness, Brown-ness, or Asian-ness, and that this understanding then accurately informs how one's (singular) race interacts with other representations. The model itself gets challenged when a person invokes multiple and simultaneous racial representations: which racial representation should a multiracial Irish and Japanese student reference to understand her gendered and class positions, for instance? Is she "classed" as Irish and "gendered" as Japanese? Often, critical theoretical racial models push students to represent themselves in such problematic ways. In what ways would a homosexual orientation inform how she performs Irish, Japanese, White, Asian, or other representations of herself? How might these performances change if she grew up in Atlanta versus Kyoto? If one conceptualizes race as a set of performances, race pedagogy needs to provide students with opportunities to not just account for their multiple representations, but to problematize those representations as fixed. And further, praxis requires scaffolding to help students think through key moments for invoking particular performances and integrating feedback regarding how such performances are "read" and for whom they serve. By mapping multiracial representations onto the above model, conceptualizations of race as static and "fixed" break down, demanding a deeper understanding of the fluidity (and social construction) of race and other categories.

A mixed race analytic becomes particularly valuable in demonstrating a necessary interpretation of race as fluid and "alive" at any given moment, prompting deeper reflection on the performative nature and opportunities that exist for justice-centered praxis. As race pedagogy in CRT and CWS seeks to increase critical consciousness of one's own position(s) and sites of privilege and oppression, multiracial representations require a complex assessment of intersections as active, shifting, and bound up with the environments (which are also active and shifting) in which one operates. Indeed, a mixed analytic provides rich opportunities to theorize race by accounting for simultaneous conflicts, sites of agency, harmony and synchronicity rather than oppositional or separate posturing of distinct, separate and fixed racial identities.

IMPLICATIONS: RESPONSE AND RESISTANCE

Given the latest iteration of colorblind ideology in mainstream discourse—that we have entered a postracial society—CRT and CWS provide excellent foundations on which to counteract such claims. A great deal of this postracial rhetoric comes from both neo-conservative and neo-liberal discourses that either maintain colorblindness, or promote self-congratulatory ideology that because of President Obama's election, U.S. society can collectively move beyond race (Joseph, 2009; Wise, 2009). However, Obama's situational identity assignment as sometimes "just Black" versus sometimes "biracial" deserves much deeper scrutiny. Activist scholars, students, and leaders should be particularly aware of the times and contexts in which Obama's racial assignment changes, and for whom his multiracial identity serves. For instance, Obama is sometimes touted as the "multiracial savior" that can bridge racial divides, and with whom many different kinds of people can identify. And yet, simultaneously, Obama's racial "flexibility" in his multiracial Blackness also results in a media-induced dissonance and anxiety regarding who he *really* represents. That is, despite his multiracial appeal, there is also a public uneasiness about where his racial loyalties lie.

CRT and CWS provide opportunities to analyze how power and privilege are deployed, subverted, and repositioned for various constituencies in the context of Obama's racial assignment(s). While Obama is held up as a role model for monoracial students of color as well as multiracial students, educators can still provide analytical guidance for understanding how his multiracial history provides new, largely unheard, mixed race narratives.

And further, a mixed race analytic offers cues to consider how and why Obama's history and politics are overwhelmingly read through racialized narratives (in contrast to the primary historical narratives of his 43 White, male, presidential predecessors). Such attentiveness can certainly be extended into classroom and higher education contexts in which participants take a more holistic inventory of their various racialized representations operating within discourse and performance.

For instance, Leonardo (2009) reminds us that, "Whiteness is the attempt to homogenize diverse White ethnics into a single category (much like it attempts with people of color) for the purpose of racial domination" (p. 171). Indeed, cultural, historical, and anthropological scholars warn that mixed race polities have a danger of being "taken up" into Whiteness rather than actively pushing against it, naming its contours, and aligning with antiracist practices (Brodkin, 1998; Bonilla-Silva & Embrick, 2006; Jacobson, 1998; Davis, 1991). With thoughtful CRT and CWS praxis however, a mixed analytic can offer practical opportunities to burst open the homogenizing process—deciphering and tracing ethnic histories—as a strategy to dismantle White racial domination. It is an opening up of ethnic categories and conversations, but also an account of the present day experiences of living in liminal in-between spaces. By recognizing mixed representations, practitioners cannot rest only or wholly on ethnic historical narratives or binary-driven, "static" social constructions of race.

Movement toward mixed race pedagogy is valuable precisely because race and ethnicity discourses are so often conflated within education. Reviewing the ways in which ethnic Hispanics (who are not a race according to current U.S. census categories) get racialized through immigration, housing, and language policies for instance, can illuminate the problematic conflations of race and ethnicity. Further examples of this conflation highlight how African immigrant students with varied ethnic histories are assigned to the same racialized "Black" category as African American students in U.S. education policies. To neglect such conflations leaves individual students (rather than policymakers) responsible for explaining or talking back to systemic injustices as evidenced through policies such as admission, recruitment, and support in higher education institutions. When we have these kinds of conflations in discourse and policy, White racial supremacy is not interrogated, and the nuances of ethnic discourses get swallowed up into racialized categorizations, thereby undermining the complex strengths, opportunities, and approach of utilizing ethnic discourse as a teaching praxis in the first place.

Though racial categorizations offer meaningful utility to understand how White racial supremacy operates, an over-reliance on monolithic racial categories *alone* to interpret and explain racism is insufficient. Returning to the "Black Feminist Statement" from the Combahee River Collective

(1994), both CRT and CWS scholars have drawn lessons from these theoretical pioneers—namely, that race and racism cannot be decoupled from other forms of oppression. However, despite theoretical advances in CRT and CWS that account for the insidious and often unmarked operation of White racial supremacy, the vast majority of scholarship in these fields still rests on taken-for-granted assumptions of what race and racial categories are, and should be (as singular and monolithic). If a Black Feminist Statement were re-written today—over 30 years since the initial Combahee River Collective—would it reflect and account for more complex interpretations and understandings of race categories? Would it acknowledge the nuances and fluidity of Blackness, Whiteness, Asian-ness, and Brown-ness *alongside* interlocking oppressions of class, gender, and sexuality? Would the definition and interpretation of what a Black feminist *is* look any differently? Unfortunately, scholarship within both CRT and CWS have too often relied on *presumed* racial identity politics (and categories) as tools for analysis. Though identity politics offer valuable and necessary opportunities for solidarity political action, race scholars and educational leaders must be attentive to those voices that are marginalized by the politics themselves, and seek to dismantle pedagogy that replicates exclusionary definitions of race categories (and by extension, "who counts" in a particular category). Pedagogy that emphasizes the multiple and varied ways of representing, experiencing, and "performing" race can provide a powerful location from which to push and extend CRT and CWS foundations.

ANTICIPATING AND CONFRONTING COMPLEXITY

Throughout this chapter, I have highlighted the challenges and utility of a mixed analytic for racial pedagogy. My final discussion considers some of the challenges that can occur when moving theory to praxis. I see this exercise as both cautionary and visionary, as leadership praxes in the classroom and beyond require vigilance in understanding and responding to inevitable challenges that materialize along the way.

Perhaps the greatest challenges for engagement stem from the normative representations of power that manifest in blinding ways to those who most strongly benefit from their privilege (Frankenberg, 1993). Whiteness, patriarchy, heteronormativity, and ability are arguably hardest to "see" for Whites, men, heterosexual, and able-bodied groups, respectively. Therefore, a significant and ongoing challenge to critical pedagogy and praxis includes the engagement and interruption of hegemonic practices and conditions. CRT and CWS analyses provide clear reminders that hegemonic conditions and practices will continue to replicate and operate even within the very sites (organizations) that seek to dismantle their vigor.

Invoking mechanisms for critical analyses therefore, revolves significantly around reflexivity, or self-reflection. I will next turn to a deeper articulation of what I mean by reflexivity, emphasizing some limitations embedded in this language, and cautions related to implementation. First, the notion of reflection overwhelmingly relies on an individualized concept of self. While I suggest the engagement of self-reflective practices for critical pedagogy and organizational leadership, I also want to problematize the individualized assumptions behind reflective practice. For instance, in suggesting that participants engage in self-reflection as part of a mixed analytic, I am concerned with the assumption that one "knows" what self-reflection looks like, or how to independently invoke such practices. Not only does this problematically presume a particular skill set of how to "be" reflective, it falsely serves as a precondition for healthy participation in praxis. Such limitations exist not only for students, but also extend to administrator performances in additional higher education settings beyond the classroom. However, in privileging the role of experiential knowledge production (presuming that one can simply "showcase" what one already "knows"), practitioners should also consider the *productive possibilities* of collaborative structures and shared responsibilities for teaching and learning through *inter*dependent reflection. While participants may intend to be independently reflective about their behaviors and actions, an assessment of such practices cannot be attributed to the individual. Rather, the community in which one sits (that is affected by one's actions) is the more authentic judge of relevant efforts. Self-reflective practices then are political by nature, and thus dependent on a group for both engagement and assessment. By framing reflexivity as a co-constructed process rather than an individualized assessment, leadership and pedagogy are opened up to new possibilities and arrangements (as well as risks) —through collaborative politics, alignment and disagreement, and shared, public assessments of justice-centered efficacy. Through mixed praxes, "self"-reflections are intrinsically transitory and change-worthy, thus inviting opportunities for growth, learning, and transformation for all participants involved.

To conclude, I want to revisit the limitations of language as both a driving concern and pedagogical opportunity. In developing and privileging a mixed analytic, I have discussed the strengths and limitations of using racialized categories for teaching and learning about the oppressive structures of racism. On the one hand, the philosophical underpinnings of CRT explicate the need for racial realism as an analytical category in legal and educational analyses. Monoracial language in CRT draws upon the historical and contemporary dimensions of legalized White supremacy to help assess the disparate impacts of institutional and systemic policies on specific, racialized populations. However, given the multiplicity within these populations and the reality of a growing self-identified multiracial population, the modes for engaging critical pedagogy demand continuous attention and productive responsiveness to the audience it serves. Indeed, the linguistic term "multiracial" can problematically erase some of the significant disparities in conditions between and among varying mixed representations. Precisely because language regarding racial taxonomies and other categories is limited, critical mixed praxes demand a collaborative approach to understanding and analyzing those social conditions that structure collective lives (in ways that are often muted through strictly monoracial language). Not only is the contemporary audience of learners complex, a mixed analytic helps to identify and engage this complexity in ways that deepen an analysis on hegemonic systems and one's relationship to them. While dialogue and language are necessary components to address and understand interdependent relationships, their inherent limitations demand innovative engagement regarding the organizational arrangements in which we teach and learn. Recognizing the conditions of where and how to leverage a mixed analytic within critical pedagogy will serve higher education institutions well as they continue to grapple with twenty-first century dynamics of racism and newly emergent manifestations of oppression.

REFERENCES

Bell, D. (1992). *Faces at the bottom of the well: The permanence of racism.* New York: Basic Books.

Bonilla-Silva, E., & Embrick, D. G. (2006). Black, honorary White, White: The future of race in the United States? In D. Brunsma (Ed.), *Mixed messages: Multiracial identities in the "color-blind" era* (pp. 33–48). Boulder, CO: Lynne Rienner Publishers, Inc.

Brodkin, K. (1998). *How Jews became White folks and what that says about race in America.* New Brunswick, NJ: Rutgers University Press.

Bush, M. (2004). The here and now. In M. E. L. Bush (Ed.), *Breaking the code of good intentions: Everyday forms of Whiteness* (pp. 1–53). Lanham, MD: Rowman & Littlefield Publishers, Inc.

Clark, C., & O'Donnell, J. (1999). Rearticulating a racial identity: Creating oppositional spaces to fight for equality and social justice. In C. Clark & J. O'Donnell (Eds.), *Becoming and unbecoming White: Owning and disowning a racial identity* (pp. 1–9). Westport, CT: Bergin & Garvey.

Combahee River Collective (1994). A Black feminist statement. In M. Schneir (Ed.), *Feminism in our time: The essential writings, WWII to the present* (pp. 175–187). New York: Vintage Books.

Crenshaw, K. (1995). Mapping the margins: Intersectionality, identity politics and violence against women of color. In K. Crenshaw (Ed.), *Critical race theory: The key writings that formed the movement.* New York: New Press.

Crenshaw, K. (2002). The first decade, critical reflections, or "a foot in the closing door". *49, UCLA Law Review,* 1343–1392.

Davis, F. J. (1991). *Who is black? One nation's definition.* University Park: Pennsylvania State University Press.

Delgado, R. (1989). Storytelling for oppositionists and others: A plea for narrative. *Michigan Law Review, 87,* 2411–2441.

Derman-Sparks, L., & Phillips, C. (1997). *Teaching/learning anti-racism: A developmental approach.* New York: Teachers College Press.

DiAngelo, R. (2004). *Whiteness in racial dialogue: A discourse analysis.* (Doctoral dissertation, University of Washington, Seattle).

Dixson, A. D., & Rousseau, C. K. (2005). And we are all still not saved: Critical race theory in education ten years later. *Race, Ethnicity, and Education, 8*(1), 7–27.

Frankenberg, R. (1993). *White women, race matters: The social construction of Whiteness.* Minneapolis: University of Minnesota Press.

Freire, P. (1970). *Pedagogy of the oppressed.* New York: Continuum.

Gillborn, D. (2005). Education policy as an act of White supremacy: Whiteness, critical race theory and educational reform. *Journal of Education Policy, 20*(4), 485–505.

Giroux, H. A. (2007). Introduction: Democracy, education, and the politics of critical pedagogy. In P. McLaren & J. L. Kincheloe (Eds.), *Critical Pedagogy: Where are we now?* (pp. 1–5) New York: Peter Lang Publishing, Inc.

Harper, S., Patton, L., & Wooden, O. (2009). Access and equity for African American students in higher education: A critical race historical analysis of policy efforts. *The Journal of Higher Education, 80*(4), 389–414.

Harris, C. (1993). Whiteness as property. *106, Harvard Law Review,* 1707.

Jacobson, M. F. (1998). *Whiteness of a different color: European immigrants and the alchemy of race.* Cambridge, MA: Harvard University Press.

Joseph, R. L. (2009). "Tyra Banks is fat: Reading (post-)racism and (post-)feminism in the new millennium. *Journal of Critical Studies in Media Communication, 26*(3), 237–254.

Ladson-Billings, G. (1992). Culturally relevant teaching: The key to making multicultural education work. In C.A. Grant (Ed.), *Research & multicultural education: From the margins to the mainstream* (pp. 102–118). Bristol, PA: The Falmer Press.

Ladson-Billings, G., & Tate, W. F. (1995). Toward a critical race theory of education. *Teachers College Record, 97*(1), 47–68.

Lea, V., & Sims, E. J. (2008). Imaging Whiteness hegemony in the classroom: Undoing Oppressive practice and inspiring social justice activism. In V. Lea & E. J. Sims (Eds.), *Undoing Whiteness in the classroom: Critical educultural teaching approaches for social justice activism* (pp. 185–202). New York: Peter Lang Publishing, Inc.

Leonardo, Z. (2009). *Race, Whiteness, and education.* New York: Routledge.

Lynn, M. (1999). Toward a critical race pedagogy: A research note. *Urban Education, 33*(5), 606–626.

McIntosh, P. (2001). White privilege: Unpacking the invisible knapsack. In P. Rothenberg (Ed.), *Race, class, and gender in the United States: An integrated study* (5th ed., pp. 163–168). New York: Worth Publishers.

Omi, M., & Winant, H. (1994). *Racial formation in the United States: From the 1960s to the 1990s* (2nd ed.) New York: Routledge.

Renn, K. A. (2004). *Mixed race students in college: The ecology of race, identity and community on campus.* SUNY: Albany.

Ringrose, J. (2007). Rethinking White resistance: Exploring the discursive practices and psychical negotiations of 'Whiteness' in feminist, anti-racist education. *Race, Ethnicity, and Education 10*(3), 323–344.

Roediger, D. (1998). *Black on White: Black writers on what it means to be White.* New York: Schocken Books.

Sandoval, C. (2003). U.S. third world feminism: The theory and method of oppositional consciousness in the postmodern world. In R. Lewis & S. Mills (Eds.), *Feminist postcolonial theory: A reader* (pp. 75–99). New York: Routledge.

Sleeter, C. E., & Bernal, D. D. (2004). Critical pedagogy, critical race theory, and antiracist education: Implications for multicultural education. In J. A. Banks & C. A. M. Banks (Eds.), *Handbook of research on multicultural education* (2nd ed., pp. 240–258). San Francisco: Jossey-Bass.

Solórzano, D. (1998) Critical race theory, racial and gender microaggressions, and the experiences of Chicana and Chicano scholars. *International Journal of Qualitative Studies in Education, 11*, 121–136.

Solórzano, D., & Yosso, T. (2002). Critical race methodology: Counter-storytelling as a analytical framework for education research. *Qualitative Inquiry, 8*(1), 23–44.

Taylor, E. (1999). Critical race theory and interest convergence in the desegregation of higher education. In L. Parker, D. Deyhle, & S. Villenas (Eds.), *Race is... race isn't: Critical race theory and qualitative studies in education* (pp. 181–204). Boulder, CO: Westview Press.

Taylor, E. (2000). Critical race theory and interest conversion in the backlash against affirmative action: Washington state and initiative 200. *Teachers College Record, 102*(3), 539–560.

Thompson, A. (2003). Tiffany, friend of people of color: White investments in anti-racism. *Qualitative Studies in Education, 16*(1), 7–29.

Thompson, B. (1999). Subverting racism from within: Linking White identity to activism. In C. Clark & J. O'Donnell (Eds.), *Becoming and unbecoming White: Owning and disowning a racial identity* (pp. 64–77). Westport, CT: Bergin & Garvey.

Wise, T. (2005). *White like me: Reflections on race from a privileged son.* New York: Soft Skull Press.

Wise, T. (2009). *Between Barack and a hard place: Racism and White denial in an age of Obama.* San Francisco: City Lights Books.

Yancy, G. (2004). *What White looks like: African-American philosophers on the Whiteness question.* New York: Routledge.

Yosso, T. J., Parker, L., Solorzano, D. G., & Lynn, M. (2004). From Jim Crow to affirmative action and back again: A critical race discussion of racialized rationales and access to higher education. *Review of Research in Education, 28*, 1–25.

CHAPTER 9

WHO'S ZOOMIN' WHO?

A Critical Race Analysis of Florida's Public High School Graduates

Terri N. Watson
The City College of New York

Jennifer Sughrue
Southeastern Louisiana University

> *You came to catch*
> *You thought I'd be naïve and tame*
> *You met your match*
> *I beat you at your own game*
> —Aretha Franklin, 1985

Who's Zoomin' Who? is soul singer Aretha Franklin's first platinum recording. Debuting in the summer of 1985, its title track is an ode to tricksters. In this cautionary tale the antagonist finds that the tables have turned and he, the hunter, has become the prey. Much like the antagonist in the Queen of Soul's classic song, the State of Florida misled its citizens to believe that it is graduating a higher number of students ready for the workforce or for post-secondary education than is really the case. The State is now being

---

Confronting Racism in Higher Education, pages 181–203
Copyright © 2013 by Information Age Publishing
All rights of reproduction in any form reserved.

confronted by policy research that demonstrates the inequities resulting from years of politically driven but poorly developed education policies.

This chapter serves to narrate a portion of Florida's public education story. It begins with a description of the perceived inequity promulgated by Florida education law and policy that defines a public high school graduate differently than what has been articulated in the No Child Left Behind Act (NCLB, 2008). This is followed by an overview of Critical Race Theory (CRT) and an explication of Critical Race Realism (CRR) as a methodological framework. The next section explains the empirical research that investigated how Florida defines and calculates the number of graduates its school districts produce and how those numbers compare with calculations by other accepted formulas. The statistical results of the study are then explained through Critical Race Realism.

INEQUITY EMBEDDED IN POLICY

America's history is riddled with race-based injustices (Bell, 1980, 1987, 1992; Dubois, 1903). The Trail of Tears, the Watts Race Riots, and the internment of Japanese Americans are evidence of systemic injustices levied against people of color by majority populations who control government institutions. Public school systems too bear this shame (Dubois, 1935; Ladson-Billings & Tate, 1995; *Roberts v. Boston*, 1850; Woodson, 1990). Despite dozens of litigation efforts and reform measures (*Brown v. Board of Education*, 1954; Elementary and Secondary Education Act (ESEA), 1965; Goals 2000: Educate America Act, 1994; *Griffin v. County School Board of Prince Edward County*, 1964; No Child Left Behind Act (NCLB, 2001; *Plessy v. Ferguson*, 1896), the nation's public schools remain inherently separate and unequal. The gross inequities found in public schools across America are promulgated by policies and practices that continually marginalize the most susceptible populace, children of color (Darling-Hammond, 2006; López, 2003).

The No Child Left Behind Act (NCLB) (2001) was intended to close the achievement gap characterized by students' racial, economic, disabilities, and academic standing. After 10 years of implementation, questions have been raised regarding the efficacy of NCLB (Freeman, 2005; Hollingsworth, 2009) and the lack of consistency in the means used to assess student achievement (Balfanz & Legers, 2004; Hall, 2005; Pinkus, 2006). Specifically, there is cause for concern as to how state-level graduation rates obfuscate the impact of broad definitions and race-based calculations of the nation's public high school graduates (Greene & Winters, 2006; Orfield, Losen, Wald, & Swanson 2004).

As graduation rates for Black and Hispanic children continue to fall short of their White counterparts, many educational activists have attempted to clarify the definition and calculation of a public high school graduate (Greene, 2001; Greene & Forster, 2003; Greene & Winters, 2005, 2006; Seastrom, Hoffman, Chapman, & Stillwell, 2005; Swanson, 2003, 2004; Warren, 2005). Investigating how states define and calculate their graduates brings transparency to the true nature of the rate of graduation in each state and elucidates the differences in graduation rates among different groups of students.

As of 2009, Florida publishes three differing calculations of its public high school graduates. The first is Florida's Self-Reported Method (FSRM), which counts all diploma recipients regardless of when or by what means they have earned their diploma. This calculation includes students who earn standard four-year diplomas, students who earn special diplomas, and students and adults who earn state-issued GED certificates. The second method of calculation is designed to adhere to NCLB. In this approach Florida only includes students who receive standard four-year diplomas and GED certificates (FNCLB). The third calculation aligns with a 2005 agreement reached with the National Governors Association (NGA). With this, the Florida Department of Education (FLDOE) includes students who receive standard 4-year and special diplomas in its calculation of its public high school graduate. This approach is indicated by the acronym FNGAC, which stands for Florida NGA Calculation (FLDOE, 2008).

The variations found in Florida's calculations of its public high school graduation rates create discrepancies, confusion, and controversy (Dorn, 2006; *Schroeder*, 2008). For instance, the research on over-identification of children of color in special education programs throughout the nation (Artiles, Klinger, & Tate, 2006; Shealey, Lue, Brooks, & Mccray, 2005) would suggest that the FSRM and FNGAC graduation calculation methods would exaggerate the graduation rates of students of color by including special diplomas in the count. Hiding special diplomas within the graduation rate deflects public scrutiny from the problem of over-identification of students of color in special education programs and from a more accurate representation of the number of students of color receiving a standard high school diploma.

Florida's inclusion of students and adults who earn state-issued GEDs in their FSRM and FNCLB calculations is egregious because it misrepresents the number of students who are truly prepared for employment or further education. It also undermines the economic development of Florida because students who do not earn a standard diploma suffer negative economic consequences, as do the communities in which they live (Amos 2008; Heckman & LaFontaine, 2008; McKinsey & Company, 2009). In addition, it obfuscates the true rate of graduation of those students who are ready to enter post-secondary education and/or the workplace.

The study discussed in this chapter investigated the premise that Florida's policy on graduates and graduation rates may present contrary reports of how many and which students graduate from high school on time and with a standard diploma, and if those reports have a significant negative impact on the graduation rates of students of color. Florida's graduation rates and graduation rate calculation methods for academic years (AY) 2004-08 were ascertained and then analyzed using the lens of CRR, a methodology founded in Critical Race Theory (CRT). This study was intended to inform the current debate surrounding the definition and calculation of a public high school graduate.

An Overview of CRT and CRR

CRT is a derivative of the Critical Legal Studies (CLS) movement (Crenshaw, Gotanda, Peller, & Thomas, 1995; Leiter, 2002) and is founded in the discourse of Derrick Bell (1980, 1987, 1992). CRT recognizes race as a social construct that is oftentimes used to rationalize social order (Omni & Winant, 1994). As an aspect of critical research, CRT proposes race-based perspectives to challenge traditional modes of inquiry and to promote a social justice agenda (Crenshaw et al., 1995).

African American and Latina/o scholars adopted CRT in their collective efforts to remedy the challenges students of color experience in America's public schools. Ladson-Billings and Tate (1995) formally introduced CRT to the field of education in order to provide a fundamental and primary understanding of how racial discrimination permeates and impairs the educational experiences of children of color. CRT presupposes educational policies and practices as inequitable and unjust in regards to students of color as political, social, and historical realities posit the normalization of inequitable, unjust, and racist practices levied against people of color by majority populaces (Crenshaw et al., 1995; Ladson-Billings & Tate, 1995). For clarity, Table 9.1 illustrates the five basic tenets of CRT, which underscore this study.

Along with America's students, educational policy research has too suffered at the long-reaching arms of racial discrimination and prejudice cemented by segregation (*Griffin*, 1964; *Plessy*, 1896; *Roberts*, 1850) and preconceived mental models (Larson & Ovando, 2001). For scores of years, educational policy research has painted a picture of public education but, in large part, has failed to acknowledge the ever-present, if concealed, discrimination that has produced paler hues in its color palate. As a result, critical race scholars have expanded CRT to include methodologies that serve to inform and construct research agendas that aim to deconstruct hegemonic policies and practices in education (Ladson-Billings & Tate, 1995).

TABLE 9.1   5 Basic Tenets of Critical Race Theory (CRT)

CRT Tenet	Definition	Source
Ordinariness	A stark contrast to the color-blind theory. This tenet recognizes that racism is deeply embedded in American life.	Bell (1980)
Interest Convergence	The interest of Blacks will only be accommodated when it converges with the interests of Whites.	Bell (1980)
Social Construction	Race is used by the majority culture as a social, economic, and educational barrier for people of color.	Omni & Winant (1994)
Differential Racialization	Focuses on the way in which different people of color are marginalized to fit the master narrative.	Delgado & Stefancic (2001)
Legal Storytelling	Counter-narratives that frame an experience or policy outcome that is contradictory to the master narrative.	Delgado & Stefancic (2001)

Tate (1993) first used a CRT methodology in educational research to critique state-mandated standardized testing, which he believed to contain racial undertones. In his argument, he called for the use of culturally relevant pedagogy along with culturally sensitive curriculum for students of color in urban classrooms.

Solórzano and Yosso (2002) urged education-based scholars to incorporate CRT in their research analyses both in and out of the classroom. They proposed a CRT methodology for educational research that:

1. foregrounds race and racism in all aspects of the research process,
2. challenges the traditional research paradigms, texts, and theories used to explain the experiences of students of color,
3. offers a liberatory or transformative solution to racial, gender, and class subordination,
4. focuses on the racialized, gendered, and classed experiences of students of color, and
5. uses the interdisciplinary knowledge base of ethnic studies, women's studies, sociology, history, humanities, and the law to better understand the experiences of students of color (Solórzano & Yosso, 2002 p. 24).

These scholars argued that CRT methodologies were needed to challenge education scholarship that were absent the concept of racism and its marginalization of students of color during the educational processes (Solórzano & Yosso, 2002).

From this, CRR, as named by Houh (2005), emerged from this line of critique. CRR aligns with CRT's social justice agenda (Crenshaw et al., 1995) as an effective mode of inquiry that can also be used to objectively substantiate meta-narratives. CRR employs CRT tenets with empirical social science research to analyze public policy and to generate pressure to change racist policies (Parks, 2006). This methodological framework employs empirical data to:

1. expose racism where it may be found
2. identify racism's effects on individuals and institutions, and
3. put forth a concerted attack against racism, in part, via public policy arguments (Parks, 2006, p. 4).

The use of CRR as a methodological framework in this study is essential to unmask the codified inequities promulgated by Florida's definition and subsequent calculations of a public high school graduate. Specifically, three of CRT's tenets (social construction, ordinariness, and interest convergence) along with empirical social science data culled from Florida's Department of Education's (FLDOE) databases were selected to deconstruct Florida's graduation rate calculation methods and to explore the potential consequences for children of color.

Overview of the Study

The purpose of this study was two-fold. First, an investigation was conducted to determine whether a significant and consistent difference existed among Florida's public high school's graduation rates relative to student race and graduation rate calculation methods. Second, CRR was used to deconstruct Florida's definition and subsequent calculations of a public high school graduate in an attempt to explain the implications for students of color.

For the purposes of comparing Florida's methods of calculating graduation rates, the Adjusted Averaged Freshman Graduation Rate (AAFGR) (Greene & Forster, 2003; Greene & Winters, 2005, 2006; Seastrom et al., 2005) was selected from a well established body of research literature that compares and contrasts the various accepted methods to calculate graduation rates. The AAFGR is calculated by using longitudinal data from each district and by dividing the number of standard diploma recipients who earned their diploma in four years (represented by the term *SHSDAwarded*) in a given year by the number of (adjusted) students enrolled in grade 8 five years earlier, grade 9 four years earlier, and grade 10 three years earlier, and averaged. For example, to calculate the 2003 graduation rate for a single public school district, the following AAFGR equation (Equation 9.1) would apply:

$$\frac{AY2003SHSDAwarded}{\left(\dfrac{Grade8Fall98+Grade9Fall99+Grade10Fall00}{3}\right)} \qquad (9.1)$$

The top numerator would include only those students who earned a standard diploma in no more than 4 years. The denominator is the averaged cumulative number of students in Grades 8, 9, and 10 that proceeded the year they would graduate.

As explained previously, Florida uses different calculations for its graduation rate, depending on to whom the rates are reported. Florida's basic equation utilizes an averaged cohort approach, but the numerator differs because, depending on which of three calculations it is crunching, the number of graduates differs.

As noted in Table 9.2 below, there are four categories of "graduates" who are potentially counted in one or more of Florida's calculations. The Standard Diploma is awarded to those students who complete the required high school course of study and pass the Florida Comprehensive Assessment Tests (FCAT) on time (within four years). Students who drop out of school or who follow a non-traditional program of study in high school often acquire a General Education Certificate (GED) by sitting for the GED exam. Special diplomas are awarded to those students who complete their schooling but are unable to meet the requirements for the standard diploma. Often students with special needs who are unable to pass the FCAT or all of the required high school courses earn a special diploma. Table 9.2 summarizes Florida's graduation rate calculation methods, as well as the AAFGR, and indicates which kinds of diplomas are counted in the calculation.

TABLE 9.2   AAFGR, FSRM, FNCLB, and FNGAC Graduation Rate Calculation Methods

Graduation Calculation Method	Standard Diploma	Student GED	Adult GED	Special Diploma
AAFGR	X			
FSRM	X	X	X	X
FLNCLB	X	X		
FNGAC	X			X

Research Questions and Design

The three guiding questions for this research focused on comparing the graduation rates among White, Black, and Hispanic students using a variety of calculation methods, including the three methods the State of Florida has adopted. It is important to note that the terms Black and Hispanic were deliberately used instead of terms such as African American and Latin American because Florida's population is ethnically very diverse. Hispanic students may come from Cuba, Costa Rica, and Puerto Rico, as well as those who come from Mexico or who are native born Americans. Many non-American Black students, in the large school districts in South Florida particularly, come from the Caribbean islands, especially Haiti and Jamaica. However, Florida does not distinguish among the ethnic groups and classifies all students by simplistic racial categories.

The questions were:

1. Is there a difference among graduation rates relative to student race (White vs. Black vs. Hispanic)?
2. Is there a difference among graduation rates relative to graduation rate calculation methods (AAFGR vs. FSRM vs. FNCLB vs. FNGAC)?
3. Is there a consistent difference among graduation rates relative to student race (White vs. Black vs. Hispanic) and graduation rate calculation methods (AAFGR vs. FSRM vs. FNCLB vs. FNGAC)?

After the graduation rate calculations were performed, a Repeated Measures design and Analyses of Variance (ANOVAs) were employed to determine whether a significant and consistent difference existed among Florida's public high school's graduation rates relative to student race and graduation rate calculation methods for AY 2004–08. The study considered 12 variables generally defined as graduation rates for White, Black, and Hispanic students based on AAFGR, FSRM, FNCLB, and FNGAC graduation rate calculation methods.

Sample Size and Data Collection

Florida's public school districts, of which there are 67, were the units of analysis. Having an alpha value set at .05, a sample size of 63 public school districts were needed to yield an a priori estimated power of .80 and a medium effect. Inasmuch as all 67 districts were included in the study, this power criterion was met. This study spanned AY 2004–08, which encompassed the first 5 years of NLCB regulations and the first 4 years of the Graduation Counts Compact. Both of these policies were adopted, in part, to increase fidelity in the calculation of the nation's graduates, so it was, therefore, important to cover the years these policies were in effect.

Unlike many other states, FLDOE has a comprehensive longitudinal database that is easily accessible from its website. Relevant data for this study were found in annual reports issued by the Education Information and Accountability Services Department and obtained via the Internet.

In order to calculate the Adjusted Averaged Freshman Graduation Rate (AAFGR), student enrollment data were collected from *Profiles of Florida School Districts* (AY 2000-06) for students in Grades 8, 9, and 10 for each of Florida's 67 public school districts. The number of standard diploma recipients was obtained from the *Completer Report by District, by Diploma, by Race, by Gender,* which is published by the FLDOE (2009). The same reports were used to obtain data on students who earned special diplomas, as well as students and adults who earned GEDs for the years under study.

Statistical Analyses

Once all graduation rates were calculated, a doubly multivariate repeated measures design was conducted to determine whether difference existed among Florida's public high school's graduation rates relative to student race and graduation rate calculation method. The units of analysis were school districts, in which 196 data points were generated by the repeated measures design. Then, three ANOVAs were conducted to determine if a consistent difference existed among graduation rates relative to student race and graduation rate calculation method. The two variables, which constituted the repeated (or within Ss) variables, were student race (White, Black, and Hispanic) and graduation rate calculation method (AAFGR, FSRM, FNCLB, FNGAC). The alpha level was set at .05 for all analyses.

Descriptive Statistics

The means and standard deviations of all the tested variables compared for notable insights. Table 9.3 and Figure 9.1 illustrate the results of aforementioned descriptive statistics.

The descriptive statistics revealed the possibility of significant disparity in graduation rates, along with a surprising result. As expected, the AAFGR calculation generally produced a lower graduation rate for White and Black students than the other three methods, because not as many students would qualify as completers when using the standard diploma as the only criteria. This produces a smaller numerator, which decreases the ratio and, therefore, the calculated graduation rate. Conversely, because more stu-

TABLE 9.3 Graduation Rates by Calculation Method and Student Race

Student Race	Graduation Rate Calculation Method	Mean	Std. Deviation
White	AAFGR	66.74	10.40
	FSRM	79.79	9.21
	FNCLB	76.91	10.06
	FNGAC	76.20	10.28
Black	AAFGR	50.11	11.15
	FSRM	63.25	9.21
	FNCLB	57.26	9.12
	FNGAC	60.20	9.74
Hispanic	AAFGR	67.03	18.33
	FSRM	66.96	11.32
	FNCLB	62.83	11.40
	FNGAC	63.48	11.52

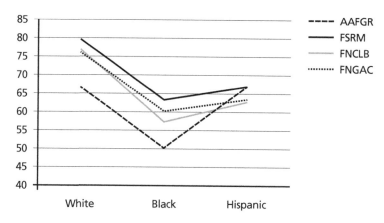

Figure 9.1 Graduation rate means by calculation method and by student race.

dents are counted as graduates under the FSRM, the mean graduation rate was higher for Whites and Blacks compared to all other methods.

The larger means for Whites, using the FSRM, FLNCLB, and FNGAC approaches, give the impression that White students are graduating in much higher numbers. In reality, there are simply larger numbers of White students completing high schools with something other than a standard diploma. The 10-point difference in means between the AAFGR and the FLNCLB calculations and the small differences in means among the FLN-CLB, FSRM, and FNGAC results suggest that many more White students are earning GEDs in place of standard or special diplomas or adult GEDs.

In contrast to White and Black student graduation rates, the AAFGR and FSRM averaged graduation rates for Hispanic students were nearly identical. In addition, the AAFGR mean for Hispanics was slightly but nonetheless higher than the AAFGR rate for Whites. This suggests that, relatively speaking, Hispanic students tend to graduate with standard diplomas and on time. Moreover, proportionately fewer leave school with a GED or special diploma compared to White and Black students.

Graduation rates for Black students were lower when compared to White and Hispanic students regardless of the method employed. The AAFGR had a lower mean compared to all other graduation rate calculation methods and the FSRM rendered the highest mean. Interestingly, the FNGAC mean is 10 points higher than the AAFGR mean and 3 points higher than the FNCLB mean, which implies that more Black students are leaving school with special diplomas in comparison to White and Hispanic students.

Analyses of Repeated Measures Design Results

Through the use of PASW version 17.02 for Windows, two statistical methods were employed to analyze the collected data. The analysis included a doubly multivariate repeated measures design and three ANOVAs. Student race and calculation methods were the main effects in each of the doubly multivariate repeated measures designs. ANOVAs were run to determine whether consistent differences existed among graduation rates relative to race and method. The outputs were used to respond to the three research questions and to test their respective null hypotheses. These analyses generated a critical perspective of the impact of Florida's race based graduation rate calculation methods on White, Black, and Hispanic students.

In respect to the first research question (whether or not there is a difference among graduation rates relative to student race), the results indicated that the with-in subjects main effect of race was significant (Pillai's Trace $= 0.79$, $F(2, 194) = 370.42$, $p < 0.001$ (partial $n^2 = 0.79$, power $= 1.00$)). In other words, there were statistically significant differences in graduation rates among the three racial categories of students.

The second research question asked if there were differences in graduation rates relative to the method used to calculate those rates. Again, a doubly multivariate repeated measures design was conducted, and the results indicated that significant differences do exist with-in graduation rates relative to graduation rate calculation methods (Pillai's Trace $= 0.86$, $F(3, 193) = 394.86$, $p < 0.001$ (partial $n^2 = 0.86$, power $= 1.00$)).

A third doubly multivariate repeated measures design was utilized to respond to the last research question, which asked if there were consistent differences among graduation rates relative to student race *and* calculation methods. Again, at an alpha level set as .05, the results revealed that the interaction effect between student race and calculation methods was significant (Pillai's Trace = 0.38, F (9, 2847) = 45.37, $p < 0.001$ (partial $n^2 = 0.125$, power = 1.00)). In other words, consistent differences do exist with-in graduation rates relative to student race and graduation rate calculation methods.

Analyses of ANOVAs

Three ANOVAs were then conducted to determine whether consistent difference existed among graduation rates relative to student race (White vs. Black vs. Hispanic) and graduation rate calculation methods (AAFGR, FSRM, FNCLB, and FNGAC). The alpha level was set at .05. Table 9.4 provides the results.

In sum, the ANOVAs affirmed that consistent differences exist among graduation rates relative to student race and graduation rate calculation methods. The salient findings in these analyses were the differing patterns of graduation rates in respect to the graduation rate calculation methods. To be specific, while the pattern of graduation rates were essentially the same for White and Black students (with the exception of a difference between FNCLB and FNGAC rates for Black students but not for White students), a significant interaction occurred among White, Black, and Hispanic students due to the drastically different profile for Hispanic students wherein the AAFGR and FSRM rates were essentially equivalent, 67.03 and 66.96.

Summary

The results of a doubly multivariate repeated measures design using student race and graduation rate calculation methods as the main effects revealed that significant differences exist with-in graduation rates relative to student

TABLE 9.4 ANOVAs for Graduation Rates for White, Black, and Hispanic Students Relative to Graduation Rate Calculation Methods

Graduation Rates	F	P	Partial n^2	Power
White	71.94 (101.04)	.001	0.19	0.99
Black	75.97 (100.86)	.001	0.19	0.99
Hispanic	3.61 (212.17)	.013	0.01	0.80

Note: Values in parenthesis presents mean squared error.

race ($p < 0.001$) and graduation rate calculation methods ($p < 0.001$), and relative to student race and graduation rate calculation methods ($p < 0.001$). Last, the results of three ANOVAs confirmed that consistent differences exist among graduation rates relative to student race and graduation rate calculation methods. The profile for Hispanic students was noted, in particular, as the AAFGR and FSRM were essentially equal, causing a significant interaction.

DISCUSSION OF THE FINDINGS: A CRITICAL RACE REALISM PERSPECTIVE

The narratives of Douglass (1845), DuBois (1903, 1935), and Woodson (1990) detailed Black America's resolute belief in public education as a means to the American dream. However, their testaments voiced the struggles people of color were forced to contend with as they attempted to become self-reliant and full members of American society. These stories are particularly poignant because of their context in a nation allegedly founded on the principles of freedom, equality, and justice for all. What Black Americans and other people of color have faced is the duality of the American promise of equality with the reality of permanent and pervasive discrimination, even in the public school house. Woodson (1990) labeled what happens in the public education system as the deliberate *miseducation* of the Negro by White America. It is not difficult to extrapolate this phenomenon to other students of color.

As a result of these stories and the documented history of government sanctioned discrimination, scholars of color created CRT in an effort to reconcile these dichotomous and racialized realities (Bell, 1980, Crenshaw et al., 1995). CRT, as a tool, challenges terms like equity and adequacy (Alemán, 2007). Investigating the embedded discrimination in education policy and law provides insight for educational leaders who struggle for social justice in America's public schools.

To this end, CRR, a methodological framework founded in CRT, was employed to illustrate the effects of FLDOE's race-based graduation rate calculation policies. In the following sections, the empirical findings are juxtaposed to three of CRT's tenets (social construction, ordinariness, and interest convergence) to demonstrate how FLDOE's approaches to calculating graduation rates are contradictory to the intent NCLB (2008), which promised to narrow the achievement gap and to improve the academic outcomes of *all* students.

Social Construction

As a fundamental tenet of CRT, *social construction* suggests that race is a man-made ideal that serves a societal purpose (Crenshaw et al., 1995; Delgado & Stefancic, 2001; Omni & Winant, 1994). In America, hegemonic practices were founded to affirm and maintain White racial dominance. As Decuir & Dixson (2004) averred, "racist hierarchal structures govern all political, economic, and social domains. Such structures allocate the privileging of Whites and subsequent Othering of people of color in all arenas" (p. 27). In relation to CRR, the principle of social construction is inherent in policies, including those for education, and can be deconstructed to expose hegemonic ideals along with outputs that fuel the idea of a White racial hierarchy.

Critical Race Realism's use of empirical analyses makes it particularly useful for understanding the implicit bias in Florida's definition of a high school graduate and its methods of calculating graduation rates. When the graduation rates for Florida high school students are calculated using the AAFGR, which only counts students who have earned a standard diploma in 4 years, and then are compared to the three equations adopted by Florida, which inflate the number of graduates by including those who have earned something other than a standard diploma, social construction becomes evident.

As previously explained, Florida chooses to calculate graduation rates in three different ways. These methodologies do not adhere to NCLB's definition of a graduate as it restricts graduates to those who earn a standard diploma in 4 years. They do, however, all indicate that White students graduate at higher rates than Hispanic and Black students. For instance, based on FSRM, FNCLB and FNGAC graduation rate means, White students outperform Hispanic and Black students by as much as 10% and 16%, respectively (see Table 9.4). Thus, FLDOE's calculations produce a statistically significant difference in graduation rates among White, Hispanic, and Black students, socially constructing a racial hierarchy.

Based on Florida's calculations, White students appear to attain the best rates of graduation, constructing the superiority and privilege of Whites. Black students, on the other hand, have the lowest graduation rates. This constructs Blacks as the least able and least privileged group. The reported graduation rates for Hispanic students are slightly higher than Blacks, but statistically lower than Whites, leaving the social impression or construction that there is a differentiation in their academic achievement and social standing relative to White and Black students, which may be attributed unwittingly and solely to race. This leads the casual observer to believe that Whites are more successful at completing high school, which perpetuates the image of White students as better prepared for work or postsecondary education and of students of color as second best. As such, underlying racist causes of the achievement gap are not considered and children of color remain marginalized in Florida's classrooms.

The scenario is made all the more suspicious when the AAFGR means for all three groups are compared. When all alternative diploma structures are stripped away, as the AAFGR method does, Hispanic students, on average, graduated at a higher rate with standard diplomas than White students for AY 2004-08. Exposing this fact might generate political fallout and challenges to the entrenched notion of White supremacy in public schools for two reasons.

First, it would change the nature of the conversation about who is struggling, who is succeeding, and why. The manner in which Florida defines a high school graduate and the methods by which Florida calculates graduation rates obscure the reality that considerably fewer students, regardless of their race or ethnicity, leave high school with a standard diploma. No longer would it be a simple matter to associate academic success as only a White phenomenon.

Second, if White parents and other privileged stakeholders discover that there is as much as a 13% discrepancy between Florida reported graduation rates and those generated by the AAFGR, they may become enraged that they have been misled by the reports of graduation rates that portray a brighter future for White students. They may lose confidence that politicians will protect their interest in maintaining the status quo, that is, their position of superiority in the "race to the top."

Feeling their political, social, and economic dominance might be threatened, White Floridians might insist that lawmakers and the FLDOE do something to improve academic achievement. No longer could the majority say it is only students of color who cannot finish school prepared for a productive future. The social construction of race would be shaken by the notion that students of color can outperform Whites on an indicator of educational outcomes, such as graduation rates.

Ordinariness

Ordinariness is a central tenet of CRT. Based on the principle of ordinariness, many CRT theorists believed that racism "is ordinary, not aberrational" (Delgado & Stefancic, 2001, p. 7). In other words, racism is entrenched and perpetual; however, it is not always overt, rendering it complicated to address. Years ago, signs over many public and private institutions in this country read *Whites Only* and *separate but equal* was the legal doctrine of the era. This made racism easily identifiable. Nowadays, however, racism in schools is masked by "neutral" educational policies that appear to provide equal educational opportunity to all children. Racial disparities that are evinced by the achievement gap, dropout rates, special education identification, and graduation rates are explained away as unintended consequences or the result of social conditions, such as dysfunctional families and poverty.

Racism, however, is alive and well. Racism's effects, in fact, can be found in the nation's segregated, post-segregated, and currently re-segregated public school systems (*Roberts v. Boston,* 1850; *Brown v. Board of Education,* 1954; Orfield & Lee, 2006; *Parents Involved in Community Schools,* 2007). Kozol's (2005) 5-year study of 60 public schools in 11 states found that despite the promise of *Brown* (1954) many public schools in America's urban areas serve primarily communities of color, and in addition to being separate and unequal, lack the necessary physical facilities, teaching staff, and funding to meet the academic needs of its students.

The results of this study bear out the suspicion that Florida's law and policy on graduates and graduation rates, while neutral on their face, function to obfuscate complex problems in schools and to subordinate students of color. An analysis of mean graduation rates derived from FNGAC and FNCLB calculations (see Table 9.4) revealed that Black students receive significantly more special diplomas in comparison to Hispanic and White students. This finding substantiates what research literature asserts; that there is an over representation of Black students in special education programs (Artiles et al., 2006; Shealey et al., 2005), which may deny them access to a standard diploma. It leads to the conclusion that Florida educational leaders, including those who legislate, have failed to or have refused to effectively address underlying problems, such as over-identification of students of color in special education, which, in reality, denies students of color, (particularly Black students) equal educational opportunities.

Consider Florida's mission for its K–20 public education system, which proposes to "increase the proficiency of all students within one seamless, efficient system, by allowing them the opportunity to expand their knowledge and skills through learning opportunities and research valued by students, parents, and communities" (Florida Department of Education, 2008). To facilitate this objective, FLDOE prides itself on establishing rigorous academic goals and objectives for traditional and nontraditional students. These goals and objectives are outlined in FLDOE's *Next Generation PreK–20 Education Strategic Plan* and are intended to increase and improve student participation in post-secondary institutions, which includes students who graduate from career, technical, and GED certificate programs.

However, students who receive special diplomas do not benefit from the open door policies afforded to standard diploma and GED recipients at Florida's public universities and community colleges (Beech, McKay, & Pankaskie, 2005). An investigation of FLDOE's databases revealed a policy brief that indicated that far less than the estimated 10% of Florida's high school graduates who receive special diplomas and participate in post secondary education complete their course of study (Reder, 2007). If students of color, particularly Black students, are being over-identified for special education programs and are increasingly likely to receive special diplomas instead of standard diplomas, then their opportunities to attend post secondary institutions are diminished substantially. Again, the ordinariness of racism underpins the lack of a response by the state legislature to remedy the tendency of public schools to award special diplomas to Black students as a convenient yet subversive method to count them as school completers. On the face of it, they are counted as graduates, inflating the true rate of graduation, but on the backside of it, Black students are not afforded the same opportunities to attend college or other post-secondary institutions.

Likewise, the GED stands in stark contrast to a standard high school diploma. As demonstrated in the literature, students who receive GEDs do not reap the expected benefits of a high school graduate in terms of participation in post-secondary institutions and lifetime earnings. Heckman and LaFontaine (2008) reported, "the most significant source of bias in estimating graduation rates comes from including GED recipients as high school graduates" (p. 2). Specifically, a GED certificate was found to be of little significance to its recipients with most earning the equivalent to that of a high school dropout (Orfield et al., 2004); who, it is estimated, based on AY 2007-08 alone, cost Florida $25,349,857,813 in potential earnings (Amos, 2008). Also, a study conducted by Tyler (2005) found that a GED did not improve the labor market for males of color as it did for Whites.

Inherent in the promise of NCLB was the belief that people of color would receive equal and equitable educational experiences and opportunities in America's classrooms. The inclusion of GED recipients in Florida's graduation rate calculation methods (FNCLB) undermines the intent of NCLB and serves to conceal Florida's broken promise as evidenced in its AAFGR rates, which are alarmingly low for Black students.

What is most important to this discussion, however, is that the ordinariness of racism in Florida's schools is manifested by graduation rate policies that hide their disparate impact on students of color. Florida legislators and policymakers continue to disregard the educational needs of these students and thereby limit those students' post secondary education and career options. As such, Florida's definition and subsequent calculations of a high school graduate are racist. They maintain the status quo and perpetuate the inequities of an educational system that does not address the academic needs of Florida's Black students.

Interest Convergence

Bell (1980) asserted that White America only acts on behalf of people of color if it is to their benefit. He labeled this theory as *interest convergence*. The results of this study could be utilized to argue for further improvement in the educational opportunities for students of color by exposing the disservice that is paid to White students by the methods Florida uses to calculate graduation rates.

When one compares the AAFGR and FNCLB mean graduation rates, it becomes evident that White students received more GEDs in comparison to both Black and Hispanic students. To explain, the difference between the AAFGR and FNCLB means for White students is more than 10%. The difference in means for Black students is a little more than 7%. This disparity exemplifies how FLDOE's response to NCLB may have encouraged unintended consequences by masking the dismal educational outcomes of Florida's White students, as well as those for Black students.

It is unclear why NCLB has approved different definitions of a graduate upon request by the states, but it is evident that it serves no productive purpose, at least in Florida. All students are poorly served by adding GEDs to the count of high school graduates. However, it could be argued that White America is beginning to wake up to the long entrenched policy manipulations that obscure the completion rates in America's high schools.

Until recently, the nation has paid little attention to its graduates, particularly those of color (NCLB, 2008; NGA Compact, 2005; U.S. Secretary of Education... Announces, 2008). The lack of uniformity and accountability in calculating the nation's graduates has garnered considerable attention recently, as states and school districts are finding themselves in the hot seat for using dubious means to report student performance on standardized tests and for obscuring how graduation rates are calculated (Heilig & Darling-Hammond, 2008; *Schroeder*, 2008). Consider the general public and its lack understanding of how graduation rates are determined. It is easy to believe that one simply counts the number of students who graduate with a diploma and divide it by the number of students in the senior class. This is conceptually far different from the equations popularly used by policymakers and researchers and it leaves untouched the lack of awareness about special diplomas and other means of leaving school with a "diploma" in hand.

One could argue that White America's recent interest in the calculation methods and accountability for the nation's graduates is a far cry from selfless. Based on the tenet of interest convergence, the nation's lawmakers and policy implementers' sudden concern is promulgated by the fact that many of the current graduation rate policies and calculations serve to promote a citizenry that is inadequately prepared for post secondary education, meaningful employment, and a living wage. In other words, the federal call to action to improve public education is based more on self-interest than on an altruistic concern for historically underperforming groups. It serves the interest of White America to increase unadulterated graduation rates of White children to maintain its superior standing in business, politics, and society. It is equally important to the nation that all students are adequately prepared to lead industry and to improve the economy in our highly competitive global environment.

CONCLUSIONS

What is apparent in Florida, based on FLDOE's graduation rates (FSRM, FNCLB and FNGAC), is that the public is led to believe that Florida's high school graduates have acquired the appropriate skill sets, which allow them to seek further academic and vocational opportunities. The fact of the matter is large numbers of graduates, particularly White and Black students, are leaving school with GEDs or special diplomas and, in so doing, are ill prepared for their future. This was indicated in literature (Reder, 2007; Tyler, 2005), which confirmed that a GED or special diploma places students at risk of failing to participate in post-secondary educational opportunities or meaningful employment.

Clarity and precision are needed to evaluate how the variables that affect graduation rates, such as inadequate funding, inadequately prepared teachers, and poverty, impact Florida's students. At this time, Florida's stakeholders are unable to accurately appraise the quality of education found in public schools throughout the state as FLDOE's graduation rate calculation methods do not subscribe to the definition and calculation of a public high school graduate promulgated by NCLB (2001). Instead, the FSRM, FNCLB, and FNGAC propagate inaccurate and biased educational outcomes, which serve to conceal the true status of high school graduation rates in Florida and to hinder the academic achievement of *all* of Florida's students. In particular, they continue to inadequately address the achievement gap between White students and students of color. Most importantly, it maintains the social construct of race, which delegates Whites to the top of the academic and social hierarchy, and reinforces stereotypical myths that Hispanics and Blacks cannot compete with Whites in the educational arena.

Accordingly, by implementing uniform graduation rate calculations and monitoring student progress, Florida can elucidate the problem of low graduation rates and can make an astute investment in education in order to promote a successful economic future for its citizens and for itself. Increased graduation rates for all students coupled with post-secondary education and/or vocational training equals a healthy economy and a country with fewer social ills.

Moreover, with the rapid growth of the percentage of students of color and with the state and national need for those students to be successfully educated, it is in the interest of policy makers, first, to support an accurate calculation of graduation rates and, second, to remedy the conditions that hinder the academic success of *all* students. If self-interest is indeed a motivator, and clearly the fact that White students in Florida are not earning standard diplomas at the rate that the current calculation methods allege, then it is certainly in the self-interest of White Floridian policymakers to advocate increased educational quality in all Florida public schools. Failure to do so will lead to a continued decline in the economic strength of the states and the nation.

In the past, educational policies and practices have been enacted, repealed, revised, or reauthorized when a travesty of justice or crisis is revealed (see Elementary and Secondary Education Act, 1965; Gun-Free Schools Act, 1994; Individuals with Disabilities Education Act, 1975; No Child Left Behind Act, 2001, 2008; Safe and Drug-Free Schools and Communities Act, 1994). Florida's public school system, based on its definition and subsequent calculation methods of a public high school graduate, is inundated by race-based inequities. And while the majority of U.S. Supreme Court justices may believe that the federal constitution is color blind (*Parents Involved in Community Schools v. Seattle School District No. 1*, 2007), there is no such guarantee in education policy. To argue that educational policies are race neutral is to ignore the fact that such policies seldom have race neutral outcomes or impact and belies the question— *Who's zoomin' who?*

REFERENCES

Alemán, E. Jr. (2007). Situating Texas school finance policy in CRT framework: How "substantially equal" yields racial inequity. *Educational Administration Quarterly, 43*(5), 525–528.

Amos, J. (2008). *Dropouts, diplomas, and dollars: U.S. high schools and the nation's economy.* Washington, DC: Alliance for Excellent Education.

Artiles, A. J., Klinger, J. K., & Tate, W. F. (2006). Representation of minority students in special education: Complicating traditional explanations. *Educational Researcher, 35*(6), 3–5.

Balfanz, B., & Legters, N. (2004). *Locating the dropout crisis: Which high schools produce the nation's dropouts.* Baltimore, MD: Center for Research on the Education of Students Placed At Risk, Johns Hopkins University.

Beech, M., McKay, J., & Pankaskie, S. (2005). *High school diploma options for students with disabilities.* State of Florida Department of State.

Bell, D. A. (1980). Brown vs. Board of Education and the interest-convergence dilemma. *Harvard Law Review, 33*, 1–34.

Bell, D. A. (1987). *And we are not saved. The elusive quest for racial justice.* New York: Basic Books.

Bell, D. A. (1992). *Faces at the bottom of the well: The permanence of racism.* New York: Basic Books.

Brown vs. Board of Education of Topeka, Shawnee County, Kan. 347 U. S. 483, 74 S. Ct. 686 (1954).

Crenshaw, K. W., Gotanda, N., Peller, G., & Thomas, K. (Eds.). (1995). *Critical race theory: The key writings that formed the movement.* New York: The New Press.

Darling-Hammond, L. (2006). No Child Left Behind and high school reform. *Harvard Education Review, 76*(4), 642–647.

DeCuir, J., & Dixson, A. (2004). "So when it comes out, they aren't that surprised that it is there": Critical race theory as a tool of analysis of race and racism in education. *Educational Researcher, 33*(5), 26–31.

Delgado, R., & Stefancic, J. (Eds.). (2001). *Critical race theory: An introduction.* (2nd ed.). New York: New York University Press.

Dorn, S. (2006, June 29). *Inflation of official Florida graduation rates: A short paper released on line June 29, 2006.* Retrieved June 20, 2008, from http://www.shermandorn.com/mt/archives/Inflated-Florida-Graduation.pdf.

Douglass, F. (1845). *The narrative of the life of an American slave.* New York: Vintage.

DuBois. W. E. B. (1903). *The souls of Black folks.* New York: Vintage.

DuBois. W. E. B. (1935) Does the negro need separate schools? *Journal of Negro Education, 4*(3), 328–355.

Elementary and Secondary Education Act, 20 U.S.C. §§ 6301 – 8962 (1965).

Florida Department of Education. (2008, November). *Florida public high school graduation rates, 2007–08* (Series 2009-5D). K-20 Education Code (2008). Tallahassee, FL: Department of Education. Retrieved June 6, 2008, from http://www.fldoe.org/eias/eiaspubs/ word/gradrate.doc

Freeman, E. (2005). No child left behind and the denigration of race. *Equity & Excellence in Education, 38*, 190–199.

Goals 2000: Educate America Act, Pub. L. No. 103–227 (1994).

Greene, J. (2001, Winter). *High school graduation rates in the United States.* The Manhattan Institute and the Black Alliance for Educational Options. Retrieved June 6, 2008, from http://www.manhattan-institute.org/ html/cr_baeo.html

Greene, J., & Forster, G. (2003). *Public high school graduation and college readiness rates in the United States.* Education Working Paper No. 3 Manhattan Institute for Policy Research. Retrieved June 6, 2008, from http://eric.ed.gov:80/ERIC-Docs/ data/ericdocs2sql/content_storage_01/0000019b/8 0/31/9a/7e.pdf

Greene, J. P., & Winters, M. A. (2005). *Public high school graduation and college-readiness rates: 1991–2002.* New York: Manhattan Institute for Policy Research [Online]. Retrieved June 6, 2008, from www.manhattaninstitute.org/html/ewp_08.htm

Greene, J. P., & Winters, M. A. (2006). *Leaving boys behind: Public high school graduation rates.* New York: Manhattan Institute for Policy Research [Online]. Retrieved June 6, 2008, from www.manhattan-institute.org/pdf/cr_48.pdf

Griffin vs. County School Board of Prince Edward County, 377 U.S. 218, 84 S. Ct. 1226 (1964).

Gun-Free School Act, 20 U.S.C. §§ 8921 –8923 (1994).

Hall, D. (2005). *Getting honest about grad rates: How states play the numbers and students lose.* Washington, DC: The Education Trust [Online]. Retrieved June 6, 2008, from http://www2.edtrust.org/NR/rdonlyres/C5A6974D-6C04-4FB1A9FC-05938CB0744D/0/GettingHonest.pdf

Heckman, J. J., & LaFontaine, P. A. (2008). *The declining American high school graduation rate: Evidence, sources, and consequences.* National Bureau of Economic Research. Retrieved July 28, 2009, from http://www.nber.org/reporter/2008number1/heckman.html

Heilig, J. V., & Darling-Hammond, L. (2008). Accountability texas-style: The progress and learning of urban minority students in a high-stakes testing context. *Educational Evaluation and Policy Analysis. June 2008,* Vol. 30, No. 2, 75–110. Retrieved November 29, 2008, from http://epa.sagepub.com/cgi/reprint/30/2/75

Hollingsworth, L. (2009, Winter). Unintended educational and social consequences of the no child left behind act. *Journal of Gender, Race, and Justice Individuals with Disabilities Education Act Amendments,* 20 U.S.C. § 1400 *et seq* (2004).

Houh, E. (2005). Critical race realism: Re-claiming the antidiscrimination principle through the doctrine of good faith in contract law, *University of Pittsburgh Law Review, 66,* 45.

Individuals with Disabilities Education Act, 20 U.S.C. §§ 1400–1450 (1975).

Kozol, J. (2005). *The shame of a nation: The restoration of apartheid schooling in America.* New York: Crown Publishers.

Ladson-Billings, G., & Tate, W. (1995). Toward a critical race theory in education. *Teachers College Record, 97*(1), 47–68.

Larson, C. L., & Ovando, C. J. (2001). *The color of bureaucracy: The politics of equity in multicultural school communities.* Belmont, CA: Wadsworth.

Leiter, B. (2002). American Legal Realism. U of Texas Law, Public Law Research Paper No. 42. Retrieved February 9, 2009, from http://ssrn.com/abstract=339562.

López, G. R. (2003). The (racially neutral) politics of education: A critical race theory perspective. *Educational Administration Quarterly, 39*(1), 69–94

McKinsey & Company. (2009). *The economic impact of the achievement gap in America's schools.* Retrieved February 1, 2009, from http://www.mckinsey.com/client-service/socialsector/achievement_gap_report.pdf

National Governors Association Compact. (2005). *Graduation counts: A compact on state high school graduation data.* Washington, DC: National Governors Association. Retrieved June 6, 2008, from http://www.nga.org/Files/pdf/0807GRADCOUNTS.PDF

No Child Left Behind Act, Public L. 107 -110 (2001).

No Child Left Behind Act of 2001, 20 U.S.C. § 6319 (2008).

Omni, M., & Winant, H. (1994). *Racial formation in the United States: From the 1960s to the 1990s.* New York: Routledge.

Orfield, G., & Lee, C. (2006). Racial transformation and changing nature of segregation. *Civil Rights Project. Harvard University,* 1–41.

Orfield, G., Losen, D., Wald, J., & Swanson, C. B. (2004). *Losing our future: How minority youth are being left behind by the graduation rate crisis.* Joint release by the Civil Rights Project at Harvard University, the Urban Institute, Advocates for Children of New York, and the Civil Society Institute [Online]. Retrieved June 6, 2008, from www.urban.org/UploadedPDF/410936_LosingOurFuture.pdf

Parents Involved in Community Schools v. Seattle School District No. 1, 551 U. S. 701, 127 S. Ct. 2738 (2007)

Parks, G. (2006, November). Critical race realism: Towards an integrative model of critical race theory, empirical social science, and public policy. *bepress Legal Series.* Working Paper 1886.

Pinkus, L. (2006). *Who's counted? Who's counting? Understanding high school graduation rates.* Washington, DC: Alliance for Excellent Education.

Plessy v. Ferguson, 163, U. S. 537, 16 S. Ct. 1138 (1896).

Reder, S. (2007). *Adult education and postsecondary success: National commission on adult literacy policy brief.* New York: Council for Advancement of Adult Literacy.

Roberts v. Boston, 59 Mass. (5 Cush.) 198 (1850).

Safe and Drug-Free School -Free School and Communities Act, 20 U.S.C. §§4601 – 4665 (1994).

Schroeder vs. The Palm Beach County School Board, No. 50208CA007579XXXX-MB (2008).

Seastrom, M., Hoffman, L., Chapman, C., & Stillwell, R. (2005). *The averaged freshman graduation rate for public high schools from the common core of data: School years 2001–02 and 2002–03* (NCES 2006-601). U.S. Department of Education. Washington, DC: National Center for Education Statistics.

Shealey, M., Lue, M., Brooks, M., & McCray, E. (2005). Examining the legacy of Brown: The impact on special education and teacher practice. *Remedial & Special Education, 26* (2), 113–121.

Solórzano, D. G., & Yosso, T. J. (2002). Critical race methodology: Counter-storytelling as an analytical framework for education research. *Qualitative Inquiry, 8*(1), 23–44.

Swanson, C. B. (2003). *NCLB implementation report: State approaches for calculating high school graduation rates.* Washington, D.C.: The Urban Institute. Retrieved June 6, 2008, from http://www.urban.org/publications/410848.html

Swanson, C. B. (2004). *Graduation rates: Real kids, real numbers.* Washington, D.C.: The Urban Institute.

Tate, W. F. (1993). Advocacy versus economics. A critical race analysis of the proposed national asssessment in mathematics. *Thresholds in Education, 19*(1–2). 16–22.

Tyler, J. H. (2005, July). *Evidence from Florida on the labor market attachment of male dropouts who attempt the GED.* Retrieved September 8, 2008, from http://www.ncsall.net/fileadmin/resources/research/ged_fl_rb.pdf

United States Department of Education. (2008). *No child left behind – 2008: Summary of final Title I regulations.* Retrieved November 16, 2008, from http://www.ed.gov/policy/elsec/reg/title1/summary.pdf

United States Secretary of Education Margaret Spellings Announces Department Will Move to a Uniform Graduation Rate, Require Disaggregation of Data. (2008, April 1). Press release. Retrieved July 8, 2008, from http://www.ed.gov/news/pressreleases/2008/04/04012008.html

Warren, J. R. (2005). State-level high school completion rates: Concepts, measures, and trends. *Education Policy Analysis Archives, 13*(51). Retrieved March 20, 2008, from http://epaa.asu.edu/epaa/v13n51/

Woodson, C. G. (1990). The mis-education of the Negro. Trenton, NJ: Africa World Press. (Original work published in 1933).

CHAPTER 10

NEITHER LATINO NOR WHITE ENOUGH

Educational Experiences of Meso Hispanic, Meso American, Urban, and Suburban Public High School Students

Paula Marie Gallegos
University of Colorado Denver

INTRODUCTION

Because Hispanics are the fastest growing racial and ethnic group in the US, and because the majority of Hispanic students enrolled in urban public school districts (Fry, 2005), and because Hispanics graduate at a rate between 52% and 64%, it is imperative to examine educational success and failure within Hispanic students and the high schools Hispanics attend to improve academic outcomes.

Current data reporting on Hispanics is ambiguous. Hispanic is an overarching term used to group many different Spanish speaking nationalities and races. With such a large and diverse grouping, educational data col-

Confronting Racism in Higher Education, pages 205–251
Copyright © 2013 by Information Age Publishing
205

lection and reporting are vague. When the U.S. Department of Education reports data about Hispanics, the data are unclear because of differences in language and citizenship. The census bureau groups citizens and non-citizen, monolingual Spanish speakers and non-Spanish speakers, which skews the data that is used in educational decision making, funding, and research. Data reported by an assortment of agencies are general (similar to that of the census bureau), and are not helpful in pinpointing specific problems with Hispanic student academic achievement. Gaps in data, specifically between Spanish speaking and non-Spanish speaking Hispanics, have lead to ineffective attempts to create and implement forms to eradicate the educational achievement gap of Hispanics. One such attempt was the No Child Left Behind (NCLB) legislation (Escamilla, Chavez, & Vigil, 2005).

Escamilla et al., (2005) were convinced that an achievement gap did not exist for English Language Learner (ELL) Hispanics if the data were disaggregated between Spanish speaking and non-Spanish speaking Hispanics. Escamilla et al., (2005) examined problems with policy, reporting, and paradigms of ELLs in public elementary schools in Colorado to explain the achievement gap. Although their intent was to debunk state reports that ELLs were the cause of the Hispanic achievement gap, their investigation of the data told another story. Escamilla et al., disaggregated the data between Spanish-speaking and non-Spanish-speaking Hispanic urban public school third-graders and found Spanish-speakers out performed White English-speakers on all of the 2004 third grade Colorado Student Assessment Program (CSAP) tests (math, reading and writing). The Spanish speakers took the CSAPs in Spanish and the English speakers took the test in English. Although not directly stated, the test data shows that Spanish-speakers also outperformed their non-Spanish speaking Hispanic counterparts through a comparison of Escamilla et al.'s data to overall Hispanic student data (the Hispanics who took the test in English) and White student data as reported by DPS for the same year.

Prior to this study, research of this nature had not been conducted on non-Spanish-speaking Hispanics at any level and specifically not at the secondary level in Colorado. To study this specific segment of the Hispanic population, I classified non-Spanish-speaking Hispanic secondary students as Meso Hispanic Meso American secondary students: in the middle, or between languages and cultures.

Because Hispanics attend predominantly urban public schools (Fry, 2005), Meso Hispanic Meso Americans in urban public high schools were studied to identify factors of academic success and failure. A critical race theory (CRT) framework in conjunction with history and literary theory endorses the examination of student experiences in a broader context for greater understanding of success. Too many times, data or research studies are not useful in the course of decision-making and the daily administration of public secondary schools. The goal of this study and its methods was to make data user friendly for urban public high school teachers and administrators as well as to recognize and give voice to this specific subgroup of Hispanics—Meso Hispanic Meso Americans.

Theoretical Framework

The way in which I approached academic success for Meso Hispanic Meso Americans was through my history. It is important to disclose that the approach for this study permits me utilizing my knowledge and experiences as a Meso Hispanic Meso American urban public high school graduate and urban public secondary school teacher as well as a non-Spanish-speaking Hispanic to bring personal and original perspective to data collection and analysis. Empirical data are explained as the experiences of the participants as well those of the researcher (Tesch, 1990). My Meso Hispanic Meso American lens aided my process from research questions to analysis and guided focus to topics specific to education that a non-Hispanic and non-educator might not identify as important. This also allowed me to add local educational context from 10 years of experience and from my viewpoint as a graduate, teacher, and researcher to round out the empirical data.

Current research narrates the needs of an increasingly diverse Hispanic, Latino, and Mexican population in public education, and the failures that are predominantly caused by linguistic issues, the effects of poverty, and parenting. However, Meso Hispanic Meso Americans who are citizens, who do not speak Spanish, cannot be classified as *linguistically and culturally diverse* because they have been U.S. citizens for generations, are not new or of the first generation immigrant population and are not in poverty, are a growing subgroup within the Hispanic population that have not been studied specifically and whose needs have not been addressed through current reforms.

One of the goals of researching Meso Hispanic Meso Americans is to change the thinking about Hispanics and educational failure. *Postmodernism,* a more specific ideological perspective, embraces change through changing thinking rather than initiating action. Postmodernism critiques ideologies of the past to change present day thinking (Macey, 2000). Postmodernism perspectives in education emerged in the 1960s and 1970s with the basic tenets that *claims* must be considered within the context of the world in which they are studied, and multiple perspectives in class, race, gender, and other group affiliation must be represented to change thinking (Creswell, 1998).

Changes in thinking are facilitated when multiple perspectives from multiple groups are presented. Multiple perspectives are necessary in postmodernism to counter the *meta-narrative* or *universal* stories that have guided educational policy and reform to this point. Meta-narratives and universal stories have been told over and over and are held to be true by the general public regardless of social condition or group affiliation. These narratives and stories about minorities and marginalized population conceal and perpetuate contradictions, oppositions, and hierarchies that oppress marginalized people and blame them for their failures educationally, socially, and professionally. These narratives and stories continue to (and are designed to continue to) oppress minorities and perpetuate the hierarchies that oppress these marginalized groups (Creswell, 1998; Ogbu, 1978).

One movement that started to change how people view and understand marginalized groups is Critical Race Theory (CRT). CRT started as a legal movement to study and change the relationship among race, racism, and power (Delgado & Stefancic, 2001). CRT has a broad perspective and scope including history, ethnic studies, economics, and civil rights. But unlike civil rights, which has an incrementalist approach to change, CRT focuses on the foundations of social order such as equality, legal reasoning, enlightenment, rationalism, and neutrality in applying the principles of constitutional law. These foci have been applied to education to understand issues of discipline, tracing, curriculum, and how the educational system determines intelligence and achievement (Delgado & Stefancic, 2001). Change through a critical theoretical approach such as this comes from comprehending the underlying order of social life. It involves exposing assumptions, critiquing research orientations, critiquing the knowledge base, and through these critiques revealing the effects on teachers, schools, students, and beliefs of public education (Creswell, 1998; Macey, 2000).This approach is recognized as beneficial for marginalized groups and was the framework used to guide this study. Focus was placed on the domination, alienation, and social struggle of minorities and marginalized people through a critique of society—as represented by the public education system.

An *historic* approach also guided the formation of this study. *Historicism,* the theory that social and cultural phenomena are determined by history (Macey, 2000), was incorporated as an approach to view and investigate the problem of academic failure of Hispanic students. Historicism suggests that history should help point to the root of the problem, or at least to a few key factors, while emphasizing that time and people play an important role in the formation of the phenomena—in this case academic achievement.

History has shown us, and CRT articulates, that within the social system of the US, race and racism are foundational to the structure of our system— racism is ordinary and normal, everyday, and experienced by most people of color (Delgado & Stefancic, 2001; Haney Lopez, 1994), and racism is hard to cure or address (Delgado & Stefancic, 2001; Haney Lopez, 1994). CRT also maintains that neither racism nor the system that perpetuates racism, are challenged or eradicated if there is an *interest convergence* for both elites and working-class people—each group is getting something out of the deal. Additionally, CRT postulates that race is a product of social thought and relations; not fixed, not biological, not genetic, but rather constructed from categories invented and destroyed by those in power in our society, endowing marginalized people with socially created negative pseudo-permanent characteristics (Delgado & Stefancic, 2001; Haney Lopez, 1994). Public education also has this social structure; Change will come from changing the narratives that change the negative characteristics socially assigned to marginalized people. CRT puts forth the notion that minority status presumes a competency to speak about race and racism because it is a daily lived experience for minorities and marginalized people; narratives of marginalized people must come from marginalized people. CRT encourages the minority voice to tell stories to make their experiences and histories known to their White counterparts to change the narratives for and of both groups.

The application of CRT is used to help understand the social situation of public education and change it through understanding how the public education system organizes itself along racial classification and linguistic lines. With this focus, phenomenology was chosen as the vehicle to gather data on the phenomena of success.

In this way, this study was framed so as to examine factors that influence Meso Hispanic Meso American student academic success. Schools, teachers, teaching, teacher practices, parental involvement, and learning are the focuses of this inquiry. Oriented toward action, this study is ontological in nature, so that by examining the nature of the high school experience for Meso Hispanic Meso Americans, the nature of their reality is identified and established through words and voices of multiple participants (Creswell, 1998). One goal was to turn those words into narratives to change the current realities of public education for Meso Hispanic Meso Americans so that they gain more access to opportunities and resources as well as to improve success for this group in the public education system.

Also, because specific data collection has not been completed on the SES of Meso Hispanic Meso American students, it is not known exactly where Meso Hispanic Meso Americans are socioeconomically. Census data suggest that many are thought to be middle class. If true, this group is not being addressed by current research or reform. In this regard, Fernandez (2002) endorses this research approach because data collected on Hispanics in the last two decades has provided an adequate amount of quantitative indicators on academic failures, but not on success. He also advocates that more research needs to be conducted on success rather than failure, and that qualitative research can provide a more descriptive picture for improving education for Hispanics than statistical information.

Conceptual Framework

As an urban public secondary teacher, I felt I was not getting enough information from current research or district professional development to help improve academic outcomes for my students. I researched educational theory to supplement my practice and felt that my teaching had improved, but was still limited. As an English teacher, I implemented practices in my classroom based on literacy and emotional intelligence research: the results were great. I began to research theory in a variety of fields to be even more effective with my students within the confines of NCLB and state laws concerning curriculum and data reporting. Theories from social sciences and law to literacy theory were chosen and organized to guide my research on Meso Hispanic Meso Americans based on informal results I had observed and documented in my classroom. The conceptual constructs of Historiography and Historicism, Erasure, Defamiliarization, and CRT were combined to explore and study the lives of Meso Hispanic Meso Americans. This framework was designed to support the goals of giving voice to this marginalized population, validating the existence of this group, and improving educational outcomes for this group whose stories have not been told before, whose lives have been invisible, erased, not recognized, or silenced, and who are part of a larger minority group that historically has been marginalized in the United States. These concepts together were designed to uncover and highlight data in ways—anti-reductionistic, narrative, extended consideration, altering viewpoints to project possible meanings, counter stories—that have not been used before with this group and are not necessarily used in educational research, or in this combination.

Because marginalized populations historically have been uncomfortable discussing the forces that oppress them (Fine & Weis, 1998), this study focuses on the discovery of positive experiences in participants' educational and personal lives. That is not to say that negative experiences and emotions were not entertained or discussed, but the goal was to discover factors that transcended the forces that have marginalized and oppressed them in education.

Given the scope of this study, I focused on the retelling of educational related events that were in the consciousness of participants to create a narrative of meaning and meaningful events that then could be linked to a path of success for Meso Hispanic Meso American public secondary education students. Events, stories, and vignettes told by the Meso Hispanic Meso American students are deemed meaningful to their success because of their reasons for telling the stories and because they are remembered. Their narratives shed light on the teacher and family interactions that were linked to participant paths of success. Thus, the phenomenon of interest in this study is success: the meaning of the educational experiences for Meso Hispanic Meso American students during high school that promoted academic success, resulting in high school graduation and matriculation to college.

To make sense of the retellings, a *historiographic* methodology was utilized to aid in the examination and understanding of the essences of experiences. Historiography, the study of historical writing and the writing of history, employs historical discourse and narrative to transform a list of historical events into narratives. Historiography prefers narratives as a vehicle to tell history because narratives (a) are translatable without fundamental damage to meaning, (b) are transcultural and transhistorical, and (c) create a meta-code that transmits messages about the nature of reality using many codes that cultures use to endow experiences with meaning. History without narration is incomplete, blind, or absent (Croce, 1909; Kant, 1963; White, 1986).

Historiography, like CRT, sees the use of narration as an effort to describe an experience of the world in language, continually substituting meaning for the events recounted. The practice of historiography dictates that nonfiction narration must possess structure, an order of meaning, to convey meaning. In this way, historiography was used to organize data and retell Meso Hispanic Meso American histories. Historiography also recognizes that the absence of narrative, narrative capacity, or refusal to narrate is the absence of meaning. Non-narratives and anti-narrative modes of representation also exist in, and throughout, history as well as in our present day society. The absence, refusal, and anti-narrative modes are a form of erasure and silencing of histories. Examining non-narratives was as important to creating new narratives as looking at the narratives provided by participants.

This erasure theory was also contemplated when examining and considering data, because the act of erasing, deleting, omitting, or ignoring data or information to change the appearance or interpretation of history (Derrida, 1976; Kaomea, 2003) could be providing an incomplete picture of Hispanic academic achievement. Erasure can also be the removal of indigenous people from their land, erasure of their economic ways of life, the erasure of culture through assimilation into the dominant culture, or the collapsing of many races and ethnicities into one general description like "Hispanic" while erasing the others (Haney Lopez, 1997; Kaomea, 2003). These two scenarios of erasure, and the acknowledgment of erasure, guided my activities to construct new narratives and context for established narratives of Hispanic academic achievement to complete and retell participant narratives.

The practice of erasure on Meso Hispanic Meso Americans in public education has been specifically through the condensing of immigrants and non-immigrants, Spanish-speakers and non-Spanish-speakers, Mexicans, Chicanos/as, and Spaniards into one group and creating one achievement narrative for all. This narrative does not allow for the targeting and addressing of specific needs for specific subgroups of Hispanics. To overcome this erasure of Meso Hispanic Meso Americans from public education discourse and reform, defamiliarization was integrated to deeply examine the history of Hispanics in education as unearthed through the use of an erasure framework and the narratives of Meso Hispanics Meso Americans in secondary public education as collected through this study.

Shklovsky (1965) describes the act of defamiliarization as the act of changing an observer's perception from *automatized* and blunted to one of lingering examination. The act of defamiliarization is practiced in literature and art where devices are used to keep reader's and viewer's from getting through material too rapidly. Defamiliarization causes confusion, makes the text or art unfamiliar, and attracts a longer, deeper perception of the material for a greater appreciation and understanding (Shklovsky, 1965). Defamiliarization includes tools such as imagery, figurative language, cadence, and word play. Kaomea (2003) describes using defamiliarization tools on marginalized and oppressed peoples as a way to peel back the familiar dominant appearances and narratives to expose previously silenced information (Adams, 1999; Castagno, 2008; Fine & Weis, 1998).

Furthermore, the intent of using defamiliarization techniques to examine student success is to examine dominant, master narratives that have explained Hispanic academic failure and success up to this point. Examination of the master narrative against those narratives told by Meso Hispanic Meso Americans of this study brought to light contradictions in data that helped dispel myths and misunderstandings associated with Hispanic academic failure.

Finally, CRT was applied to narratives to examine issues of race and power in the high school setting as described by participants, as a framework to explore different possible interpretations of previously collected education data, and to propose new or different educational decision making that will aid Meso Hispanic Meso American students to be successful in public secondary education.

Narrative

As mentioned earlier, narratives were the predominant form of data collection. Narratives are important to acknowledging the existence of Meso Hispanic Meso Americans, validating their presence in the US, and changing how others see them and other Hispanics. To dislodge others from their normative universes, *nomos,* narratives must be well-told stories that describe the realities of the Meso Hispanic Meso American students (Delgado & Stefancic, 2001). Only through engaging stories can researchers hope to encourage others to understand and empathize with the plight of Meso Hispanic Meso Americans and other marginalized minorities. Marginalized minorities are people who do not possess power and privilege in society and are oppressed by those who do have power and privilege. Through a common understanding we can bridge the gap between educators and Meso Hispanic Meso American students and their parents to improve the educational conditions, reforms, and outcomes for this group.

Because educational reform is data driven, data is collected and presented to explain academic failure so as to prescribe an intervention to correct the failure. Much literature frames failure by comparing performance of Hispanic students to the dominant culture—Whites. Narratives then take on a slant that benefits educational institutions and places the responsibility of failure with Hispanics or within the Hispanic community (McDermott &Gospodinoff, 1979). Throughout history, the historical consciousness is specific to western prejudice that presumes the superiority of the dominant culture (White, 1973). By framing the data in this light, Hispanics are viewed as incapable or as less intelligent than Whites. For this reason, defamiliarization and historiography methods helped to scrutinize current, local, educational narratives of Hispanic achievement to uncover the context of the local educational agency achievement narratives, and reporting. Comparisons were then made between student participant narratives and agency narratives. Although I am studying individuals, I do not examine them in accordance with Husserlian phenomenology (1931) in which the students are analyzed without consideration of the world around them. Instead, I scrutinized student experiences keeping in mind that the world around them influenced in part how they act, as in Heiddegerian phenomenology (Cerbone, 2006).

METHODS

Phenomenology

Phenomenology uses narrative as a primary data source. Phenomenological narrative protocol requires a descriptive approach so that the phenomenon speaks for itself (Cerbone, 2006; Moustakas, 1994) to determine the experience's meaning for the individual. Phenomenology, combined with CRT, facilitates this process, empowering the Meso Hispanic Meso American population by allowing their voices to be heard completely and thoroughly, not reducing their lives to numbers or generalizations (Delgado & Stefancic, 2001; Fernandez, 2002).

Phenomenological methods start by exploring collected narrative stories in rough description: using the words participants use to describe their experiences, not using research terminology (Moran, 2000; Morse, 1994; Moustakas, 1994; Pollio, Henley, & Thompson, 1997; Sokolowski, 2000). In using phenomenological methods, my attention was centered on the participants' knowledge, experience, consciousness, intentionality, intuition, and perception of experiences. The data process specifically utilized the phenomenological methods of narrative retellings, imaginative variation, and reflection (Moran, 2000; Moustakas, 1994; Pollio et al., 1997; Sokolowski, 2000).

Through these methods, meaning is derived from first person accounts, interviews and narratives (Moustakas, 1994; Seidman, 2006) of life and experiences understood against the backdrop of the whole experience. In identifying meaning for a phenomenon, an investigator should examine the whole, then through the parts draw relationships between experiences, and summarize related experiences into global themes (Pollio et al., 1997; Sokolowski, 2000). Phenomenology helps researchers uncover and derive general or universal meanings—essences and structures of experience that are common to all humans (Cerbone, 2006; Moran, 2000; Moustakas, 1994; Seidman, 2006; Sokolowski, 2000; Velmans, 2000). The *phenomenological interview* is the way to gather data to describe human experience as lived and described by individuals (Pollio et al., 1997). Interviews close together in time with open-ended questions are recommended. And, as shown by Coburn and Nelson (1989) through a study of American Indian children, open-ended survey questions supplemented with extended answer interview questions gain considerably rich data. Similarly, methods by Werner (1984), Geary (1988), Phelan et al., (1992), Ogbu and Simons (1998), and Howard (2003) also support the use of the phenomenological interview to describe the meaning of human experiences.

Once stories were collected through the interview process, meaning was unearthed through the examination and interpretation of experiences as well as the emotions tied to those experiences and events. This is why looking at factors that can be attributed to success other than intelligence, was important in this study (Csikszentmihalyi, 1990; Goleman, 1995). Phenomenological methods work to probe the conscious knowledge of participants about their experiences and how those experiences create meaning. Building meaning from descriptions of experiences involves consideration of human horizons. Horizons are perceptual experiences and background as well as environmental influences that construct the reality of experiences. Horizons are all those things that affect how humans see objects in the world and how people react to and with the world (Cerbone, 2006; Moran, 2000; Moustakas, 1994; Pollio et al., 1997; Seidman, 2006; Sokolowski, 2000). Examining horizons creates a complete picture of experience to expose the meaning for the researcher. The researcher needs to be careful not to impose her horizons on the participants' experiences, and so bracketing is practiced.

Bracketing is a subtractive process to remove biases that can distort interpretations (Pollio et al., 1997). But, theorists point out that understanding and meaning are created in the context of the human experience, and so true bracketing does not examine experience in isolation. The procedure of bracketing helps to overcome researcher limitations. To bracket and provide the best understanding of meaning, a researcher can (a) provide a personal statement as consideration for why she is conducting the research so that her horizons are considered in the meaning, (b) use words of the participants rather than technical terms or words of the researcher, and (c) interpret findings of a group, not one individual, to validate data (Pollio et al., 1997). Furthermore, Moustakas (1994) adds that bracketing aids a researcher in looking at phenomenon naively and freshly through a purified consciousness that improves the identification of meaning and understanding.

After considering horizons and bracketing when handling the data to find meaning, researchers also must then acknowledge participants' intentions. *Intentionality* is an awareness directed towards objects; every experience or act of consciousness is connected to an object and is a conscious relationship to that object (Sokolowski, 2000). Pollio et al., (1997) agrees with Husserl's (1931) assessment of consciousness in that consciousness exists within the context of *something*, so experiences need to describe the connection to the objects and not make judgments about how it appears, or the objects, but about the meaning of it all. It is also important for a researcher to *epoche*, or take no position about an experience, holding at bay whatever colors the experience (Moustakas, 1994).

After the interview and all considerations are made on how to engage the data, the researcher completes *reduction*. Reduction describes in textural language what is seen: external objects, internal acts of consciousness, the experience, and the relationship between phenomenon and participant. Finally, *imaginative variation* is employed as a reflective and personal process to "check" for additional meaning. Many methods can be used to accomplish this reflection; for this study, a combination of historiography, examination for erasure, defamiliarization, and CRT were used.

Population

The study population attended and graduated from secondary public schools in Colorado from various school districts along the Front Range.

Additionally, the target population for this study was Meso Hispanic Meso American college juniors and seniors attending one of three urban public institutions of higher education in the Denver metropolitan area. Junior and senior status for participants was preferred to freshman and sophomore status students because most students who drop out of four-year colleges and universities drop out in the first two years. College students drop out at a rate of 34% after freshman year, 30% after sophomore year, 18% after junior year, and 8% within the senior or subsequent years. And, Hispanic college students and African American students have the highest dropout rates of college freshman and sophomores and of all students combined (*Post-Secondary Access and Success in Colorado*, 2006). Furthermore, to participate in this study students could not be fluent in Spanish or have learned Spanish as a first language. Students had to have self-identified as Hispanic, Latino/a, Chicano/a, or Mexican American at their local institution of higher education and had to have been born to two parents of Hispanic background. To control for culture and language identity, students who identified as the above races, but were of mixed race, were not considered for this study.

Data Collection

Interviewing provides context to a person's behavior allowing researchers better understanding of behavior and actions. Interviewing is most appropriate for data collection to understand the meaning of experiences because it is consistent with a human being's ability to make meaning through the use of their language (Seidman, 2006; Vygotsky, 1986). In-depth phenomenologically based interviewing uses open-ended questions; the purpose is to build on and explore the answers to the questions (Seidman, 2006). Reconstruction of events rather than memories of events is significant to the analysis of meaning; memory can be faulty, but reconstruction of events recovers greater details for better analysis of meaning.

Phenomenological methods dictate that to collect a sufficient amount of data and to allow participants time to reflect on events and topics discussed in interviews, each participant needed to be interviewed three times one week apart (Cerbone, 2006; Moran, 2000; Moustakas, 1994; Seidman, 2006; Sokolowski, 2000). The focus of the first interview was the life history of the individual and to establish the context of the high school experience. The goal was to have participants reconstruct their earliest experiences in high school and among their family. The focus was on their experiences as a student, and any related situations leading up to starting high school, including middle school, through high school graduation. The second interview focused on the details of the experiences: the participant reconstructed the *concrete details* of the lived experiences in high school. Because humans have close to 30,000 events in an eight-hour day, the goal of the second interview was to reconstruct as many details, no matter how incomplete, of the experiences. It was important to stay away from opinions and focus on the details of the experiences upon which opinions are built (Moustakas, 1994; Seidman, 2006). Therefore, my job was to reconstruct all the details of the experiences. To place the details of experience within a social context, participants' were asked about relationships with teachers and family. Two ways in which data were collected during this interview were through the reconstruction of one day from beginning to end or through anecdotes or vignettes about specific school experiences.

The third interview was to encourage participants to reflect on their stories told, and the meaning their experiences held for them. This interview addressed the connections between emotion and intellect, and home life and school life. Questions about the connection were about how they felt, their understanding of success and learning, and how they see themselves (Seidman, 2006).

Guiding Questions

Guiding questions that directed data collection were designed to solicit narratives about success. Questions were based on a review of the literature, on secondary academic success, and on pilot studies, formal and informal, conducted with secondary students at the secondary school where I taught. Questions were formed to probe the Meso Hispanic Meso American public secondary student consciousness to determine the importance of experiences in relation to success based on social structures as identified by social science and educational research. Figure 10.1 establishes levels of context and influence on the student participants as emphasized by research. Interview questions were asked about all levels of context to understand what is filtered out by students, what is important or influential in their success, and in the end what was not important. In the final analysis, meanings were used to reflect back on this model and to recommend decision making for schools, teaching and teacher practices, parents, learning, and college readiness.

As seen in Figure 10.1, the context for the study of public high school academic success for marginalized groups such as Hispanics includes factors that have already been established as influential on academic outcomes for all students. These factors include societal influences, teacher expectations, teaching practices, parent and family influences,

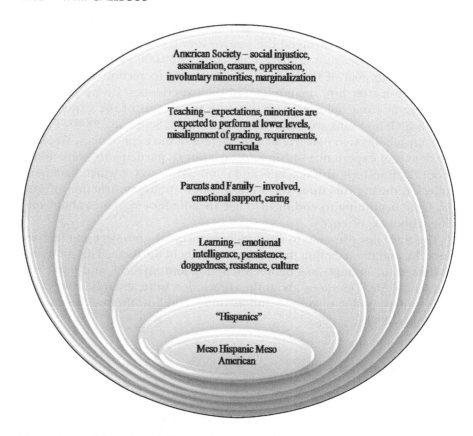

Figure 10.1 Educational Success Lens.

mainstream learning theory, and marginalized group learning theory. Together, these factors also function as a set of assumptions concerning the nature of the Meso Hispanic Meso American students' human existence in secondary public education, and so framed how I viewed data and organized it for analysis and synthesis.

This model helped focus the inquiry and directed where to look for information. It also provided enough structure to keep me from imposing my beliefs about the phenomenon under investigation: yet, it also gave me flexibility to be open and receptive to everything the participants said—to be naïve. Here is where the phenomenological methods on intuition, imagination, and universal structures helped to discern the structures that underlay the experiences of participants (Cerbone, 2006; Moran, 2000; Moustakas, 1994; Pollio et al., 1997).

Research Questions

1. When it comes to secondary education, what really matters to Meso Hispanic Meso American students?
   A. What educational experiences are most meaningful to Meso Hispanic Meso American students?
   B. What impact do parents and teachers have on academic success?
   C. What explains Meso Hispanic Meso American academic success?
2. What is the Meso Hispanic Meso American student's path to success?
   A. What helps Meso Hispanic Meso American students succeed academically?
   B. If not, what hinders learning and/or academic success?

Analysis

Once the framework and questions were set, and data collected, several theories guided how I viewed the data and narrated the results. Through the theory of transaction (the process of assigning meaning to text or other materials through the interaction between the material and the reader or observer), Rosenblatt determined that knowledge does not reside in either the material/text nor in the human being, but that meaning is created and only exists within and through the interact between humans and materials (Rosenblatt, 2005). I applied this idea in the data analysis process for two purposes. First, consideration of data in social sciences is subject to criticism because of its subjective nature; to account for and explain data as truthfully as possible, this process was applied to all narrative data. The interaction between the participants and me, and between me and the data, needed to be considered in the analysis. Secondly, the interactions between the participants and their classmates, participants and their school administrators, participants and their teachers, as well as interactions between participants and their parents also need to be considered when determining meaning because of the interaction: these events did not stand alone. The goal was to consider all influences on data to better understand the data. The interactions the participants had with adults during their high school experiences were what created meaning and strung together these meanings to construct an understanding of their experiences.

Process

I began with text data and ended with a narrative. My goal was to obtain snapshots of experiences, describe the meaning of experiences for the participants, and cluster the experiences to two to three central themes or essences (Creswell, 1998; Moustakas, 1994). Knowledge and truth were the goals, in that truth is defined as an interpretation that is made in a specific sociohistorical context (Pollio et al., 1997).

I also practiced bracketing to keep from imposing my personal biases, preconceived ideas, and conceptual biases so as not to distort meaning and interpretation (Creswell, 1998; Moustakas, 1994; Pollio et al., 1997). Bracketing was done in a positive way as discussed by Merleau-Ponty (2006) and Heidegger (1962) in that I did not place myself as a neutral observer, but rather acknowledged biases (my background as a Meso Hispanic Meso American public high school student and teacher) while analyzing and allowing for the interpretation to come from the data rather than an a priori framework (Pollio et al., 1997).

I then employed imaginative variation to seek other possible meanings through the process of imagination, varying of perspectives, different points of view, or differing roles (Moustakas, 1994). Husserl (1931) sees imaginative variation as a play of fancy where the researcher brings different ideas together to "birth" new ones. He explains that humans can find in *phantasie* the potential meaning of something that makes the invisible visible. Structures or conditions must be revealed and must be shown to exist for other things, such as essences or meanings, to appear along with imaginative variation. As described earlier, phenomenological reduction was also used to transform facts to essences. Kockelmans (1967) speaks of the process of reduction and imaginative variation together as "making the researcher move from static facts to an arena of ideas and possibilities" (pp. 24–36). In this arena, understanding the general meaning of a phenomenon becomes more than just putting facts together to describe an event, but rather giving a picture of the influences on the event and how they shape or create meaning.

Once I had completed bracketing and imaginative variation, I carried out horizonalization of the data by listing all words, phrases, or expressions related to or relevant to the experience (Moustakas, 1994) of success. Listing all *horizons* of success was to list all that was seen, felt, or heard during the experience. Listing all horizons placed all data with equal importance for consideration of the meaning associated with and that shaped the experience (Moustakas, 1994). Horizonalization initially lines up all data so that each piece of datum has equal importance for determination of relevance—that it is necessary and sufficient to understand the experience. If a piece of information is deemed not necessary to understanding the experience, it was eliminated. Because another goal of this study was to present data in an anti-reductionist form, not many pieces of information were eliminated. If a piece of data was found to be irrelevant to the experience, repeated, vague, or overlapping, the data were reduced or eliminated. All data was tested for relevance, clarity, overlapping, and repetition so that clustering and thematic classification was precise.

Horizonalization was conducted in two ways. After all interviews were transcribed, pieces of the interviews—horizons of success—were extracted. Each horizon was categorized based on success with teachers, parents, or learning. After all data were considered and listed, a review of horizons was completed to check for vague or repeated horizons. Some data were combined or deleted. Other data were separated into two or more horizons and new categories created. New categories were topics brought up by participants during the course of the three interviews: the two new categories were schools and college readiness.

Horizonalization Example

Rebecca, a female urban public high school participant, spoke passionately of her experiences ditching high school in ninth grade. She talked of the ditching in ten different instances and in ten different contexts. Although noted during the interviews, it was not until later examination of Rebecca's stories as a whole, and then in part, that the meaning of this experience began to take shape. I first placed each description of a high school experience for Rebecca in a handwritten horizontal list. Because the phrase, "I thought someone would come running after me" drew my attention as an important indicator of intentionality, I created *ditching* as a theme to discover for Rebecca. As I contemplated the meaning behind Rebecca wanting someone to chase after her, I poured over all her data again looking for other indicators that might add to the meaning of this experience.

What I found was that this experience, in her freshman year, set the context for the rest of her experiences at this school. This experience of "not being chased . . . no one caring about me," became the object with which all her experiences were understood, remembered, and acted against—her intentionality. Using imaginative variation, I categorized other experiences with ditching as related to her intentionality, and then organized all experiences around "not being chased," an essence, and how they related to the ditching experience. In this organization, the data showed that "not being chased" was at the center of almost all of Rebecca's high school experiences. I then looked for experiences that might help understand the initial ditching and found that her grandmother's death between Rebecca's 8th and 9th grade years was the greatest indicator for Rebecca's change of intentionality in high school. Before high school, Rebecca went to a magnet middle school, was identified as gifted and talented, and did well in school. Piecing together the experiences in a way to understand experiences and the everyday life of Rebecca was the goal of this exercise.

Using imaginative variation again to change the point of view, one can re-examine Rebecca's story from the viewpoint of an administrator. An administrator could argue that Rebecca's intentionality towards school influenced her actions, and that her actions could be part of the "normal" teenage experience, and they should be handled by the parents. From a parental point of view, parents could argue that the school administration and district's actions (or lack of action) caused her to experience "erasure." That created this intentionality or aided in its development and caused more ditching behavior. If she was seen as a problem student because of credit loss and ditching, those views could have perpetuated an administrator's desire, lack of desire, or inability to act on the ditching.

Once I identified the lack of school administration "caring" as a theme through Rebecca's narratives, I looked for similar experiences with the other participants. In looking at others' experiences, I found that this type of uncaring attitude by administration was expressed exclusively by urban public high school students, and not at all by suburban public high school students. After this realization, I shifted examination of experiences and clustering of themes into urban and suburban groups. Some themes were common to both groups, while others were clearly located with one group or the other.

After this process, phenomenological methods of imaginative variation and reflection were applied again to Rebecca's narrative to explore more points of view to aid in finding structures or conditions of that experience that gave added meaning. Any perspective was possible and was allowed to enter my consciousness. After contemplating legislation, achievement data, and local newspaper articles about Rebecca's school, I practiced phenomenological reflection again to eliminate possibilities that were not supported by any of these other data sources.

Imaginative Variation and Phenomenological Reflection Example

Looking at Rebecca's experiences around ditching for a fourth time, had she not talked about ten experiences related to ditching, and had she not discussed ditching at every interview, and had I not reflected and examined the interviews several times, I might have missed the importance, reduced the meaning, or erased the narrative all together. Reflection forced me to carefully examine the meaning and support it with several pieces of data and points of view.

To gather other points of view, I employed imaginative variation again to test the data against state and district achievement reporting as a point of view. I researched district attendance and testing policies, district attendance data, attendance data for Rebecca's school, testing performance data, principal retention data, and other historical information about her school during her years of attendance. I found that there were not then, and still are not today, attendance policies that compel students, parents, or administrators to keep students in school other than a state compulsory attendance law. Some schools in this district had individual policies that were aggressive, but Rebecca's school was not one of them. A recent local newspaper article reported on how the current principal was disciplined for a "too aggressive" attendance policy. Additionally, her school was often in the local paper about problems of attendance, achievement, and problems between the district and the teachers. I also found that the principals at this school left their position at a rate of every 18 months, the principals stayed between one and two years, over the last 10 years. Finally, since the data collection of standardized testing as mandated by NCLB, Rebecca's school had been (and still is) rated as low performing every year. The data collected as part of my imaginative variation exercise reinforced Rebecca's experiences and essences of her experiences in high school and thus validated the meaning and essence.

Although not all experiences, meanings, or essences needed this amount of imaginative variation, it exemplifies the process and care taken here. Additionally, this process closely aligns with the historiography process to give context, added viewpoints, and voice to all accounts of history.

RESULTS

Participants

What follows is a short summary of findings about Meso Hispanic Meso American academic success. The original study was much more extensive in scope; here I address a small piece specific to schools, teaching, learning, and small part of parent influence.

All participants attended and graduated from a Colorado public high school, some suburban and some urban. All participants did not speak Spanish as a first language and did not speak Spanish fluently even though several had learned it in school. Participants were between the ages of 20 and 33 years. Three of the participants were male, Edward, Mario, and Miguel, and four were female, Maya, Bianca, Julie, and Rebecca. All had junior or senior credit status in a bachelor's degree program at one of three urban colleges or universities in the Denver metropolitan area.

As established through this study, the typical successful Meso Hispanic Meso American public high school graduate graduated with a diploma, achieved a cumulative grade point average (GPA) of between 2.5 and 3.5, and achieved a composite ACT score between 20 and 32, which is close to (or above) the national average of 21.1. Colorado's average ACT score for 2009 was 20.8. Participant ACT scores were above the state averages for Hispanics, which was at a composite score of 13 for 2007, 15 for 2008, and 17.6 for 2009 (ACT Profile Report, 2009). Rebecca was the only successful Meso Hispanic Meso American participant without ACT test scores. She was not allowed to take the ACT test during her junior year of high school because she was classified as a sophomore by credit attainment at the time of state ACT testing.

All Meso Hispanic Meso American student participants participated in some sort of extracurricular activity or sport while in high school, and all, except Mario, participated in at least two academic organizations. Four participants also worked part-time jobs for two to three years of high school. Working was not a necessity for the family or student. These students worked to have certain luxuries not afforded by their parents, such as cellular phones, cars, and car insurance.

"Hispanic" Failure: Graduation and Drop Out Rates

The context for this study in 2009 was that the national dropout rate was defined and measured as the percentage of 16- to 24-year-olds who were not enrolled in school and had not earned a high school credential. This number declined from 14% in 1980 to 9% in 2007. Hispanic dropout rates from 1980 (35.2%) to 2007 (21.4%) have decreased considerably. But, as seen in Table 10.1, Hispanic drop out rates are double that of the total population (Colorado Department of Education, 2000–2009d).[1]

Conversely, graduation rates for Colorado (see Table 10.2) show that Hispanics lag behind Whites. Additionally, of all minority groups Hispanics have the highest high school drop out rate.

Suburban Meso Hispanic Meso American High Schools

Part of phenomenological methods is to create composite descriptions that compile narrative descriptions of events, people, and places. Participants were asked to recall what helped them be successful, or to discuss what hindered their success. What follows are composite descriptions of

TABLE 10.1   Colorado Hispanic Dropout Rates

Year	Hispanic	Total Population
1997–1998	6.3%	3.5%
2002–2003	4.2%	2.4%
2005–2006	8.2%	4.5%
2006–2007	8.0%	4.4%
2007–2008	6.6%	3.8%

Note: Colorado Department of Education, 2000–2009d.

TABLE 10.2   Colorado Graduation Rates

Year	Hispanic	Total Population
1996	59.6%	77.7%
2000	65.0%	80.9%
2003	69.6%	83.6%
2006	56.7%	74.1%

Note: Colorado Department of Education, 2000–2009a,b,c.

schools, teachers, and Meso Hispanic Meso American high school students as described by participants.

A typical Meso Hispanic Meso American suburban high school was welcoming, fun, employed good teachers, had well organized events that recognized academic achievement through a variety of celebrations, and provided opportunities for Meso Hispanic Meso American students to access pre-collegiate courses and post-secondary options. The school was *stable.* Stable was operationally defined by participants as consistent, reliable, practicing traditions and routines, and predictable. Additionally, when asked about the school schedule, suburban high school students had clear opinions that their school schedule did not affect them. Their days and classes were seamless, or they commented that their school schedule helped them learn and create a place for them to succeed and have fun. Participants agreed that a good schedule provided time for students to access teachers regularly for academic help during ACCESS period—a late start day, one day a week, with 90 minutes of time for academic enrichment and/or remediation.

The composite Meso Hispanic Meso American suburban high school had a student body comprised of a large White population on average of 80% or more, up to 2% African American, and between 6% and 7% Hispanic. The school achieved average to high standardized test scores as compared to the nation and Colorado as compared to a 20 composite ACT score and proficient or advanced on all CSAP tests, an average graduation rate of 74.1% total students, and an average college matriculation rate of 66% (Colorado Department of Education, 2000–2009a,b,c; School Digger, 1980–2009). According to a review of high schools' own websites, this composite suburban school would offer between 34 and 42 different extracurricular activities for students in academics, performing arts, community service, and specific student interests.

In the suburban setting, all suburban school schedules were blocked, 90 minutes to 120 minutes, or the equivalent of two class periods together, and had curricula that were aligned for cross content and team teaching. In literature and U.S. history, for example, teachers taught the same subject for multiple years (if not decades). Participants' siblings, friends, and friends' siblings had the same teachers years later, and they emphasized academics, but also provided a wide variety of electives, and flexibility for students to take a variety of classes as well as the ability to make up failed classes within a traditional classroom setting.

ACCESS time allowed suburban Meso Hispanic Meso American public high school students extra time with teachers for assistance in specific content areas, time to "just hang out" and bond with teachers or other students, time to "hang out with friends," time to "hang out in the library," complete homework or group projects, or for academic and extracurricular club meetings. All suburban Meso Hispanic Meso American student participants' schools had an ACCESS period and all attended ACCESS and found it helpful in getting through high school. Three of four said that they enjoyed the ACCESS time and benefited academically from it. Furthermore, students verified that their suburban high school schedule did not change once during the four years they attended their specific high schools.

Urban Meso Hispanic Meso AmericanHigh Schools

The composite profile of an average Meso Hispanic Meso American urban public high school is less welcoming and less fun as an institution. Meso Hispanic Meso American students of urban public high schools tended to form their own "fun" outside of school. Participants talked of socializing at raves, coffee shops, and other venues as opposed to school. Urban students did not speak of school as a place where they enjoyed friends; this narrative was absent, a non-narrative, for urban students. Urban students had friends at school, but did not enjoy school with friends as suburban students attested to.

The urban composite high school had a high minority population, low standardized test scores, lower attendance rates than suburban school, much lower graduation rates, and low college matriculation rates. Few opportunities to be recognized for academic success existed at urban public high schools, and opportunities talked about by urban students were awards sponsored by outside organizations, or were one-time awards at the end of the four years in high school, not before.

The school schedule and curricula inhibit learning and academic achievement as well as the completion of credits. The urban school schedule often changed. Bell schedules changed with each new principal. On average, 70% of new high school principals leave the principal position within five years, more than 20% leave after the first year and urban school principals turn over at a higher rate than suburban principals (Fuller & Young, 2009). Additionally, urban school schedules did not provide time during the regular school day to access teachers for additional help. Participants talked about how the school schedule changed every year and how they liked block scheduling, how they learned more in block classes, but that 45 minute classes were the reality in urban public schools. Furthermore, because of specific needs for urban at risk populations, regular bell schedules were disrupted often by testing, guest speakers, field trips, sports, cultural celebrations, intervention pull-outs (attendance interventions, parent conferences, conflict resolution), academic intervention (GEARUP, CU succeeds, Colorado Uplift), and clinic calls for inoculations and physicals.

If a student failed a class, the student was assigned to credit recovery to recover the credits for that core content area class which was needed for graduation per district and state requirements. Credit recovery was a computer aided online course the students worked on independently and was self-paced. Generally, thirty to fifty students were housed in a computer lab with one teacher or paraprofessional to assist. The recovery class was scheduled the next year, and the student continued to take a regular sequence of classes in the classroom even though they did not master the content of a prerequisite class. In many cases, the student was unable to complete the in-class course as well as the credit recovery course. For those schools that do not have credit recovery, students who fail a core graduation requirement were required to repeat the course in-class until they passed or recovered credit at a separate intervention school or summer school.

Moreover, policies also change with a change of principal and often create confusion, especially for students who have failed classes, or have deviated from the traditional comprehensive school graduation sequence of courses. New principals can change academic interventions, credit recovery programs, and policies that allow for students to earn credit. All of this contributes to the instability and unpredictability of the school in the eyes of a Meso Hispanic Meso American.

Lastly, the urban public high schools offered between 13 and 20 extra-curricular activities for students in areas of academics, fine arts, and sports.

Teaching

For all Meso Hispanic Meso Americans, suburban and urban, teaching and teachers were important to their success. Meso Hispanic Meso American students depended on and valued their teachers. The average successful Meso Hispanic Meso American student had a strong relationship with at least one teacher. Their relationship consisted of mutual respect. They were friends, they talked about everything including politics, boyfriend or girlfriend issues, and of course academics. Meso Hispanic Meso American students understood the teacher's effort in planning for class and for challenging students. Meso Hispanic Meso American students also understood the challenges teachers faced and had to overcome to be good to students.

According to Meso Hispanic Meso Americans, teachers who taught well took a book or curriculum and internalized it, added their knowledge and experiences, and then shared it with the students. A respectable teacher did not hold anything back, the teacher was not afraid of the Meso Hispanic Meso American student knowing everything she knew. The teacher made differentiated lessons and activities, and understood the Meso Hispanic Meso Americans' academic level at all times. Not only did the "good" teacher always know where the student was academically, but she paid attention and adjusted expectations based on the students' circumstances. The teachers always knew when something was wrong, or when the Meso Hispanic Meso American student did not complete the homework. The good teachers respected students enough to not "call them out" when they had not done their homework. The teacher let the student know that they knew the student was not performing, but always respected the student in public. Later on, the teacher always found time to track down the student and ask about changes in personality or other concerns. Good teachers also had high energy and cared about the things the students did. They were more like the students than a parent or "elder." Although both suburban and urban schools had good teachers, the number of good teachers was considerably fewer in the urban schools.

Pre-collegiate and post-secondary opportunities existed at the urban public high school, but they were less in tenor and volume than at the Meso Hispanic Meso American suburban public high school. Meso Hispanic Meso American suburban female students did not worry about taking or passing advanced placement classes. They felt that waiting and taking these classes in college was appropriate. Meso Hispanic Meso American male students also did not over emphasize the importance of college or AP classes, but did take them while in high school. This view seems counter to that of other racial groups, teachers, school administrators, school districts, and institutions of higher education. Educational institutions push students to take more advanced classes to gain exposure to more difficult content and rigor. Educators want students to complete college classes before graduating high school so that college is easier and less expensive as well because administrators are judged on these numbers for their school performance framework established through NCLB. Advanced placement classes are also pushed so that students can gain acceptance into college or receive scholarships due to their academic record. Studies have proven that a correlation exists between access to AP courses and college success, but for Meso Hispanic Meso American students, that was not a consideration. They were living in the moment and doing what they could to be successful in high school. They did not fear the future, they did not worry that college would not happen; they just needed to take one step at a time and master high school before mastering college. They were happy they completed high school, and they knew they would go on to college, they never questioned completing school. Time did not bind them; they were not in a rush. And, according to district level data, AP courses were offered at the three urban public high schools where urban participants attended, but only one urban participant was given access to those courses.

Compilation Meso Hispanic Meso American Student

Getting It Done: Non-Traditional Is Just As Good

One concept that even surprised this secondary educator and researcher was the concept that Meso Hispanic Meso American students defined college-ready much differently than educators. Educators get buried in the tasks of performance reporting, research, curriculum, assessments, getting students ready to go to college, and yet we forget about being "high school ready." We have been shown through research (Conley, 2009) that this preparedness will serve students once in college and will facilitate success there. The Meso Hispanic Meso American participants were not worried about being college ready. Even though they wanted to attend college, they did not worry about it or share in the urgency of educators. They focused on getting done with high school and not getting caught up in the practice of college readiness. Julie and Maya both made deliberate decisions not to take an AP or accelerated course in return for having a "good" high school experience. They still matriculated on to college, both graduated college within two semesters of this study, and both currently hold jobs within their degree field.

Rebecca and Miguel were clear that just finishing high school was what was important. They emphasized that there was time after high school to think about college; there are alternate routes other than AP courses, early application, early admissions, high ACT scores, and traditional universities. Mario pressed the importance of balancing family and education. He took classes part-time and online so that he could spend time with his family and he expressed his belief of that balance when he said, "Education is a part of life and life is education," the two go together; one does not wait on the other.

Essences of Experience

The essence of the experiences surrounding successful Meso Hispanic Meso American students are the largest encompassing descriptions of what was at the heart of the success phenomenon, what mattered the most to the participants which allowed them to be successful—focusing on learning, teaching, and parents. All experiences, descriptions, themes, and synthesis of ideas are best represented by four essences: acceptance, respect and relationships, social justice, and challenge.

Acceptance at School

Whether a Meso Hispanic Meso American was talking about a teacher, a school and its culture, a parent, or a situation, they wanted to be accepted. Participants talked about "loving" their school or feeling "betrayed" by their school. The discussion of what they thought of their school highlighted what it was they wanted from the school. Regret over what Rebecca and Miguel did not get is about what they wanted. The tone of the discussions was not about entitlement. The participants were not angry, they were upset and longed for a responsive school even years later.

Rebecca and Miguel talked of negative attention and that the administration did not really care about them and other students. Again, the fact that they were looking to the administration suggested that they sought out attention and recognition and did not receive it. They sought out recognition because they respected the institution of education. Urban students did not feel validated at school. Rebecca did not feel accepted or valued because she was not "chased" when leaving school during the school day; she was not even questioned or talked to by advisors. Miguel did not feel accepted because of accusations of cheating and because of low teacher expectations of him. Mario made a distinct observation that he was only respected in IB courses, not regular courses. The suburban students all felt validated by school adults, all received access to opportunity and courses, all received recognition of their achievements, and all felt their teachers cared for them.

On a similar note, urban students Miguel and Mario spoke of not being accepted at school, and of many experiences when they were seeking help from teachers, when engaging teachers about grading, and of a discussion with a classmate who ultimately expressed negative beliefs of Hispanics. These accounts are only common between these two, so I began to look at common contexts for this treatment. Both young men attended urban high schools, but what stood out most were their age, common language, dress, and "racial" features. Miguel and Mario both displayed a stronger Chicano presence than other participants. Miguel had long dark wavy hair he wore in a ponytail as where Mario had a shaved head. Both participants had facial hair in the form of a goatee. They dressed in what could be described as "worn" clothes in styles that are "common" to Chicano populations. Based on Rist's (2000) study of the affect of appearance on teacher belief of ability to learn, it is possible that Miguel and Mario had such issues because of their appearance.

Julie, Bianca, and Rebecca talked of not belonging with the "other" Hispanic students. The other Hispanics spoke Spanish, were English language learners (ELLs), or were "more" Mexican than them. These other Hispanics students teased or ridiculed the three participants about not speaking Spanish, about their accents when trying to speak Spanish, about their light skin color, or about their lack of Hispanic culture. The female Meso Hispanic Meso American females were called "Guerita" and were told, "... you are not Latino enough."

Acceptance at Home

All participants talked of characteristics they liked in parents. They liked parents that did not judge them, that understood them, and that listened to them. Participants wanted parents to accept them for who they were flaws and all. And, most participants admitted to their flaws and wanted their parents to take them as they were. Edward had also mentioned that, "Parents should let their kids know they look up to them." Participants needed to know that their parents respected them. Maya and Bianca both recalled experiences where their mother pointed out, through words or actions, a flaw in them, or the way they were leading their life, and through the accusation, blamed the girls for the flaw. These instances stood out in the girls' experiences of high school as important. These experiences could have hindered success, but did not because the girls had their fathers as the "supportive and accepting" parent. Participants also enjoyed when parents participated in school functions, listened to their children talk about school, and had daily discussions with the child. These acts were viewed as acts of acceptance by the Meso Hispanic Meso American students.

Respect and Relationships: Acceptance in the Classroom

Meso Hispanic Meso American students were very vocal about their desire and need for respect from those who taught them. Participants liked and enjoyed learning from teachers that had and shared their content expertise with the students. The participants also respected a teacher who put out extra effort for lessons and activities in class. The participants respected teachers that not only prepared for class, but also added their own knowledge to the lesson, and then asked the students to add their knowledge through class discussions. Additionally, students respected those teachers who unrestrictedly shared their knowledge with the students; the Meso Hispanic Meso Americans saw this sharing as an act of respect toward them, and saw it as the sharing of "the person" not just facts.

Teachers also earned participants' respect when they showed their knowledge of the individual student. Teachers who had their finger on the pulse of the student—their abilities and needs—showed respect through their knowledge of the student. And, if the teacher did this for all students, not just some, the Meso Hispanic Meso American student participants saw this as a sign of respect for students as a whole, and that their teacher did not play favorites—another sign of respect. The participants enjoyed when a teacher "really knew" them; who they were and where they were in their lives. The most respected teachers were described as "seeing me," "paying attention to the students as people" on a daily basis, watching for changes and then asking about their situation. And, with almost every participant, they referred to their favorite teachers as "friends." Many times, they acknowledged that this is taboo and non-traditional, but nonetheless, they preferred this form of relationship with their teachers.

Participants also suggested that when they felt comfortable at school, it was because they had the respect of the teachers, staff, and the administration. They were respected as students, for showing up every day, for doing what they should do, and for being "good kids." Respect was also seen by Meso Hispanic Meso American student participants as a reciprocal relationship rather than as a mentor-mentee type relationship. Mario spoke about how reciprocal relationships were motivational for student and teacher. He described how when his teachers believed that he could be somebody, they taught him more. This belief made him feel involved in and a part of his learning, so he worked harder.

Social Justice

Another essence of many narratives was social justice. Fixing the wrongs of society was at the core of mattering for students at the most at-risk schools or in the most at-risk situations. It was important that education be above, or all together separate from society and its ills as expressed by urban students. All participants saw education as the one avenue of change. Education was an opportunity provider. They saw the education system as a place where a child should be allowed to make mistakes and take those opportunities to "build the person." Discussion evolved around how schools do not treat students fairly, but instead mirror the social injustices of society.

When talking of social injustices, Mario shared that he preferred the online courses because of their anonymity; he was just like anyone else. He said that in online courses, "A grade is a grade; it cannot be manipulated by the teacher and his issues." This comment, and others, exemplifies the distrust in the evaluative and grading practices of teachers. Mario wanted to be judged on his intelligence alone, but his narratives showed that in face to face situations he was judged on aspects other than his intelligence (Rist, 2000). In face to face courses, professors verbally confronted Mario, and he saw these confrontations as interfering with his educational process. Mario was angered and upset by these events because he understood that the issues brought up by the professor were not related to the course, and in the end created obstacles to his passing the course. Mario added, "The professor's issues are a waste of my time."

Additionally, social justice to improve academic outcomes for Meso Hispanic Meso Americans was narrated as "believing in" and "expecting a lot" from the students regardless of how they dressed, how they wore their hair, how they spoke, if they were "bad," or where they lived. Meso Hispanic Meso Americans saw social justice as access to rigorous courses, access to college testing that was paid for by school districts, and access to opportunities to "turn themselves around."

Rebecca, Miguel, and Mario found experiences where teachers had low expectations of them as meaningful to their failure and success. Teachers would use worksheets or independent reading as the primary or only instructional method. These urban Meso Hispanic Meso American students did not experience this type of teaching as a rule, but they did experience it more often than the suburban students and did discuss these experiences with great frequency throughout all three interviews. For example, Rebecca spoke about how she felt the "low expectations of Hispanic students allowed teachers to not teach."

> I know there were instances when I thought the teacher was like referencing the book. Like, I'm like, "Can't you just give me the book and I can read it myself," you know. And I think its cause a lot of times they put teachers, maybe it has to do with like being short staffed on teachers and teacher shortage, so people are teaching in areas that they really don't [know]. . . . So, I'm just like, oh, "You're just teaching what I could have read and let's just cut out the middle man here and just give me the book."

Additionally, Miguel spoke about how, for a variety of reasons, the work he did in geometry class was not about geometry and consisted of worksheets without instruction from the teacher.

> I went into those upper classes, but the teachers in the class that they placed us into, that junior year when I was taking geometry, the teachers were either not teaching the students period, or doing other things that they wanted to do. Like in my geometry course, he wouldn't assign us any homework from the book. He would give us worksheets that had nothing to do with geometry and we'd be like, why is he giving us this when we should be studying from the book . . . ?

Because of these teaching practices, these students often had to "teach themselves." In addition to teaching themselves, Miguel and Mario faced direct opposition to learning. Miguel, for example, was punished for seeking assistance in class, and Mario had constant confrontations with one instructor. Both experiences were viewed as injustices because the *attacks* were not about intelligence or ability, but about their physical appearance. Although neither Miguel nor Mario articulated the essence of the problems, they attributed the aggression to race and ethnicity. Mario talked about having to retake a class a second time because of difficulties with the instructor the first time.

> This is the second time I've took calculus. The first time I took it was with a professor and I didn't agree with him. I didn't like him at all, so I ended up dropping the class. I like this course [the online calculus course] cause of that [being online]. . . . A lot of people's issues are a waste of my time. Half the time when I did go to his class, I would sit there and I would be like, "I could be doing this at home," so I would leave his class and maybe that's probably the reason me and him didn't get along.

> And the funny thing about it is I'm still taking, I'm taking his class online now. And I put in his comments there, "I would rather much take your classes online 'cause I didn't want to have to deal with you in person, you need to be humbled," I told him. He'll probably remember me, but my grades are there so he can't manipulate the grades, so I don't care what he thinks of me.

Miguel recalled how he was "picked on" because of his ethnicity in two different classes.

> I had to teach myself. I didn't learn from the teacher, because he wasn't teaching us directly as Mexicans as people. He wasn't giving us the attention that he would give the other students, the Caucasian students directly. So it was an indirect, how would you say it, a subliminal, that's what I was talking about, a subliminal treatment towards us.

> [Another] one of the teachers had accused me of cheating in his class. I asked [another student], "You know, I don't remember this formula, could you help me remember this formula?" And she had grabbed the test book and said, "Yeah, here's the formula, do this and this and then the transformation on the equation." And I said, "Okay." So then I started working on the problem, when the teacher came over and asked me, "You know, Miguel, you're cheating, blah blah blah." And I was like, "No, no, you talk to the student here and she'll vouch for me." And [during this time] students in the front of the class were exchanging answers, literally, handing each other their test booklets and exchanging answers, and I was like, "wait a second." They were two Caucasian students, I was a Hispanic student, Mexican, and she was a Caucasian student and it's a good thing I turned to her and asked her because she was kind enough to say, "No, he had asked me just for a formula."

Moreover, Rebecca was denied access to educational resources to recover credit and take the ACT test because she fell behind in credits. Rebecca did not say that she felt this denial of access was due to her race or ethnicity, but she did suggest that denial was due to being labeled a "bad student" and because the school she attended was in a "predominantly Hispanic low-income neighborhood."

The urban Meso Hispanic Meso American students of this study were clearly different from their suburban Meso Hispanic Meso American counterparts in that they all recounted times in their high school education where "we taught ourselves."

Challenge

Challenge as defined by research (Bruner, 1961; Conley, 2009; Dewey, 1997; Dweck, 1986; Vygotsky, 1986) includes providing material above grade level and beyond previous knowledge but with a zone of development, using methodologies that extend thinking, providing activities that deepen understanding, utilizing assessments with proper and timely feedback, and standardization. Differentiation helps create challenge while avoiding frustration. Differentiation helps meet content standards through different pacing or narrowing of the content. Differentiation facilitates growth and growth facilitates success.

All participants agreed that *challenge* was important. To truly challenge students, teachers must know the students' abilities and continually share that knowledge with the students. Suburban and urban magnet school Meso Hispanic Meso American students knew how they were ranked in relation to other students, ahead or behind others in the class, and were clear that their teacher knew where they stood as well. All Meso Hispanic Meso American participants were clear that good teachers (their favorite teachers) always knew where they were in terms of understanding the content. The teachers then differentiated and challenged each Meso Hispanic Meso American student according to her or his specific level and need.

In this regard, Edward talked of his AP Spanish teacher making entire worksheets just for him and one other student to specifically address their needs. He also talked of how his anatomy teacher scaffolds her assignments with individual instruction and personal direction in addition to class instruction. Edward admits that had his teachers not differentiated material and skills for him, he might not have succeeded to major in pre-med or Spanish. "I probably would have graduated and gone on to college regardless, but I may not have been as far along. I may have had less skill and confidence, or I may have chosen a different major."

Teachers were the catalyst for challenge, not curricula or access to rigorous courses. Challenge came from teachers in the form of (a) not letting the student give up (Edward, Maya, Rebecca), (b) tutoring after school, outside of class, on the teacher's time (Edward, Maya), (c) being creative with class and grading policies to engage and encourage students (Maya),

(d) knowing when a student was having life challenges and adjusting grading and classroom policies (Mario, Bianca), and (e) being a role model for "Hispanic" students and the embodiment of success (Edward, Maya, Bianca). So, when I speak of challenging Meso Hispanic Meso American students, educators need to acknowledge that differentiation and teachers are the two major components for challenging these students; what is more important is the teacher, not the course or content.

To conceptualize the idea of challenge for Meso Hispanic Meso American students, it is necessary to understand that participants found challenge necessary for learning. But, participants also agreed that other factors that must be addressed, and which play a more important role in Meso Hispanic Meso American student learning are (a) having a connection with the teacher(s) emotionally and professionally to build trust (Cornelius-White, 2007; Keddie & Churchill, 2005; Pomeroy, 1999), (b) teaching must be differentiated to compensate for lack of foundational knowledge due to cultural differences, (c) teachers and schools must be flexible in their policies for the demonstration of knowledge (Brice Heath, 1983; Gutierrez-Clellen & Pena, 2001), and (d) schools and districts must recruit and employ teachers of similar race and ethnicity and with similar backgrounds as the Meso Hispanic Meso American students to serve as role models for students (Zirkel, 2002).

RESEARCH QUESTION ONE

When it comes to secondary education, what really matters to Meso Hispanic Meso American students? To answer this question, I address the most meaningful educational experiences of my participants, paying attention to emotional intelligence, identity, parents, the impact of a parent on a student's academic outcomes, and how Meso Hispanic Meso Americans defined and identified success through their narratives of learning, doggedness, and several aspects of teaching.

What Matters Most

Complementary to Dewey (1997), Bruner (1961) explains through his research that learning occurs when children are taught to use and use heuristics independently and practically: constraint location questioning, patterns to organization, and recall of information. Although I discussed learning situations to a great extent with the participants, understanding how they learned was not as easy. Participants were asked several times and in different ways to identify which practices they enjoyed, which methods of studying they liked, and which methods they incorporated into studying routines. Finally, they were asked which teaching and learning methods they felt were most successful in their opinion. Overall, the participants talked about the practice of trial and error, rote memorization and repetition to gain control over content, note taking, visual learning, class discussion, and group work. The work that participants felt gained them the most learning was independent work (reading, reviewing, and writing) and class discussions (understanding another person's thinking).

The organization, storage, and recall of information was a process that most participants struggled with, but found that they could better organize complex ideas after participating in discussion-formatted classes. Specifically, Bianca and Rebecca talked of how others' ideas and life experiences helped them understand social science ideas and retain those ideas for easier recall.

Contrary to their active practice of schema building, all participants except one expressed their success at learning during high school in terms that characterized them as secondary learners (Rist, 2000) when it came to organization of information for storage and recall. Several participants indicated they would "not ask questions," "not want to mess up in class," so they did not practice skills in class. They would listen and take notes, but not join in the discussion. They would present when they had to (Edward), and they would avoid tests when possible (Maya).

Additionally, every student spoke about how at least one teacher in their high school career taught without engaging them—passive teaching. Mario, for one, remembered being lectured at, Rebecca and Miguel talked of worksheets for class instruction, and Julie and Maya remember not understanding math or statistics, but the teacher did not slow down or go back to review, re-teach or differentiate in any way. Most of these behaviors were expressed by participants of suburban schools and by female participants.

All but two participants, Mario and Julie, articulated that they needed to hear and see the thought processes of the instructor. They needed an overhead projection and simultaneous narration of the content by the instructor to learn. Pre-designed outlines, notes, and diagrams distributed before the lecture with overhead projections and narration together netted the most learning for these two. Edward and Mario talked about learning through repetition and accessing multiple resources.

Doggedness

Aside from teaching and learning, a key trait that Meso Hispanic Meso American participants displayed through their narratives about high school was doggedness. Doggedness can be closely linked to persistence and is defined as the sheer desire to achieve (Bruner 1961). Goleman

(1995) also refers to doggedness as the traits of enthusiasm and persistence in the face of setbacks. Enthusiasm is not a word I would use to describe what Meso Hispanic Meso American experienced and how they perceived their experience. Enthusiasm implies that although there is a setback, a person continues forward because she perceives a benefit at some point. As narrated by participants, the perception that there would be a future benefit was perceived but not expected. Participants were keenly aware that if they did not persist in education that there would be little offered by society. Keeping in mind the social status of these students, I redefine doggedness for marginalized groups as the sheer desire to achieve and persistence in the face of no perceived benefit. Additionally, because participants were not "excited" about the setbacks, and did not possess an altruistic desire to achieve, words like resistance, resilience, opposition to oppression, and oppositional better describe Meso Hispanic Meso Americans' "enthusiasm."

To further expand on Goleman's (1995) definition, doggedness is more narrowly defined as persistence in the face of acts of God or random acts of inconvenience, suggesting that the types of setbacks are natural. Setbacks as described through Meso Hispanic Meso American participant narratives can neither be called random or acts of God. Setbacks the participants experienced included acts of racism, aggression, isolation, and low expectations to no expectations. These acts by adults at public high schools, which were setbacks to the participants, are not natural or random, but specific socially constructed acts of oppression and marginalization. To expand and redefine the term doggedness for marginalized groups like Meso American Meso Hispanics is to define doggedness as "persistence in the face of random or intentional socially constructed setbacks, and socially constructed obstacles that were intentional acts of marginalization with a perceived notion that no benefit will come of the persistence and that the act of persistence is active resistance to marginalization and oppression rather than enthusiasm."

Obstacles

In the face of obstacles, more often at the highly Hispanic populated schools than others, participants possessed qualities of doggedness on a daily basis. And, all participants, with the exception of Mario, displayed sheer doggedness in their educational setting. Their frustrations were high and with many reasons to quit school, they persisted against ridicule (Rebecca— regularly being corrected or 'called out" by classmates about her speech), isolation (Bianca—not Latino enough and not White enough), conflicts (Mario—with teachers, Bianca and Rebecca—with other students), denial of access to educational opportunities (Rebecca and Miguel), critiques of character (Miguel), and low expectations (Rebecca and Miguel). Their frustrations point to educational institutions as an obstacle, in that the high volume and tenor of college requirements cause Meso American Meso Hispanics to fall behind and constantly fight to catch up academically to their White counterparts (Edward, Julie, Miguel, and Rebecca). Keeping in mind the new definition established here, the quality most closely associated with Meso Hispanic Meso American public high school success is doggedness based on these participant's stories and experiences. I also assert that participant social resistance is doggedness and that they persist to overcompensate for social injustices.

Teacher Practices

The outlook of optimism that aided some Meso Hispanic Meso Americans came from family involvement, some from the school itself, and some through teachers. Teachers can develop or squash student optimism. Teachers are essential to academic success—the practices and beliefs teachers embody. Goodlad (1983), Skinner (1984), and Dweck (1986) understand that teaching is the moment-to-moment sharing of resources from teacher to student, and that teachers must respond to students' questions in real time, in class, or during the school day. If teachers had fewer tasks to perform in the school day, they could spend more time with students, accelerating student learning to improve at a greater rate. In this regard, all participants were exact in their description of good teaching and teachers—that good teaching included allowing for student discussion in class, that good teachers talked to the students, and that the good teacher made time for students, outside of and in class. For example, Bianca, Rebecca, and Julie appreciated when the teachers shared their thoughts, beliefs, and knowledge of content that helped them learn the material.

Further, several participants understood that teachers who were not considered "good" were not necessarily "bad," but that the "bad" teachers had been beaten down by administrators, tasks, and the school system. They pointed to rules, policies, or burnout as reasons why teachers built walls around themselves and kept the students out. Conditions like large class sizes, lack of teaching materials and textbooks, not enough planning time, assessments, data reporting to administrators, confines of curricula, pressure to pass and graduate more students every year, and the fear of accusations of inappropriate relationships with students all conflicted with teaching and learning and caused teachers to become less effective or even "bad." Edward also acknowledged that success in his Spanish class would not have happened if the class had been a large class of thirty or more students to one teacher. He admitted he knew that thirty or more students in a class was typical in public high schools, but this was not the case in his AP Spanish course.

Teaching and Learning

Another aspect of good teaching as shown by Young, Wright, & Laster (2005) determined that varying learning styles and instructional methods for African American students improved their academic outcomes. When discussing teaching and learning, all participants expressed similar preferences for a variety of learning styles and instructional methods. Although they experienced a variety of instructional methods, many of the participants preferred lectures with visual displays of content—heuristics, displays of thinking—schema, and a preference for independent learning. They all stated that three or more methods for one learning task were necessary to master the content. Additionally, a few female participants liked group work (Bianca, Julie, Maya).

As a way to express what they liked for instructional methods, Mario, Miguel, and Rebecca talked of what "did not work" for them. Mario talked about "waiting out my time" and not getting much use out of class time. He needed more challenge and differentiation. Rebecca was frustrated when a method did not go beyond reading from a textbook. She could have done this work on her own and she did not see it as a practical use of her time either. Specific instructional practices the three mentioned that did not aid in their success were "we were always writing"—no variety; they always completed worksheets—no differentiation or "imagination or authenticity," and the teacher "just regurgitated what the text book stated."

Another method that teachers used that Meso Hispanic Meso American students felt did not help them was "tracking." Rist (2000) showed that grouping students by ability level is discriminatory as did Echevarria, Vogt, and Short (2008) who found that differentiating instruction happened in negative ways, and that student grouping often occurred based on *belief* of student ability rather than actual performance of ability. Meso Hispanic Meso American participants of this study negatively felt the effects of differentiated grouping or tracking mostly in highly populated Hispanic urban high schools. Miguel spoke directly to being placed in various classes randomly with no expectation of work. Mario's and Miguel's schools exhibited traits of tracking most often through inconsistent or no grading policies, low expectations, and an inconsistent or double standard of expectations. Negative effects of grouping were in the classroom, but also were exercised through the counselor's office and district policies. In the end, participants did suffer the long-term effects of negative tracking, but they overcame tracking through doggedness and parent support at home enough to graduate high school and matriculate to college.

Teacher Expectations

Rist (2000) as well as Clifford and Walster (1973) uncovered a relationship between student physical factors and teacher expectations of the student which manifested into grouping or tracking of students based on physical traits rather than intelligence. For a child to be aware that he or she received negative or differential treatment because of specific physical traits, the child must be self-aware enough to understand teacher verbal and non-verbal cues (Weinstein et al., 1987). In this case, these Meso Hispanic Meso American participants were not only aware enough in high school; they were hyper-aware. They knew how and what every teacher felt about them and for the most part why the teacher felt it. To combat the effects of differentiate grouping or tracking, the participants divided the teachers into "those who liked them" and "those who did not," and they focused on and worked more closely with those who liked them. Meso Hispanic Meso American students would then spend a great deal of time with the teachers who liked them, and this time resulted in better grades (Bianca, Edward, Julie, Maya, Mario, Rebecca) and staying in school (Rebecca). This tactic of making friends with teachers was to overcome being different—not Spanish speaking—and the challenge of finding a social group with which to belong. For these Meso Hispanic Meso Americans, because of self-identified differences between them, their classmates, and their teachers, they had become very good at developing relationships where they could feel accepted and succeed in high school.

Physical factors were not directly addressed in this study, nor did any such factors come up during interviews directly. But, Miguel and Mario both mentioned how they look different, "more minority looking," and they mentioned how their appearance played some role in their educational experiences. Mario and Miguel looked more ethnic and possessed more racial characteristics in their dress, grooming, and language than did the other participants. Miguel wore his hair long and braided with facial hair, and Mario touted a shaved head and goatee.

Schools

Policy shifts, shifts in curriculum, feelings of being pushed out, feelings of invisibility, not feeling a part of the school, and feelings of being less worthy of services than other students were all identified as reasons why

Hispanics drop out of high school (Fernandez & Shu, 1988; Zanger, 1993). With the exception of Miguel and Rebecca, the two Meso Hispanic Meso Americans at highly Hispanic urban public high schools, the participants felt welcomed and valued as much as White students and other minority students at school.

At the highly Hispanic urban public high schools, Rebecca recalled and spoke directly of policy shifts every year, of a constant rotation of principals during her four years at her high school, being invisible when it came to ditching, and feeling like she was less worthy of services than other students at her school due to falling behind in credits. She also felt less worthy of attention, expectations, and services than other students at other schools in other districts because students from other high schools spoke about how they were treated well and received free services such as ACT classes and awards.

Miguel stated feelings of not belonging to the school community as well as feelings of less worthiness concerning the lack of time and attention the counselors and teachers gave to him. Thus, I conclude that because of these feelings Rebecca and Miguel did suffer effects of dropping out (withdrawal, ditching, hopelessness, and gang affiliation)—Rebecca said it, Miguel joined a cliqué—yet they overcame these negative effects to graduate high school. Although they are deemed successful per my definition, of the seven participants, all three urban Meso Hispanic Meso Americans are on a longer path to complete a four year degree, whereas, all the suburban students have graduated since the completion of this study.

Role Models

Zellman and Waterman (1998) found that minority group teachers tend to be more proactive in involving parents of minority groups in the educational process, as well as serving as role models for minority students (Zirkel, 2002). Although this topic was not a question asked during the three interviews, it did come up in conversations with participants. Edward talked several times of a connection he had with a teacher who was very similar to him—racially, ethnically, and socially. That connection was a factor in his success in the AP Spanish class and in Spanish acquisition. His connection with his teacher compelled him to continue with AP Spanish and eventually succeed in all Spanish classes. Edward also had another good connection with his orchestra teacher. He connected with her through similarities in culture, values, and beliefs. Conversely, Miguel declared that he did not like that any of the counselors were like him in his high school, and that few teachers were like him. Participant narratives point to the importance of having teachers, counselors, and administrators of the same race and ethnicity as role models, and that these roles models did facilitate success. At a minimum, racially or ethnically similar adult role models comforted Meso Hispanic Meso American students. Unfortunately, White teachers comprise 95% of the teacher workforce in urban public school districts where 56% of the student population is minority (Colorado Department of Education, 2000, 2008).

STUDY IMPLICATIONS

Implications for schools, administrators, teachers and parents of public high school Meso Hispanic Meso American are that small changes can improve academic outcomes and create situations which facilitate academic success. First, at the school level, what was learned from suburban Meso Hispanic Meso American students was that the school structure, how the school day was organized, routines, and consistency in every aspect of how the school was run, benefited students and promoted success. Administrators of urban public secondary schools need to reconsider the structure of their schools, from scheduling to teacher rules and required tasks. To improve success for Meso Hispanic Meso Americans, urban public secondary schools need to work to retain administrators, and develop a culture of success through developing and promoting (a) teacher expectations, (b) students expectations, (c) routines, (d) processes for recognizing achievement, (e) capacity within the school through cross content team teaching, and (f) retention of teachers to provide consistency and the building of culture. Also, schools that serve Meso Hispanic Meso Americans and other marginalized groups must work hard to provide and secure a safe environment for learning at school, separate from society, rather than as an extension of society.

TABLE 10.3   Educational Staff Data for Colorado

	Ethnic Group	Females	Males	Percent of Total
2000	American Indian	216	72	0.06%
	Asian	255	94	0.08%
	African American	499	211	1.6%
	Hispanic	1888	835	6.0%
	White	29,300	10,100	90.0%
2008	American Indian	not available	not available	0.0%
	Asian	424	164	3.0%
	African American	519	231	1.0%
	Hispanic	2566	897	7.0%
	White	34,007	10,977	89.0%

Note: Colorado Department of Education, 2000, 2008.

The schools of the participants in this study that consistently and equitably applied these policies helped Meso Hispanics Meso American students be successful. Schools that instituted a block schedule with cross content and collaborative teaching aided in Meso Hispanic Meso American participant understanding of content. Schools whose schedule provided time for students to access teachers during the regular school day for extra help aided in content mastery and the building of relationships that produced academic achievement and avoided dropping out for Meso Hispanic Meso Americans. Moreover, schools that required fewer administrative tasks of teachers or where teachers put the students first, allowed teachers to be more effective, and freed them to spend more time with students. The teachers were able to differentiate more, and had more time to spend with students to create a community for learning and success. All of these factors benefited Meso Hispanic Meso Americans who had less capital outside of school to support the educational process.

Administrators also need to be keenly aware of and address the issue of class size and its effect on learning: Smaller class sizes are more beneficial according to the finding of this study as well as other research (Biddle & Berliner, 2002; Finn & Achilles, 1990; Nye & Hedges, 1999; Nye, Hedges, & Konstantopoulos, 2000). Bell schedules and time on task also need to be adjusted to allow for more time for marginalized populations (not language learners) to absorb concepts along with the practicing of skills for better understanding. Clearly, English language learners need extra time to acquire language along with content, but what I want to point to more clearly is the difference between language learning Hispanics and Meso Hispanic Meso American Hispanics. Meso Hispanic Meso Americans need extra time in class not to acquire the language of English, but to acquire all of the background knowledge and ambiances of the English language. It is presumed because Meso Hispanics Meso Americans speak English that they are as well equipped as their White counterparts to participate in class based on the assumption that being born in the United States and being raised to speak English as a first language provides a basis of knowledge for learning. But, because they are not integrated or allowed to be a full participants of White society—Meso American—they do not have the background knowledge that Whites provide and receive in their racial and ethnic groups. Bianca, Julie, and Rebecca spoke specifically to the point that they needed more time to understand basic concepts that "seemed" to come more quickly to their White counterparts. They felt that the cross-curricular classes helped build a bridge between content and their lack of prior knowledge and that that process took more time than a 45 minute class allowed.

Furthermore, school districts need to be consistent, meaningful, and purposeful when creating and changing educational policies. Policies need to allow for non-traditional paths to graduation as well as non-traditional paths for college readiness. District administrators need to be consistent across schools, time, and programs (IB, regular, night school) when implementing new policies. Districts need to implement policies that "build the student" while still serving the needs of specific student groups and promote success. Giving schools more site-based control over policy implementation to address the needs of the specific community they serve also promotes success. If school districts and schools can do this, Meso Hispanic Meso Americans will succeed at greater rates.

Considering the findings of this study, I fervently disagree with educators' and school districts' long-held definitions and the values associated with college-readiness, and suggest they examine and reassess what *readiness* means and looks like in multiple ways for multiple types of people (Adelman, 2006; Conley, 2008; Goldrick-Rab, 2006; Kuh, 2007). Even though the participants for this study were selected because they had made it to college and were statistically likely to complete a four-year degree, these statistically unlikely college candidates, while in high school, were not necessarily college-ready, but ended up college-successful.

Like some students in this study, my current students do not like the "rigor" in school. They describe wanting to do well at "high school stuff" before doing well at "college stuff" and are stressed about taking Post Secondary Educational Options (PSEO) college courses and advanced placement courses while in high school. From what they say, they feel trapped, and they feel pressured to take the classes or be looked down upon by adults in the building and even worry about being thrown out of school. The net effect is that these students are being turned off to college before they even get through their junior year of high school. Yet, my study points to ways in which high schools can in fact encourage Meso Hispanic Meso American and other students to aspire to higher levels of education.

Teachers, as testified by participants and much recent local and national press, are essential to student success (Brophy& Good, 1986; Rockoff, 2004). Districts and administrators need to recognize the importance of teachers and that the greatest resources for the students are teachers. But good or great teachers cannot do the job without proper support. Teachers need to have more time with students and spend less time on administrative tasks—professional development, assessment training, standardized testing and assessments, data reporting, and focus teams and groups. It is also apparent that teachers need to spend more time than currently allowed with students to build relationships. Meso Hispanic Meso American participants also pointed to the need to provide teachers with more time to plan and prepare for class. Not only did the participants identify time as important to instruction, but also expertise in the content area. Students expressed a need for teachers who were experts because that person taught better and was willing to share their knowledge. Participants noticed that these expert teachers not only taught well, but also were good at building relationships with the students, and they treated the students as people, not children. That confidence and respect exuded by the expert teacher improved academic outcomes for the participants of this study.

Participants also cited not wanting mentors in high school, but wanting adults in their lives that respected them, that they could joke with, who would create limits for them, and who would not judge them. Adults in the building who took on traditional "mentor" roles were seen as condescending and controlling. The students needed someone who truly cared about them.

Finally, parents need to be aware that judgment or the representation of judgment hurts their relationship with their child. This was especially true for female Meso Hispanic Meso Americans in this study. Simple daily discussions with their parent mattered, helping with homework mattered, but general "book knowledge" did not matter at all. Attending school or athletic activities was about showing respect for the child. Participants simply wanted to know a parent cared. Meso Hispanic Meso American participants also wanted and valued parents who set limits for them.

SUMMARY

How Did They Succeed?

I would like to provide a final statement about each participant, in relation to their success as discovered through this study. These Meso Hispanic Meso Americans are incredible people and have succeeded against the odds. In the end, I determined Rebecca to be not resilient in the traditional sense, she was at-risk, but her success was attributed to her sheer doggedness. Miguel as well was dogged, and at-risk, but he was more traditionally resilient by relying on his non-traditional peer group, the cliqué, for his network of support. Mario was not at-risk but did have to be persistent through many obstacles. Edward, Julie, and Bianca were not at-risk, but were persistent because of familial support. Maya was one suburban student who was at-risk; she had some family network support, but she also had peer network support, and a school network of support, mostly though policy and programs.

Success Redefined

How were these dogged, persistent, and at-risk students successful? Even though I defined success at the beginning for this study as graduating from high school, matriculating to college, and completing enough credits to achieve a junior or senior status at a four-year institution of higher education, and used that definition as a framework to examine the success of Meso Hispanic Meso American students, student narratives have caused me to re-examine this definition, as well as the general academic definition of success. And, although defining success was not a research focus at the onset of the study, it evolved out of the data analysis process.

To redefine academic success for Meso Hispanic Meso American students it means (a) having good people in your life who care about you—both teachers and parents, (b) valuing education as a path of transcendence, (c) knowing or recognizing your limitations and working through or within those limits, (d) showing you care, and (e) never giving up hope—exercising doggedness, persistence, and resilience.

According to student participants, success was defined as (a) the ability to negotiate the public-education system, (b) possessing the belief that even a system that does not recognize you as a specific minority and does not provide appropriate services, can nonetheless help you, (c) study all the time, study some more, and study more than the average student, (d) feel like a failure but keep trying, (e) feeling like you are all alone, (f) get up and do it over and over again until you have passed enough classes to graduate, (g) graduate high school, (h) matriculating to college, (i) achieving junior or senior credit status at a four-year institution, and (j) graduate with a four-year degree.

NOTE

1. 1972 was the first year in which *Hispanics* were separated from the White population for data collection purposes.

REFERENCES

Adams, N. (1999). Fighting to be somebody: Resisting erasure and the discursive practices of female adolescent fighting. *Educational Studies, 30*(2), 115–139.

Adelman, C. (2006). *The toolbox revisited: Paths to degree completion from high school through college.* Washington, DC: US Department of Education.

Biddle, B., & Berliner, D. (2002). Small class size and its effects. *Educational Leadership, 59*(5), 12–23.

Brice Heath, S. (1983). *Ways with words: Language, life, and works in communities and classrooms.* Cambridge, United Kingdom: Cambridge University Press.

Brophy, J., & Good, T. (1986). Teacher behavior and student achievement. In M. Wittrock (Ed.), *Handbook of research on teaching* (3rd ed., pp. 328–375). Washington, DC: American Educational Research Association.

Bruner, J. (1961). The act of discovery. *Harvard Educational Review, 31,* 21–32.

Castagno, A. (2008). "I don't want to hear that!": Legitimating Whiteness through silence in schools. *Anthropology & Education Quarterly, 39*(3), 314–333.

Cerbone, D. (2006). *Understanding phenomenology.* Stocksfield, United Kingdom: Acumen.

Clifford, M., & Walster, E. (1973). The effect of physical attractiveness on teacher expectations. *Sociology of Education, 46*(2), 248–258.

Coburn, J., & Nelson, S. (1989, January). *Teachers do make a difference: What Indian graduates say about their school experience.* Portland, OR: Northwest Regional Educational Lab.

Colorado Department of Education. (2000, 2008). *Staff data.* Retrieved on August 10, 2012 from http://www.cde.state.co.us/cdereval/rv

Colorado Department of Education. (2000–2009a). Assessment performance data for all schools and districts across the state. [Data file]. Retrieved from the Colorado Department of Education Web site, http://www.cde.state .co.us / index_stats.htm

Colorado Department of Education. (2000–2009b). Assessment performance data for all schools and districts across the state. [Data file]. Retrieved from the Colorado Department of Education web site, http://www.cde.state.co.us / cdereval.rs

Colorado Department of Education. (2000–2009c). Assessment performance data for all schools and districts across the state. [Data file]. Retrieved from the Colorado Department of Education web site, http://www.schoolview.org

Colorado Department of Education. (2000–2009d). Colorado Dropout Rates. [Data file]. Retrieved from the Colorado Department of Education Web site, http://www.cde.state.co.us/cdevenal/rv2008Dropoutlinks.html

Colorado Department of Education. (2008a). District profiles, post secondary information.[Data file]. Retrieved June 23, 2009, from http://wwwcde.co.us. scripts/districtprofiles/postsecondaryinfo .asp?Dist=0880&sch444

Colorado Department of Education. (2008b). Graduation rates. Retrieved from http://www.cde.state.co.us/cdereval/rvgrad1299.html

Conley, D. (2008). *Towards a more comprehensive conception of college readiness.* Eugene, OR: Educational Policy Improvement Center.

Conley, D. (2009, August). *College and career ready.* Paper presented at Denver Public Schools, Abraham Lincoln Leadership Cadre, Colorado Springs, CO.

Cornelius-White, J. (2007). Learner-centered teacher-student relationships are effective: A meta-analysis. *Review of Educational Research, 77*(1), 113–143.

Creswell, J. (1998). *Qualitative inquiry and research design: Choosing among five traditions.* Thousand Oaks, CA: Sage.

Croce, B. (1909). *Aesthetic as science of expression and general linguistic.* (D. Ainslee, Trans.). London: Mcmillian.

Csikszentmihalyi, M. (1990). *Flow: The psychology of optimal experience.* New York: Harper and Row.

Delgado, R., & Stefancic, J. (2001). *Critical race theory.* New York: New York University Press.

Derrida, J. (1976). *Of grammatology.* Baltimore, MD: John Hopkins University Press.

Dewey, J. (1997). *How we think.* Mineola, NY: Dover.

Dweck, C. (1986). Motivational processes affecting learning. *American Psychologist, 41*(10), 1040–1048.

Echevarria, J., Vogt, M., & Short, D. (2008). *Making content comprehensible for English learners: The SIOP model.* Boston: Allyn and Bacon.

Escamilla, K., Chavez, L., & Vigil, P. (2005). Rethinking the gap: High-stakes testing and Spanish-speaking students in Colorado. *Journal of Teacher Education, 56*(2), 1–13.

Fernandez, L. (2002). Telling stories about school: Using critical race and Latino critical theories to document Latina/Latino education and resistance. *Qualitative Inquiry, 8*(1), 45–65.

Fernandez, R., & Shu, G. (1988). School dropouts: New approaches to an enduring problem. *Education and Urban Society, 20*(4), 363–386.

Fine, M., & Weis, L. (1998). (Eds.) *The unknown city: Lives of poor and working-class young adults.* Boston, MA: Beacon Press.

Finn, J., & Achilles, C. (1990). Answers and questions about class size: A statewide experiment. *American Educational Research Journal, 27*(3), 557–577.

Fry, R. (2005). *The high schools Hispanics attend: Size and other key characteristics.* Washington, DC: Pew Research Center.

Fuller, E., & Young, M. (2009, Summer). *Tenure and retention of newly hired principals in Texas.* Texas High School Project Leadership Initiative Issue Brief 1. Austin, TX: University Council for Educational Administration, Department of Educational Administration, The University of Texas at Austin.

Geary, P. (1988, April). *Defying the odds? Academic success among at-risk minority teenagers in an urban high school.* Madison, WI: National Center on Effective Secondary Schools.

Goldrick-Rab, S. (2006). Following their every move: An investigation of social-class differences in college pathways. *Sociology of Education, 79*(1), 67–79.

Goleman, D. (1995). *Emotional intelligence: Why it can matter more than I.Q.* New York: Bantam.

Goodlad, J. (1983). *A place called school.* New York: McGraw-Hill.

Gutierrez-Clellen, V., & Pena, E. (2001). Dynamic assessment of diverse children: A tutorial. *Language, Speech, and Hearing Services in Schools, 32,* 212–224.

Haney Lopez, I. (Winter, 1994). The social construction of race: Some observations on illusion, fabrication, and choice. *Harvard Civil Rights-Civil Liberties Law Review, 29*(1).

Haney Lopez, I. (1997). Erasure: The salience of race to LatCrit theory. *California Law Review, 85*(5), 1143–1211.

Heidegger, M. (1962). *Being and time.* Malden, MA: Blackwell Publishing.

Howard, T. (2003). "A tug of war for our minds:" African American high school students' perceptions of their academic identities. *The High School Journal, 87*(1), 4–17.

Husserl, E. (1931). *Ideas.* (W. Gibson, Trans.). London: Gorge Allen & Unwm.

Kant, E. (1963). *On history.* (L. Beck, Trans.) New York: Bobbs-Merrill.

Kaomea, J. (2003). Reading erasure and making the familiar strange: Defamiliarization methods for research in formerly colonized and historically oppressed communities. *Educational Researcher, 32*(2), 14–25.

Keddie, A. , & Churchill, R. (2005). Teacher-student relationships. In D. Pendergast & N. Bahr (Eds), Teaching middle years: Rethinking curriculum, pedagogy, and assessment (pp. 211–225). Crows Nest, NSW: Allen & Unwin.

Kockelmans, J. (1967). What is phenomenology? In J. Kockelmans (Ed), *Phenomenology: The philosophy of Edmund Husserl and its interpretation* (pp. 24–36). Garden City, NY: Doubleday.

Kuh, G. (2007). What student engagement data tells us about college readiness. *Peer Review, 9*(1), 4–8.

Macey, D. (2000). *The penguin dictionary of critical theory.* London: Penguin Books.

McDermott, R., & Gospodinoff, K. (1979). Social contexts for ethnic borders and school failure. In A. Wolfgang (Ed.), *Nonverbal behavior: Applications and cross cultural implications* (pp.175–195). New York: Academic Press.

Merleau-Ponty, M. (2006). *Phenomenology of perception.* New York: Routledge.

Moran, D. (2000).*Introduction to phenomenology.* New York: Routledge.

Morse, J. (1994). Qualitative research: Fact or fantasy. In J. Morse (Ed.), *Critical issues in qualitative research methods.* Thousand Oaks, CA: Sage.

Moustakas, C. (1994). *Phenomenological research methods.* Thousand Oaks, CA: Sage.

Nye, B., & Hedges, L. (1999). The long-term effects of small classes: A five-year follow-up of the Tennessee class size experiment. *Educational Evaluation and Policy Analysis, 21*(2), 127–142.

Nye, B., Hedges, L., & Konstantopoulos, S. (2000). The effects of small classes on academic achievement: The results of the Tennessee class size experiment. *American Educational Research Journal, 37*(1), 123–151.

Ogbu, J. (1978). *Minority education and the caste: The American system in cross-cultural perspective.* New York: Academic Press.

Ogbu, J., & Simons, H. (1998). Voluntary and involuntary minorities: A cultural-ecological theory of school performance with some implications for education. *Anthropology & Education Quarterly, 29*(2), 155–188.

Phelan, P., Locke Davidson, A., & Coa, H.T. (1992). Speaking up: Students' perspectives on school. *Phi Delta Kappa, 73*(9), 695–696, 698–704.

Pollio, H., Henley, T., Thompson, C. (1997).*The phenomenology of everyday life.* Cambridge: Cambridge University Press.

Pomeroy, E. (1999). The teacher-students relationship in secondary schools: Insights from excluded students. *British Journal of Sociology of Education, 20*(4), 465–482.

Post-Secondary Access and Success in Colorado. (2006, January). Retrieved from http://highered.colorado.gov/publications/studies/taskforce/minoritysuccess/200601_AccessSuccess_ppt.pdf

Rist, R. (2000). Student social class and teacher expectations: The self-fulfilling prophecy in ghetto education. *Harvard Educational Review, 70*(3), 266–301.

Rockoff, J. (2004). The impact of individual teachers on student achievement: Evidence from panel data. *The American Economic Review, 94*(2), 247–252.

Rosenblatt, L. (2005). *Making meaning with text.* Portsmouth, NH: Heinemann.

School Digger. (1980–2009). *Search, evaluate and compare schools, districts, and cities.* [Data file]. Retrieved from http://www.schooldigger.com/go/CO

Seidman, I. (2006). *Interviewing as qualitative research: A guide for researchers in education and the social sciences.* New York: Teachers College Press.

Shklovsky, V. (1965). Art as technique. (L. Lemon & M. Reis, Trans.). In L. Lemon & M. Reis (Eds.), *Russian formalist criticism* (pp. 3–24). Lincoln: University of Nebraska Press.

Skinner. B. (1984, September). The shame of American education. *American Psychologist,* 947–954.

Sokolowski, R. (2000). *Introduction to phenomenology.* Cambridge: Cambridge University Press.

Tesch, R. (1990). *Qualitative research: Analysis types and software tools.* Bristol, PA: Falmer Press.

Velmans, M. (2000). *Investigating phenomenal consciousness advances in consciousness research.* Philadelphia: John Benjamins Publishing.

Vygotsky, L. (1986). *Thought and language* (A. Kozulin, Trans.). Cambridge, MA: MIT Press.

Weinstein, R., Marshall, H., Sharp, L., & Botkin, M. (1987). Pygmalion and the student: Age and classroom differences in children's awareness of teacher expectations. *Child Development, 58*(4), 1079–1093.

Werner, E. (1984). Resilient children. *Young Children, 40*(1), 68–72.

White, H. (1973). *Metahistory: The historical imagination in nineteenth-century Europe.* Baltimore, MD: Johns Hopkins University Press.

White, H. (1986). Historicism, history, and the figurative imagination. In H. White (Ed.) *Topics of discourse: Essays in cultural criticism.* Baltimore, MD: John Hopkins University Press.

Young, C., Wright, J., & Laster, J. (2005). Instructing African American students. *Education, 125*(3), 516–524.

Zanger, V. (1993). Academic costs of marginalization: An analysis of Latino student perceptions at a Boston high school. In R. Rivera & S. Nieto (Eds.), *The Education of Latino students in Massachusetts: Issues, research, and policy implications* (pp. 170–190). Amherst, MA: University of Massachusetts Press.

Zellman, G., & Waterman, J. (1998). Understanding the impact of parent school involvement on children's educational outcomes. *The Journal of Educational Research, 91*(6), 370–380.

Zirkel, S. (2002). Is there a place for me? Role models and academic identity among White students and students of color. *Teachers College Record, 104*(2), 357–376.

ABOUT THE CONTRIBUTORS

Collette M. Bloom is currently an associate professor of educational administration in the College of Education and is a research coordinator at Texas Southern University in Houston, Texas. She received her EdD from Texas A&M at College Station, Texas in the area of educational administration. Her dissertation was entitled, "Critical Race Theory and the African American Woman Principal: Alternative Portrayals of Effective Leadership Practices in Urban Schools." Her master's degree was conferred by the University of Houston in the areas of educational administration and supervision. She received her bachelor's degree from Xavier University of Louisiana in elementary education. With more than twenty-five years experience in public school education, Dr. Bloom has served in various teaching assignments, supervisory and leadership positions at all levels of education in Louisiana and Texas.

In 2003, Dr. Bloom received recognition and was awarded with a scholarship for her outstanding dissertation by the American Educational Research Association's Research on Women's Special Interest Group. Dr. Bloom is actively involved in many professional organizations, including the American Educational Research Association, American Association of University Women, University Council for Educational Administration, and The American Historical Association. With her varied experiences, Dr. Bloom continues to teach in the graduate school, publish, conduct workshops, and serve as a consultant to school districts. Her research interests include urban principal leadership development, qualitative methodologies, mentoring minority women faculty in academe, histori-

Confronting Racism in Higher Education, pages 253–257
Copyright © 2013 by Information Age Publishing

cal perspectives of African American education, and science, technology, engineering, and mathematics (STEM) teacher preparation programs.

Andre Brown, MS, is a doctoral candidate and graduate research assistant in the Department of Educational Leadership and Policy Analysis at the University of Missouri. Currently, Andre is completing his doctoral study in Higher Education. Andre's research interest includes Black racial identity development, college student development, campus climate, and the differential impact of college on students. Along with working in higher education as a diversity educator for five years, Andre has researched racial identity in Black males, masculinity in Blacks males, and the effects of race-neutral admission policies.

Bradley Carpenter is an Assistant Professor in the Department of Leadership, Foundations and Human Resource Education at the University of Louisville. His research focuses on the politics of school improvement, and implementation issues related to the Title I School Improvement Grant program; the ways in which school leaders craft and implement policies that shape how parents and communities are able to meaningfully participate in schools; how educational administration professors facilitate conversations surrounding race; and the possibilities that exist for education leaders asked to realize their role as an advocate at the state and federal levels of policymaking.

Dr. Carpenter's primary responsibilities at the University of Louisville include leadership education/development and the fostering of supportive research and mentoring relationships with leaders located within JCPS and OVEC schools.

Bradley is a former graduate fellow from The University of Texas at Austin where he received his PhD in Educational Policy and Planning.

Sarah Diem is an Assistant Professor in the Department of Educational Leadership and Policy Analysis at the University of Missouri. Her research focuses on the social and cultural contexts of education, paying particular attention to how the politics and implementation of educational policies affect outcomes related to equity and diversity within public schools. She is also interested in the ways in which future school leaders are being prepared to address race-related issues that may affect the diverse students and communities they are called to serve. Dr. Diem received her PhD in Educational Policy and Planning from The University of Texas at Austin.

Dr. Diem was awarded the 2011 Outstanding Dissertation Award by the Districts in Research and Reform Special Interest Group of the American Educational Research Association (AERA) for her dissertation, "Design Matters: The Relationship between Policy Design, Context, and Implementation in Integration Plans Based on Voluntary Choice and Socioeconomic Status."

Claire Peinado Fraczek is an Affiliate Assistant Professor in the Department of Gender, Women, and Sexuality Studies at the University of Washington, Seattle, where she also serves as an academic advisor for two interdisciplinary undergraduate programs—the Diversity Minor Program, and Education, Learning and Society Minor. She received a PhD in Educational Leadership and Policy Studies from the University of Washington, and a BA in Political Science from Stanford University. Her research draws from critical theory, cultural studies, and feminist theories to investigate organizational change in education, with a particular emphasis on the politics and implications of multiracial discourses on educational leadership. Please direct correspondence to msclaire@uw.edu.

Paula Marie Gallegos earned her PhD from the University of Colorado Denver in the department of Educational Leadership and Innovation. She conducted research on successful non-Spanish speaking Hispanic American urban public high school students and was awarded the Outstanding Graduate award for her research which was labeled "asset rich." Her conceptual and research focus was, and still includes, the study of urban public secondary education using Critical Race Theory and Social Justice frameworks.

She works as a CU Succeeds instructor. CU Succeeds is the concurrent enrollment program between UC Denver and various public school districts in the Denver metro area. She teaches Fundamentals of Communications 1011 and Introduction to Ethnic Studies 2000. She also has been a guest lecturer for various instructors at the university and has taught the teacher licensure program courses in young-adult literature.

Additionally, Dr. Gallegos is an English teacher by training and taught English for eight years before coordinating college readiness programs. She is a College Readiness Coordinator at Abraham Lincoln High School in Denver Colorado for Denver Public School District 1. Her job includes developing and coordinating concurrent enrollment programs with local community colleges and universities, coordinating the advanced placement program, ACT testing and ACT preparation courses, professional development around college readiness, professional learning community leadership, and college counseling for students.

Dr Gallegos' volunteer work includes tutoring high school students, college counseling for high school students and college dropouts, coaching girls' tennis at Abraham Lincoln High School, and organizing support groups for first year college students, as well as for doctoral students through the Doctoral Students of Color (DSOC) through the University of Colorado Denver. She also provides dissertation support to students in the Social Justice and Diversity Lab at the University of Colorado Denver.

Chad Everett Kee has been a student affairs practitioner at universities in North Carolina, South Carolina, and Washington, DC for approximately ten years. He earned his master's at the University of North Carolina at Charlotte and is currently pursuing a PhD in educational leadership and policy studies at Iowa State University. Prior to entering the PhD program, he has been involved in summer-bridge programs designed to support academic success and preparation for minoritized populations in postsecondary education. In addition, he has been involved in teaching sociology courses, and facilitating learning opportunities that promote cultural competency and social justice. His research interests center on Critical Race Theory, educational equality within schools from Kindergarten to College, social justice education, and educating for personal and social responsibility.

Tamara Nichele Stevenson, EdD, is the postdoctoral teaching fellow in Speech Communication at Westminster College of Salt Lake City, Utah. She previously served as a Visiting Assistant Professor in Educational Leadership at Miami University–Ohio. She recently earned a doctorate in Educational Leadership and a Graduate Certificate in Community College Leadership from Eastern Michigan University in 2012. Her research interests include Critical Race Theory, Racial Battle Fatigue/racial microaggressions, campus racial climate, community college teaching, learning, and leadership, faculty/professional development issues, and qualitative research methods. This chapter is excerpted from her doctoral dissertation.

Jennifer Sughrue is an associate professor at Old Dominion University. Her research interests span educational law, finance, policy, and politics. She is particularly enthusiastic about critical theory as it relates to inequities in educational opportunity for diverse student populations.

Terri N. Watson, PhD, is a Barbara Jackson Scholar and Dean of Students at Florida Atlantic University Schools. Her research centers on Critical Race Theory, social justice, and equitable educational outcomes for all students.

Brandon L. Wolfe, PhD, is the Assistant Director of Student Activities and Leadership Development at Alabama Agricultural and Mechanical University (Alabama A&M). In addition to his administrative duties, Dr. Wolfe investigates the leadership challenges facing African Americans and other people of color in higher education. Specifically, his research agenda centers on two major foci: (a) assessing minority leadership and the ways it affects the institutional landscape, and (b) identifying and understanding factors that enable or inhibit the success of historically underrepresented and misrepresented populations, with a particular accent on Critical Race Theory, socialization, and persistence in postsecondary education.

Dr. Wolfe received a bachelor's degree (BA), a master's degree in adult education (MEd.), and a doctorate (PhD) in higher education administration from Auburn University. He is a member of Alpha Phi Alpha Fraternity, Incorporated and is a native of Birmingham, AL.

Evelyn Y. Young is a Program Analyst in the Department of Academic Program Development at the University of California, Los Angeles. She is working with international school leaders and teachers to develop teacher training programs and summer sessions for high school students from a cross-linguistic and cross-cultural perspective. Her research interests include Critical Race Theory, urban education, global education, and comparative educational philosophies, pedagogies, and policies.

CPSIA information can be obtained at www.ICGtesting.com
Printed in the USA
LVOW01s1307021013

354962LV00002B/3/P